P9-DMS-549

PLYMOUTH PUBLIC LIBRARY
PLYMOUTH IN 46563

Flowering Plants

A PICTORIAL GUIDE TO THE WORLD'S FLORA

GENERAL EDITOR: LEON GRAY

FROM ORIGINAL TEXTS BY

V.H. HEYWOOD, R.K. BRUMMITT, A. CULHAM, O. SEBERG

CHARTWELL
BOOKS

This edition published in 2015 by
CHARTWELL BOOKS
an imprint of Book Sales
a division of Quarto Publishing Group USA Inc.
142 West 36th Street, 4th Floor
New York, New York 10018
USA

Copyright © 2011 Brown Bear Books Ltd

All rights reserved. No part of this publication may be
reproduced, stored in a retrieval system, or transmitted,
in any form or by any means without the prior written
permission of the publisher, nor to be otherwise circulated
in any form of binding or cover other than that in which it
is published and without a similar condition being imposed
on the subsequent purchaser.

ISBN-13: 978-0-7858-3306-2

Produced by
Windmill Books
First Floor
9-17 St. Albans Place
London N1 ONX

MANAGING EDITOR: Tim Harris
DESIGNER: Lynne Lennon
INDEXER: Ann Barrett
DESIGN MANAGER: David Poole
PRODUCTION DIRECTOR: Alastair Gourlay
EDITORIAL DIRECTOR: Lindsey Lowe

Printed in China

Flowering Plants

A PICTORIAL GUIDE TO THE WORLD'S FLORA

PLYMOUTH PUBLIC LIBRARY
PLYMOUTH IN 46563

Contributors

HEB   Harvey E. Ballard, Jr., Ohio University, Athens, OH (USA)

DMB   Diane M. Bridson, Royal Botanic Gardens, Kew, Richmond (UK)

RKB   R. K. Brummitt, Royal Botanic Gardens, Kew, Richmond (UK)

MRC   Martin R. Cheek, Royal Botanic Gardens, Kew, Richmond (UK)

RJC   R. J. Chinnock, State Herbarium, Adelaide (South Australia)

AC   Alastair Culham, The University of Reading (UK)

APD   Aaron P. Davis, Royal Botanic Gardens, Kew, Richmond (UK)

DJG   David J. Goyder, Royal Botanic Gardens, Kew, Richmond (UK)

PSG   Peter S. Green, Royal Botanic Gardens, Kew, Richmond (UK)

VHH   Vernon H. Heywood, The University of Reading (UK)

DJNH   D. J. Nicholas Hind, Royal Botanic Gardens, Kew, Richmond (UK)

PH   Petra Hoffmann, Royal Botanic Gardens, Kew, Richmond (UK)

SLJ   Stephen L. Jury, The University of Reading (UK)

EJL   Eve J. Lucas, Royal Botanic Gardens, Kew, Richmond (UK)

OS   Ole Seberg, University of Copenhagen (Denmark)

GWS   G. W. Staples, Bishop Museum, Honolulu, Hawaii (USA)

MT   Margaret Tebbs, Royal Botanic Gardens, Kew, Richmond (UK)

TMAU   T.M.A. Utteridge, Royal Botanic Gardens, Kew, Richmond (UK)

PHW   Peter H. Weston, Royal Botanic Gardens, Sydney, NSW (Australia)

CMW-D   Melanie C. Wilmot-Dear (Melanie Thomas), Royal Botanic Gardens, Kew, Richmond (UK)

Leon Gray was the general editor of the fully updated edition of the classic *Flowering Plant Families of the World* (2007)—a definitive survey of the flowering plants worldwide upon which this pictorial guide is based—that was written by Vernon H. Heywood, Ph.D., D.Sc., Hon.F.L.S., R. K. Brummitt, Ph.D., Alastair Culham, Ph.D. and Ole Seberg, Ph.D., D.Sc. In addition, the following are authors who contributed to *Flowering Plants of the World* (1978), and whose contributions were drawn upon to some extent in preparing the family accounts for *Flowering Plant Families of the World* (2007).

CDC   C. D. K. Cook, University of Zurich (Switzerland)

JC   James Cullen, University Botanic Garden, Cambridge (UK)

JME   Jennifer M. Edmonds, University of Leeds (UK)

CJH   Christopher J. Humphries, Natural History Museum, London (UK)

FKK   Frances K. Kupicha (UK)

BFM   B. F. Mathew, Royal Botanic Gardens, Kew, Richmond (UK)

BM   B. Morley, Adelaide Botanic Garden, Adelaide (South Australia)

BP   B. Pickersgill, The University of Reading (UK)

GDR   Gordon D. Rowley, The University of Reading (UK)

ARTISTS

Judith Dunkley, Victoria Goaman, Christabel King

Introduction

The flowering plants (angiosperms) are the basis of the world's primary productivity on land and are perhaps the most important component of global biodiversity. Not only do they provide the crops that feed us, as well as ornamentals, medicines, poisons, fibers, oils, tannins, beverages and stimulants, herbs, and spices, but they also constitute the main structure of our terrestrial ecosystems, and the habitats for countless animals. It is not surprising that they have fascinated people for centuries and that their classification has attracted a great deal of attention and controversy.

Because of the importance of the flowering plants, a great deal of effort has been put into organizing the information about their characteristics in the form of a classification. Classification is a basic human endeavor. The basic unit of classification, and one that most people are familiar with to some degree, is the species. All species apart from their vernacular name, are referred to scientifically by a Latin name consisting of usually two words – referred to technically as binomials; thus the common foxglove is *Digitalis purpurea* – *Digitalis* being the genus name while *purpurea* indicates the species. Genera that are most similar to each other are grouped into families, their names normally ending in –aceae, such as the Ranunculaceae, the buttercup family. Some families, such as the grasses (Poaceae), the palms (Arecaceae), the composites or daisies (Asteraceae) and the umbels or carrots (Apiaceae) have such distinctive features that they have been recognized for centuries, even before formal acceptance of the family as a unit of classification. In fact the Apiaceae, with their flowers arranged in umbels, characteristic fruits and distinctive chemistry, was the first family to be formally recognized as such, under the name Umbelliferae, toward the end of the 16th century. Other families are not nearly so distinctive or easily recognizable.

This book presents a selection of flowering plant families from the comprehensive *Flowering Plant Families of the World* (2007), by V.H. Heywood, R.K. Brummitt, A. Culham and O. Seberg. It does not, however, include the information on the classification and relationships or the references to relevant literature for each family that are key features of the original work. It does not pretend to be a fully representative sample but includes many well known families and should provide a good introduction to the amazing diversity of this fascinating group of plants.

Since attempts to classify plants began, botanists have sought to discover the most 'natural' system of classification. For centuries, most of the evidence used came from the structure and appearance (morphology) of plants, later supplemented by data from new fields such as anatomy, embryology, cytology and chemistry. In post-Darwinian times, attempts were made to turn classifications into phylogenetic systems but the difficulty of interpreting the mainly morphological evidence coupled with the use of different philosophical approaches to plant classification led to the publication of a number of competing systems. In the last twenty years, dramatic changes have taken place as the result of a massive increase in the amount of morphological, structural and molecular information that have become available. Most notably DNA sequence data of thousands of species, coupled with the development of specialized software and the availability of high speed and relatively inexpensive computing capacity, has allowed new methodologies to be implemented for analysing the large sets of data to establish patterns of relationship among plants in a reproducible way. Analysis of the DNA sequence data, which are generally less subjective than morphological data, led to the recognition that the main lineages of the flowering plants closely matched groups previously recognized on pollen morphology and this led a group of botanists from around the world, known as the Angiosperm Phylogeny Group (APG), to publish the first system of classification of the angiosperms based on DNA data in 1988. As more data became available, two further versions, APG II and APG III, were published in 2003 and 2009. The 2009 version (APG III) is reproduced at the end of this book. The APG system has been adopted by botanic gardens and herbaria around the world, such as the Royal Botanic Gardens, Kew and Edinburgh, for the organization of their collections.

This new information, both morphological and molecular, has led to a considerable number of realignments such as the partial abandonment of the traditional division between the monocotyledons and dicotyledons although many botanists still prefer to retain them as in this volume; also there have been changes in the content, circumscription and number of the families recognized. This has led to some strange bedfellows such as the recent placement of the parasitic giant-flowered *Rafflesia* alongside the small-flowered spurges in the Euphorbiaceae. Since most genera and species have not yet been sampled for their DNA, their allocation to families is based on the traditional assumption that morphological similarity probably indicates phylogenetic relationship although this is by no means certain and it is likely that more surprises await us as further evidence becomes available. For example, a small family usually classified in the monocotyledons has recently been shown to belong in the dicotyledons.

Although this volume does not follow the APG system as such, it does take it into account and shows considerable agreement for many of the families, although there are also some considerable divergences. Thus no attempts have been made to organize families according to their relationships and this book simply lists the families of both monocotyledons and dicotyledons alphabetically for ease of reference. The APG III system presented on pages 268–271 will outline how the families are related to each other in that system. Those seeking further information should consult both *Flowering Plants of the World* and other handbooks such as the second edition of Takhtajan's massive *Flowering Plants* (2009) and *Mabberley's Plant-Book* (2008). Another useful source of information, although primarily for specialists, is the continually updated Angiosperm Phylogeny Website (www.mobot.org/MOBOT/Research/APweb/welcome.html) maintained by Peter Stevens at Missouri Botanical Garden, USA.

It is our hope that this beautifully illustrated book will serve as both a popular introduction to the flowering plants that contribute so much to our daily lives as well as being an encouragement to the reader to delve further into their fascinating detail.

Vernon H. Heywood

CONTENTS

THE DICOTYLEDONS

THE MONOCOTYLEDONS

Acanthus Family

A mainly tropical or subtropical family of herbs, shrubs, and climbers, but also some, occasionally large, trees, related to the Scrophulariaceae (Figwort and Foxglove family). Several species are mangroves.

Description This family comprises mostly annual to perennial herbs, shrubs, and climbers (subfamily Thunbergioideae), but occasionally they may be large trees such as *Bravaisia* in Mexico (more than 20 m high with a trunk of 40 cm diameter), while several species are mangroves (2 species of *Acanthus* in Asia and Australia, and species of *Bravaisia* and related genera in Central America).

The leaves are opposite and usually entire (may be basal to subopposite and deeply divided in *Acanthus*), without stipules, and occasionally spiny. Except in subfamilies Nelsonioideae and Thunbergioideae and in the tribe Acantheae, the leaves have cystoliths that are visible with a magnifying lens as rod-shaped structures in the epidermis.

Inflorescence bracts are often well developed and showy. The flowers are gamopetalous and zygomorphic, usually with a 2-lipped corolla or sometimes the upper lip lacking, and 2 or 4 (5) stamens. The anther structure is diverse, with the cells often being separated by a broad connective or reduced to 1 per anther. The ovary is bicarpellate and develops into a capsule with 2 to 8 (16) seeds, or in *Mendoncia* a single-seeded drupe. Except in the subfamilies Nelsonioideae and Thunbergioideae, each seed is borne on a retinaculum, which is a stiff, hooklike structure arising from the axile placenta. This feature allows the great majority of the species to be readily referred to this family.

The family is well known for the remarkable diversity of its pollen in size, shape, pores, and exine structure and ornamentation. Many genera can be characterized by a distinctive pollen type. In some larger genera, however, such as *Justicia*, there is a wide range. *Crossandra stenostachya* from East Africa probably has the longest pollen of any terrestrial flowering plant, each javelin-shaped grain being over ½ mm long and clearly visible to the naked eye.

Distribution Tropical and subtropical, well represented in the New World, tropical Africa, Madagascar, and tropical Asia, but less so in Australia; extends only sparingly into temperate regions. Only one genus, *Acanthus,* is native to Europe, and few species occur in temperate Asia and North America. The family may be characteristic of wet forests and arid regions.

Economic uses The flowers, and often the bracts, are large and showy in many genera, making them popular ornamentals in tropical gardens or in conservatories in cooler regions. The most commonly grown are *Aphelandra*, *Asystasia*, *Barleria*, *Crossandra*, *Eranthemum*, *Hemigraphis*, *Hypoestes*, *Justicia* (including *Adhatoda*, *Beloperone*, and *Jacobinia*), *Mackaya*, *Odontonema*, *Pachystachys*, *Peristrophe*, *Pseuderanthemum*, *Ruellia*, *Ruspolia*, *Ruttya*, *Schaueria*, *Strobilanthes*, and *Thunbergia*. In temperate regions, 3 species of *Acanthus* (bears' breech) are commonly grown outdoors: *A. mollis* (the leaves of which are the motif of capitals of Corinthian columns in Greece), *A. hungaricus*, and *A. spinosus*. Several species are grown as house plants including *Aphelandra squarrosa* (Zebra Plant), *Fittonia albivenis* (Nerve Plant), and *Thunbergia alata* (Black-eyed Susan).

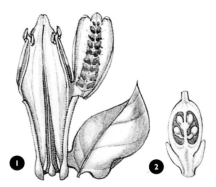

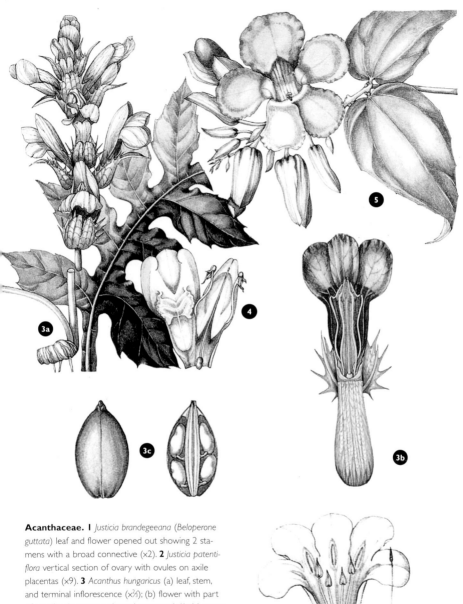

Acanthaceae. 1 *Justicia brandegeeana* (*Beloperone guttata*) leaf and flower opened out showing 2 stamens with a broad connective (×2). **2** *Justicia patentiflora* vertical section of ovary with ovules on axile placentas (×9). **3** *Acanthus hungaricus* (a) leaf, stem, and terminal inflorescence (×⅔); (b) flower with part of corolla cut away to show 4 stamens (×1); (c) ovary entire and in cross section (×1). **4** *Justicia* sp flower opened out (×3). **5** *Thunbergia grandiflora* flowering shoot (×1). **6** *Ruellia dipteracantha* (a) corolla opened out to show epipetalous stamens (×1); (b) calyx and gynoecium (×1).

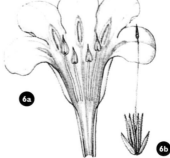

Amaranthaceae. 1 *Deeringia amaranthoides* inflorescence with fruits at the base (x3). **2** *Amaranthus retroflexus* (a) leafy shoot with flowers in axillary tassels (x⅔); (b) fruit dehiscing by lid to disperse globular seed (x6). **3** *A. caudatus* (a) flower with reddish subtending bracteoles and reddish perianth (x14); (b) seed (x14); (c) leaf (x⅔); (d) vertical section of male flower (x12); (e) vertical section of female flower (x4). **4** *Froelichia gracilis* (a) shoot with large, lateral, hairy, sterile flowers (x⅔); (b) inflorescence (x⅔); (c) vertical section of sterile flower (x⅔).

Amaranths, Celosias, and Cockscombs

The Amaranthaceae is a large family of herbs and shrubs, containing the grain amaranths of Central and South America, as well as several species of horticultural importance, such as the cockscombs (*Celosia* spp.).

Description Annual or perennial, largely nonsucculent herbs or shrubs; rarely trees or climbers. Leaves entire, opposite or alternate, and lacking stipules. The flowers are actinomorphic, bisexual or rarely unisexual, solitary or in axillary dichasial cymes arranged in spikelike or headlike inflorescences. The perianth is often dry, membranaceous, and colorless. Sometimes, the lateral flowers are sterile and develop spines, wings, or hairs that serve as a dispersal mechanism. The flowers have well-developed, dry, chaffy scales (bracteoles). Perianth segments 3 to 5, sometimes united. Stamens are 1 to 5, free or united at the base in a tube from which petaloid appendices arise between the stamens in some genera. The superior ovary has 2 to 3 fused carpels that are free from, or united with, the perianth, with 1 locule containing 1 to many ovules. The fruit may be a berry, pyxidium, or nut; the seeds have a shiny testa; and the embryo is curved.

Distribution Widespread in tropical, subtropical, and temperate regions. Most genera and species are tropical, growing mainly in Africa and Central and South America.

Economic uses The edible seeds of some *Amaranthus* species (grain amaranths) were widely used, especially in Central and South America. Several are still grown now. Some species are used as potherbs or vegetables, such as the fleshy leaves of *A. sessilis*, eaten in some tropical countries. A few species are grown as garden ornamentals, and some Celosias are grown as pot plants or tender bedding plants. The Cockscomb (*Celosia cristata*) is a tropical herbaceous annual. *Alternanthera*

species from the New World tropics are grown for their ornamental leaves, and *Iresine herbstii* and *I. linderi* (from South America) for their colorful leaves as house plants or bedding plants. *Gomphrena globosa*, a tropical annual with white, red, or purple heads, is grown as an "everlasting." Some species are reputed to have medicinal properties, and saponins are present widely in seeds of *Amaranthus* species.

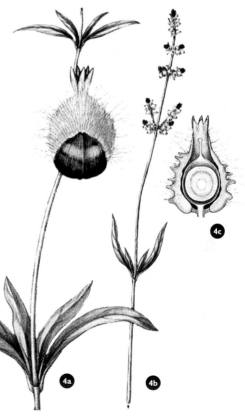

Cashew, Mango, Sumacs, and Poison Ivy

An economically important, largely tropical and subtropical family of trees and shrubs producing exudates that often turn black, which may cause severe reactions in humans.

Description Trees and shrubs—occasionally scandent shrubs, herbaceous climbers, or lianas—with resin canals and clear to milky sap that may turn black on exposure to air and is often poisonous, causing severe contact dermatitis. The irritant chemicals may be distributed throughout the plant body or concentrated in particular organs, e.g., in the fruit wall of the cashew (*Anacardium occidentale*). The leaves are alternate, rarely opposite (*Abrahamia, Blepharocarya, Bouea*), exstipulate, often pinnate, sometimes simple (*Cotinus, Anacardium,* and *Mangifera*). The flowers are actinomorphic and bisexual, or sometimes unisexual (then plants dioecious), small and inconspicuous, in terminal or axillary panicles, thyrses, spikes, racemes, fascicles, or solitary. Sepals (3–)5(–7), usually connate at the base, but free above. Petals (3–)5(–7), rarely absent, and free. Stamens 5 to 10 or more, the filaments distinct or rarely connate at the base, forming a tube. An instrastaminal fleshy receptacle (disk) is usually present. Staminodes are present in female flowers.

The ovary is usually superior (inferior in *Drimycarpus*) and comprises 1 or 3 to 5 united, very rarely free, carpels, with 1 to 5 locules, each containing a single ovule. There are 1 to 3 styles, sometimes none. The fruit is usually indehiscent and drupaceous but a diversity of unusual fruit types also occurs, such as samaras encircled by a marginal wing (*Campylopetalum, Dobinea, Laurophyllus*), samaroid with a single wing (*Faguetia, Loxopterygium*), dry syncarps (*Amphipterygium, Orthopterygium*), or achenial (*Apterokarpos*). In *Anacardium* and *Semecarpus*, the hypocarp subtending the drupe is enlarged and edible. The solitary seed may have thin endosperm, or none, and fleshy cotyledons.

Distribution The family occurs in both the eastern and western hemispheres, with a more or less equal representation in South America, Africa, and Asia. Several genera are native to temperate North America and Eurasia (e.g., *Rhus, Pistacia,* and *Cotinus*).

The family has diversified in Central and South America, southern and central Africa, Madagascar, Indochina, and Malesia. The largest genus, *Rhus*, with c. 200 species, grows in both temperate and tropical regions of both hemispheres. *Semecarpus* (c. 60 spp.) is Indo–Malesian in distribution.

Economic uses *Cotinus, Pistacia, Schinopsis,* and *Rhus* are major sources of tannins for the leather industry. The resin of *Rhus verniciflua*, native to China, is the basis of lacquer. Mastic and pistachio turpentine are produced from *Pistacia*. The family yields important fruits and nuts, e.g., cashew nuts (the swollen hypocarps) and cashew apples (*Anacardium occidentale*), pistachio nuts (*Pistacia vera*), Dhobi's nut (*Semecarpus anacardium*), the Mango (*Mangifera indica*), and the Otaheite apple, hog plum, and Jamaica plum (fruits of *Spondias* spp.).

The small berrylike fruits of *Schinus terebinthifolius* (Brazilian Pepper Tree) are used as pink peppercorns (baies roses) in cooking, and the species is a serious invasive in some parts of the tropics and subtropics. *S. molle* (Pepper Tree) is widely cultivated as an ornamental and as a shade tree in warm climates.

Other common ornamental trees include the sumacs (*Rhus* spp.) and the Smoke Tree or Wig Tree (*Cotinus coggygria*). Some genera, such as *Astronium, Dracontomelon,* and *Schinopsis*, include useful timber species (e.g., for veneers and fine furniture).

Anacardiaceae. 1 *Pistacia lentiscus* (a) shoot with imparipinnate leaves and male inflorescences (x⅔); (b) male flower with short, lobed calyx and stamens with short filaments (x10); (c) female flower with 3 spreading stigmas (x14); (d) vertical section of fruit (x4). **2** *Anacardium occidentale* (a) shoot with inflorescence and fruits, the latter swollen, with a pear-shaped stalk and receptacle with the kidney-shaped fruit below (x⅔); (b) simple leaves (x⅔); (c) male flower with a single stamen protruding (x3); (d) bisexual flower with petals removed showing all stamens except 1 to have short filaments (x4); (e) vertical section of fruit (x1). **3** *Rhus trichocarpa* habit.

Carrot Family

The Apiaceae is one of the best-known families of flowering plants, thanks to the characteristic inflorescences and fruits and the distinctive chemistry reflected in the odor, flavor, and even toxicity of many of its members.

Description Most of the Apiaceae are herbaceous annuals, biennials, or perennials, with hollow internodes; sometimes they may be stoloniferous (*Schizeilema*), rosette plants (*Gingidia*), or cushion plants (*Azorella*). Several of the herbaceous species develop some degree of woodiness, but genuinely woody, treelike, or shrubby species also exist. Examples include *Eryngium bupleuroides* and *E. sarcophyllum* of the Juan Fernández Islands, which develop a woody trunk; *Myrrhidendron* species from mountain summits above 3,000 m in Central and South America; and several shrubby species of *Bupleurum*. Several species are spiny, such as the thistle-like *Eryngium* species.

The leaves are alternate, without stipules, and the leaves usually dissected (ternate or variously pinnate). Entire leaves are present in *Bupleurum*, often with parallel venation.

The main inflorescence present in the Umbelliferae is a simple or compound umbel, sometimes modified and reduced to a single flower, as in some *Azorella* spp. Less frequent are panicles or racemes (Mackinlayoideae). In *Eryngium* (Saniculoideae), the stalkless flowers are crowded into a dense head surrounded by spiny bracts. Dichasia are found in the monotypic *Petagnia*, endemic to Sicily, Italy. The characteristic umbel is a flat-topped inflorescence in which each flower stalk (pedicel) arises from the same point on the rays (peduncles), being of different lengths to raise all the flowers to the same height. A compound umbel is one in which the ultimate umbels (*umbellets* or *umbellules*) are themselves arranged in umbels. Bracts are often present at the base of the rays of a compound umbel, forming an involucre, and bracteoles are present at the base of the umbellets, where they form an involucel. The bracts and bracteoles vary in number and size.

The flowers of an umbel and of the component umbellules open in sequence from the

Apiaceae. **1** *Eryngium biscuspidatum* shoot with spiny leaves and bracts, and flowers in a dense head (x⅔). **2** *Eryngium maritimum* barbed fruit—a schizocarp (x6). **3** *Petroselinum crispum* (a) schizocarp—comprising 2 mericarps (x8); (b) cross section of a single mericarp with a central seed and canals (vittae) in the fruit wall (x12). **4** *Psammogeton canescens* schizocarp (x8).

outer whorls to the center. Sexual differentiation in the umbels is marked in some cases, varying from genus to genus, ranging from a few male (staminate) flowers per umbel, to umbels that are composed of nothing but male (staminate) flowers. Moreover, the percentage of perfect (bisexual) flowers in the latter cases is higher in the primary umbels and progressively lower in the successive umbels, until the last umbels produced are almost entirely composed of male flowers. The degree of organization of the umbel is highly developed in some cases. In some umbels, whole flowers, which are functionally unisexual, take on the role of stamens or pistils (e.g., *Astrantia, Petagnia, Sanicula*), or the umbels take on the role of stamens or pistils in more complex inflorescences.

The marginal flowers in the umbel are sometimes irregular, as in *Daucus carota* (Carrot), *Turgenia latifolia*, and *Artedia squamata*, thus serving as an attraction to insect pollinators. The visual impact is also enhanced by an increase in the number and size of the umbellules and a closer spacing of the individual flowers. The bracts forming the involucre may also become enlarged, colored, and showy as in various *Eryngium* and *Bupleurum* species.

Most of the Apiaceae species are pollinated by a wide variety of insects—mostly flies,

The flower of the umbellifers is basically uniform, consisting of 5 white, yellow, blue, or purplish petals; 5 free stamens; a greatly reduced calyx (except in *Eryngium*); an inferior ovary with 2 carpels and 2 locules; and a stylopodium supporting 2 styles. There is a single pendulous, anatropous ovule in each locule. A feature showing considerable variation is the stylopodium—the swollen, often colorful, nectar-secreting base of the styles, which is characteristic of the family. This organ varies widely in shape, size, color, and nectar secretion.

The fruit shows quite a remarkable range of variation. It is a dry schizocarp that splits down a septum (commisure) into 2 single-seeded mericarps that normally remain for some time suspended from a common forked stalk—the carpophore (absent in the Saniculoideae)—finally separating at maturity. The fruits are often compressed, either dorsally or laterally. The endocarp may be woody (Azorelloideae, Mackinlayoideae) or not (Apioideae, most Saniculoideae). The outer surface of the mericarp normally has 5 primary ridges and between them 4 secondary vallecular ridges, all of which run longitudinally from the base to the stylar end of the fruit. In the furrows between the primary ridges, in the ridges themselves, or all over the fruit, oil ducts/cavities or resin canals are often present. Crystals of calcium oxalate may be present in the pericarp. The fruit surface may bear spines, hooks, hairs, or tubercles of various kinds; in some fruits, the lateral ridges are extended into wings. All these features are related to their dispersal strategy: variations in shape, size, color, wings, and spines are numerous; some fruits are remarkable constructions and scarcely bear any resemblance to the basic umbelliferous type, such as those of *Petagnia, Scandix*, and *Thecocarpus*. The seeds (2; 1 per mericarp) have an oily endosperm and a small embryo.

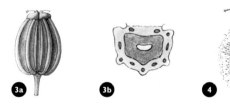

3a   3b   4

mosquitoes, or gnats, but also some of the unspecialized bees, butterflies, and moths. Self fertilization is the normal situation, and self-sterile plants are rare. Pollination is often by geitonogamy (the pistils may be pollinated by the anthers of adjacent flowers in the same umbel). One feature of the family is the small amount of hybridization—few attested records of interspecific hybrids have been recorded.

Distribution The Apiaceae grow in most parts of the world, but are most common in temperate upland areas. The 4 groups into which it may be divided have characteristic distribu-

Apiaceae. 5 *Heracleum sphondylium* (a) leaf shoot bearing large inflorescences—note the outer flowers are irregular and have deeply cut petals (×⅔); (b) regular flower from center of inflorescence (×6). **6** *Daucus carota* schizocarp with spines on the ridges (×6). **7** *Sanicula europaea* schizocarp (×6). **8** *Peucedanum ostruthium* (a) winged schizocarp (×4); (b) cross section of schizocarp (×4).

tions. The largest, the Apioideae, is bipolar but mainly developed in the northern hemisphere in the Old World. The Saniculoideae is also bipolar but better represented in the southern hemisphere than the Apioideae. The Azorelloideae grow in the southern hemisphere in South America, Australia and New Zealand, and Antarctic and sub-Antarctic islands, extending to the Canary Islands and Somalia if the genus *Drusa* is included. The Mackinlayoideae grow mainly in the South Pacific Rim, with *Centella* mainly in South Africa and 3 more species growing in southern tropical Africa; *C. asiatica* is cosmopolitan and pantropical.

About two-thirds of the species of Apiaceae are native to the Old World, but the distribution of the subfamilies in the Old and New Worlds is different, 80% of the Apioideae growing in the Old World, and 60% of the Azorelloideae in the New World (90% of these in South America), where they form a significant component of the flora of temperate southern zones. The subfamily Saniculoideae is almost evenly split between the Old and New Worlds.

Economic uses Different species of umbellifers have a wide range of uses, ranging from food and fodder to spices, poisons, and perfumery. Only the Carrot (*Daucus carota*) is a major vegetable crop and also used as animal feed, with a world production of 23.3 million megatons. The Carrot and Parsnip (*Pastinaca sativa*) are the only umbellifers of international repute as root crops, but other members of the family have been so used, whether cultivated or not, such as the tubers of the Great Earthnut (*Bunium bulbocastanum*) and the Pignut (*Conopodium majus*). In South America, Arracacha or Peruvian Parsnip (*Arracacia xanthorrhiza*), one of the "Lost crops of the Incas," is domesticated in the Andes, where it sometimes replaces potato, and elsewhere in South

Apiaceae. 9 *Centella asiatica* creeping leafy stem bearing axillary flowers (×⅔). **10** *Sanicula europaea* leafy shoot and inflorescences (compound umbels) (×⅔). **11** *Artedia squamata* winged schizocarp (×3). **12** *Mackinlaya macrosciadea* (a) petal and stamen (×12); (b) flower from above (×12).

and Central America. Species of *Lomatium*, the largest genus of umbellifers in the USA, have been true staple foods for several groups of Native Americans in the northwestern part of the country and in western Canada. Stems, petioles, and leaves may be used for food as in Angelica (*Angelica* and *Archangelica* spp.), Celery (*Apium graveolens*), and Lovage (*Levisticum officinale*). Herbs used for flavoring include Chervil (*Anthriscus cerefolium*), Fennel (*Foeniculum vulgare*), and Parsley (*Petroselinum crispum*). Spices derived from fruits or seeds, which contain essential oils, are numerous in the Apiaceae. Examples include Anise (*Pimpinella anisum*), Caraway (*Carum carvi*), Coriander (*Coriandrum sativum*), Cumin (*Cuminum cyminum*), and Dill (*Anethum graveolens*). Several of these are used as flavorings for alcoholic beverages, especially anise. Many umbellifers have medicinal uses, for gastrointestinal complaints, cardiovascular ailments, and as stimulants, sedatives, antispasmodics, and so on. They are also a source of gum resins and resins such as asafetida, derived from *Ferula asafoetida* and other species; another is galbanum, an oleogum resin obtained from *Ferula galbaniflua*. There are many poisonous species, the most celebrated being Hemlock (*Conium maculatum*). A few umbellifers are grown in gardens for their ornamental value. Examples include *Eryngium giganteum* and various cultivars, *Astrantia* (Masterwort), *Bupleurum fruticosum*, *Ferula communis*, and *F. tingitana*, and *Heracleum* species (hogweeds), especially the spectacular *H. mantegazzianum* (Giant Hogweed).

Oleander and Milkweed Family

Apocynaceae is a large, widespread family of woody and herbaceous plants, now including the families Asclepiadaceae and Periplocaceae, which were once recognized as separate families.

Description Trees, shrubs, woody lianas, vines, and herbs, mostly perennial but occasionally annual or even ephemeral, sometimes strongly succulent. Latex usually white, but occasionally red or yellow (e.g., *Aspidosperma*, *Strophanthus*), or clear, most notably in the succulent *Ceropegieae* (formerly *Stapelieae*). Leaves are simple and almost always entire; most commonly opposite, but frequently whorled (e.g., *Allamanda*, *Nerium*); alternate in several genera of the subfamily Rauvolfioideae and sometimes in the subfamily Apocynoideae (e.g., *Adenium*, *Pachypodium*).

Flowers are actinomorphic, bisexual, mostly 5-merous, except for the carpels. The petals are fused at least at the base, the corolla varying from rotate or shallowly campanulate to tubular or funnel-shaped, the lobes often twisted in bud and overlapping to the left or right, but sometimes valvate.

Coronal structures are often present either on the corolla or on the gynostegium, which is formed from

Apocynaceae. 1 *Vinca minor* (Periwinkle) (a) shoot with opposite leaves and solitary flower (x⅔); (b) part of dissected flower showing epipetalous stamens and thickened hairy stylar head (x3); (c) paired fruits (x1). **2** *Plumeria rubra* (Frangipani) (a) flower (x1); (b) leaf (x1).

Apocynaceae. **3** *Allamanda cathartica* (a) flowering shoot (×1); (b) dehiscing fruit (×1). **4** *Nerium oleander* (Oleander) (a) flowering shoot (×⅔); (b) dissected flower with 2 corolla lobes removed, showing the corona lobes at the mouth of the corolla tube and the apically prolonged anthers united at the tips (×1½).

the fusion of the stamens and the stylar head (the stylar head is free from the stamens in Rauvolfioideae). Stamens are inserted on the corolla tube or at its base, the filaments free or forming a tube, and the anthers often have specialized marginal wings or guide rails.

Pollen is shed as single grains, tetrads, or pollinia. The ovary is superior to subinferior, syncarpous, with 2 carpels, or more commonly apocarpous with 2 carpels (rarely more) that fuse apically to form a stylar head with the stigmatic surfaces on the underside.

Secretions from the stylar head are sticky and amorphous, or formed into 5 discrete spoonlike or cliplike structures, which assist in pollen transport.

Generally, the fruits are a pair of ventrally dehiscent follicles, but follicles are commonly single through abortion and, in *Lepinia*, up to

Apocynaceae. 5 *Periploca graeca* (a) shoot with opposite leaves and axillary inflorescence (x⅔); (b) flower with coiled corona lobes and hairy anthers (x3); (c) fruit, comprising a pair of follicles (x⅔).

5 slender follicles remain fused apically to form a cage. Drupes, berries, and capsules occur in the subfamily Rauvolfioideae.

Distribution The Apocynaceae are pantropical and subtropical, with the 2 predominantly woody subfamilies being most diverse in wetter biomes, such as the tropical rain forests and swamps of India and Malaya, and the 3 largely herbaceous subfamilies being most diverse in seasonally dry environments; a few genera in this family, such as *Vinca*, extend into temperate regions.

Economic uses Cardiac glycosides are obtained from many genera, e.g., *Strophanthus* (used locally as an arrow poison). *Rauvolfia* produces reserpine and rescinnamine (used to treat certain mental illnesses). *Catharanthus roseus* (Madagascar Periwinkle) yields 2 important cancer drugs—vinblastine and vincristine—used to treat childhood leukaemia and Hodgkins' disease. *Hoodia gordonii*, used by Kalahari bushmen as an appetite suppressant, has been commercialized for the treatment of obesity. Many members of the family are used in folk medicines. Latex or India rub-

ber is valuable and is extracted from *Hancornia speciosa*, *Funtumia elastica*, and species of *Landolphia*. *Alstonia scholaris* is an important timber tree in Southeast Asia, and wood from *Aspidosperma* is particularly resistant to decay. Ornamentals widely planted in tropical regions include *Allamanda cathartica*, *Cryptostegia*, *Hoya* (Wax Plant), and *Plumeria* (Frangipani). *Asclepias* (milkweeds), *Araujia* (Cruel Plant), *Nerium oleander* (Oleander), *Stephanotis*, and *Vinca* (periwinkles) are popular in temperate regions, as are succulent genera such as *Caralluma*, *Ceropegia*, *Orbea*, and *Stapelia*.

Apocynaceae. 6 *Asclepias curassavica* (Butterfly Plant) (a) leafy shoot with opposite leaves and extra-axillary inflorescence (x⅔); (b) flower with orange reflexed corolla lobes and yellow staminal corona obscuring the gynostegium (x3); (c) upper part of gynostegium with corona lobes removed to show anthers with thickened lateral margins forming guide rails, and triangular anther appendages curved over top of stylar head (x10); (d) pollinarium, formed of 2 pollinia linked by a pair of slender translator arms to the cliplike corpusculum (x14); (e) seed with tuft of hairs (x10). **7** *Ceropegia stapeliiformis* semisucculent shoot with a cluster of tubular trap-flowers (x⅔).

Aquifoliaceae. 1 *Ilex aquifolium* (a) leafy shoot and fruits (x⅔); (b) female flower with 4 staminodes (x4); (c) male flower with 4 stamens alternating with the petals (x4); (d) corolla of male flower opened out, showing stamens attached at the base (x4); (e) gynoecium with sessile stigma (x4). **2** *I. anomala* (a) flowering shoot (x⅔); (b) bisexual flower (x3); (c) perianth opened out, showing stamens fused to the base of the perianth tube and alternating with the lobes (x3); (d) fruit—a berry (x4). **3** *I. paraguaensis* (a) leafy shoot with fruits (x⅔); (b) fruit with wall cut away, showing 4 hard pyrenes each containing a single seed (x4).

Hollies and Yerba Maté

A widespread, but mainly tropical, family of trees and shrubby plants with characteristic toothed leaves. This family is distributed worldwide, and many species are grown for their foliage and berries as ornamentals.

Description Shrubs or small trees, sometimes scandent or epiphytic, usually evergreen, rarely deciduous. Leaves alternate; rarely opposite or nearly so; simple; often leathery; with prickly dentate margins, although heterophylly is found in some species, whereby both dentate or entire leaves occur, either on the same or on separate plants.

Flowers are actinomorphic; unisexual (plants dioecious); small and inconspicuous; white, cream, greenish-white, and yellow, in axillary cymose, racemose, or subumbellate inflorescences. The sepals are 4–5 or 6–8, valvate, more or less connate at the base. The petals are 4–5, rarely 6–9 or more, usually connate the base, less frequently distinct. The stamens are usually as numerous as the petals. Staminodes occur in the pistillate flowers and a pistillode in the staminate flowers. The ovary is superior, of (2–3)4–5 or more united carpels; as many locules as carpels, the locules with a single terminal, sometimes minute, style; the placentation is apical-axile, with 1 or rarely 2 pendulous, usually anatropous, ovules per locule.

The fruit is a drupe containing 1–6 or more hard pyrenes; seeds 1–6, with copious endosperm.

Distribution The single genus *Ilex*, with more than 400 species, has a more or less worldwide distribution, but with the greatest diversity of species in tropical South America and Asia (mainly in Southeast Asia) and with a poor representation in Africa (1 sp.) and northern tropical Australia (1 sp.).

The family extends into temperate regions of North America, Europe, and Asia, and a few species occur on the islands of the Azores, the Canaries, the Caribbean, Hawaii, Madeira, and Tahiti.

Economic uses Many *Ilex* species are grown as ornamentals (hollies) for their foliage and berries. Beverages are made from the leaves and other aerial parts of many species, most notably those of *I. paraguariensis*, which is used in Argentina, southern Brazil, Paraguay, and Uruguay to prepare a popular beverage called yerba maté. The appeal of the beverage lies in its stimulative properties, which is due to the plant's caffeine and theobromine content.

Other species are used in traditional medicines in Africa, Asia, Europe, and America. The wood of a limited number of species of *Ilex* is much valued for carving, furniture, and tools.

1a

Ivies and Ginseng

The Araliaceae is a medium-sized, largely tropical, family of mainly trees or shrubs, characterized by their often compound leaves and compound inflorescences, with small regular flowers and drupaceous fruits.

Description The Araliacae consists of small to medium, usually evergreen, trees or shrubs, occasionally climbers (*Hedera*) or rhizomatous herbs (*Aralia*). The leaves are usually alternate and often large and pinnately to palmately compound and sometimes crowded toward the end of the shoots in flushes; frequently covered with stellate or dendroid hairs; the stipules are small and poorly developed or conspicuous. In those species with a climbing habit, aerial roots are modified for clinging to the supporting structures. The inflorescences are umbels, heads, or racemes, or spikes. The flowers are actinomorphic, small, often greenish or whitish, bisexual or unisexual. The calyx is small, with 4 or 5 teeth, fused to the ovary. Petals 5–10(–12), free or partially fused. The stamens are free, equal in number to the petals, and alternate with them, and attached to a more or less fleshy, nectariferous disk, which surmounts the ovary. The ovary is inferior (rarely superior, as in *Tetraplasandra*), with the disk surrounding the styles, which are free or fused into a column. The ovary has (2–)5–10(–12) fused carpels, with (1)2–5(–10) locules, each with a single, pendulous ovule. The fruit is drupaceous, or less frequently baccate, containing 2–5 seeds, each with copious endosperm and a small embryo, rarely dry.

Distribution The Araliaceae is distributed throughout much of the world in both temperate and tropical regions, although the family is mainly tropical. In terms of generic diversity, the chief centers are located in eastern and southeastern Asia, the Pacific and Indian Ocean basins and, in terms of species, the Americas and Indo-Pacific regions.

Economic uses Economically, the family is important for the plants of the ginseng group, which include American Ginseng (*Panax quinquefolia*), Oriental Ginseng (*P. pseudoginseng*), and Tienchi-ginseng (*P. notoginseng*), whose thickened roots are the source of complex mixtures of triterpenoid saponins, which possess hormonal activity. Root extracts are reputed to have stimulant, tonic, and aphrodisiac properties. The word *Panax* is derived from the Greek *panakeia*, which means "universal remedy," hence "panacea." Chinese rice paper is obtained from the pith of *Tetrapanax papyrifera*. Medicinal extracts have also been obtained from a number of Aralia spp., e.g., *A. cordata* and *A. racemosa*. The family includes a number of ornamentals with attractive foliage, such as *Schefflera* (*Dizygotheca*) *elegantissima*, *S. arboricola*, and some ivies, in particular the ornamental cultivars of *Hedera helix* and the Canary Island ivy (*H. canariensis*). *Fatsia japonica* is a house plant and outdoor ornamental, with its glossy green leaves. Bush ivy (x *Fatshedera lizei*) is a bigeneric hybrid of the houseplant Japanese fatsia (*Fatsia japonica* "Moseri") and Irish ivy (*Hedera helix* var. *hibernica*). It is grown as a house plant or outdoor plant, often used for ground cover. Shrubby species from the genera *Polyscias* and *Acanthopanax* are grown as garden ornamentals.

Araliaceae. 1 *Tetraplasandra hawaiensis* (a) cross section of fruit (×2); (b) flower with caplike corolla, which falls off (×2). **2** *Hydrocotyle vulgaris* (a) schizocarp (×10); (b) cross section of schizocarp, showing flattened appearance, and a narrow wall (commisure) between the 2 single-seeded mericarps, each with prominent ridges (×10). **3** *Cussonia kirkii* (a) portion of stem crowned by fruiting head (×⅔); (b) part of inflorescence (×⅔); (c) fruit (×⅔). **4** *Acanthopanax henryi* (a) shoot with stipulate trifoliolate leaves, and young and mature fruits (×⅔); (b) vertical section of ovary (×3). **5** *Aralia scopulorum* pinnate leaf (×⅔). **6** *Hedera helix* (a) climbing shoot with juvenile leaves and adventitious roots (×⅔); (b) shoot with adult leaves and flowers in umbels (×⅔); (c) cross section of fruit (×2); (d) flower (×3).

Sunflower Family

The Asteraceae (Compositae) is one of the largest and best-known families of flowering plants and certainly the largest of the dicotyledonous families, with a worldwide distribution, excluding the Antarctic mainland.

Description Most of the Asteraceae are annual or perennial herbs; subshrubs or shrubs; climbers (e.g., *Mikania* spp. and *Mutisia* spp.) or lianes; small or rarely large trees; epiphytes (e.g., *Gongrostylus*, *Neomirandea*); true aquatics (e.g., *Sclerolepis*, *Shinnersia*, *Trichocoronis*) are rare. Rootstocks fibrous and fleshy, sometimes with a distinct woody perennating rootstock (xylopodium). Stem usually unarmed, rarely spiny (e.g., in most members of the tribe Barnadesioideae and in few Mutisieae); spiny leaves are relatively common and typical in the tribe Cardueae.

The Asteraceae are characterized by the presence of resin canals (in all except most members of the tribe Lactuceae) or laticifers (in all Lactuceae) and latex sacs (e.g., a few genera of Cardueae and Arctotideae). Characteristic biochemical features include the presence of the polysaccharide inulin, instead of starch, in the subterranean parts (e.g., *Helianthus tuberosus*) and fatty oils in the seeds.

The leaves are alternate or opposite, rarely whorled, and without stipules; they are usually simple, rarely compound, pinnately or palmately veined, and either sessile or petiolate, sometimes with

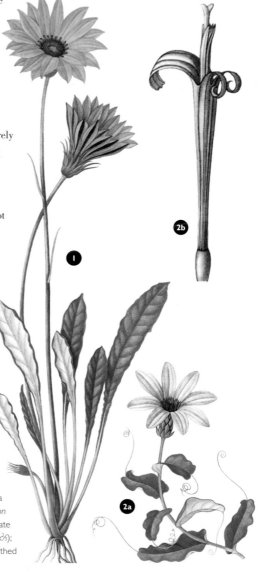

Asteraceae (Compositae). I *Gazania linearis*, a low-growing perennial herb, producing a basal rosette of leaves and terminal radiate (i.e., outer ray and inner disk florets) flower heads (capitula) that are subtended by a series of green phyllaries (x⅔). **2** *Mutisia oligodon* (a) a scrambling perennial herb, showing alternate leaves with tendrils and a terminal capitulum (x⅔); (b) hermaphrodite bilabiate floret with a 3-toothed outer lip and a 2-toothed inner lip (x3).

an expanded, sheathing or auriculate, base; they are often lobed or variously toothed, rarely succulent, rarely ending in a tendril (e.g., *Mutisia* spp.), and rarely reduced to scales and falling rapidly (e.g., *Aphylloclados*).

The headlike capitulum is one of the most characteristic features of the Asteraceae. It is an inflorescence made up of many small individual flowers (florets) and surrounded by an involucre of protective bracts. The whole structure resembles a single flower and is usually referred to as such by the layman. The capitula themselves, however, are cymosely arranged in the overall inflorescence, which is variable in size, shape, construction, number of capitula, and disposition on the plant.

Several types of capitula can be distinguished by the types, arrangement, and sex of florets within them. Homogamous capitula contain all hermaphrodite, or more rarely, all male (staminate) or all female (pistillate) florets. Unisexual capitula may be on the same plant (e.g., *Ambrosia*, *Xanthium*) or on different plants (e.g., *Baccharis*, *Gochnatia* spp., some Inuleae). Homogamous capitula may be discoid (with all florets tubular and actinomorphic), ligulate (with all florets ligulate), or bilabiate (with all florets bilabiate), and the florets are all hermaphrodite, all male, or all female. Heterogamous capitula contain outer florets that are female (pistillate) or sterile and inner florets, which are usually hermaphrodite.

Within the capitula, the florets are arranged racemosely or indeterminately, the outer opening first; this sequence may be unclear in

Asteraceae (Compositae).

3 *Cichorium intybus* (endive) (a) flowering shoot with capitula of ligulate florets only (×⅔); (b) ligulate floret (×2); (c) ligulate floret with corolla removed to show stamens inserted in the corolla tube and anthers united in a tube around the style (×4). **4** *Liatris graminifolia* (a) flowering shoot bearing discoid capitula (i.e., only with disk florets) (×⅔); (b) disk floret with a regular 5-lobed corolla (×4). **5** *Centaurea montana* leaf and terminal radiant capitulum of disk florets, the outer ones being sterile and enlarged (×⅔).

Asteraceae (Compositae). 6 *Ursinia speciosa*
shoot bearing pinnatisect (deeply cut) leaves
and radiate capitulum (x⅔). **7** *Bellis perennis*
showing basal rosette of leaves and solitary
radiate capitula (x⅔). **8** *Helianthus giganteus*
(a) female ray floret (x4); (b) hermaphrodite
disk floret (x6); (c) disk floret opened out (x6).

compound and secondary inflorescences. Morphologically, florets can be divided into 2 types: those with actinomorphic corollas that are typically disk florets in radiate capitula, or florets found throughout discoid capitula; and those with zygomorphic corollas. Florets with zygomorphic corollas are of several types: bilabiate (e.g., many Mutisieae), pseudobilabiate (e.g., Barnadesieae), rayed, or ligulate (e.g., all Lactuceae).

Predominantly, members of the Asteraceae have 5 connate anthers, forming a tube (surrounding the style), and dehisce their pollen introrsely (i.e., into the tube); rarely are there genera in which the anthers are free. The anthers may be dorsifixed (fixed to the filaments by their upper surface), e.g., subfamily Cichorioideae, with pollen grains within the anthers below the level of attachment; or basifixed (fixed at their bases), e.g., subfamily Asteroideae, with all the pollen grains above the insertion. In many cases, the anthers are elongated below the point of filament insertion and have sterile tails at the base of the thecae. The filaments are inserted basally inside the corolla tube, higher up in the tube or sometimes just beneath the sinus of the corolla lobes, and are usually glabrous, rarely papillose or even hairy; rarely are the filaments fused together (e.g., some *Barnadesia* spp.). A filament, or anther, collar (found just below the point of insertion on the anther) is formed from thicker-walled cells and may be conspicuous and diagnostic in many groups (e.g., the Eupatorieae).

Typically, the style is divided into 2 style arms, with the stigmatic surface on their inner surfaces. Both the style and style arms may be hairy, papillose, or glabrous externally. The anthers ripen and dehisce the pollen into the anther cylinder before the styles. As they mature and elongate, thick styles usually push the pollen out of the anther tube; thinner and hairy or papillose styles and style arms brush, or sweep, the pollen through the tube. The style arms may have characteristic sterile appendages, which may be well developed (e.g., the Eupatorieae). The stigmatic papillae are often conspicuous and arranged along the margins or the inner surfaces of the style arms,

or they are inconspicuous and either marginal or all over the inner surface. The style arms commonly separate in maturity to expose the stigmatic surfaces and may curve back to the pollen on top of the anther tube of the same floret to enable self-pollination if they are self-compatible.

The single-seeded fruit (the seed has no endosperm and a straight embryo) is indehiscent, nearly always dry, and is termed a cypsela as it develops from an inferior ovary and is thus surrounded by other floral tissues in addition to the ovary wall, although commonly referred to as an achene. It may be angular, rounded, variously compressed, or curved, ornamented or winged in various ways, glabrous or variously pubescent or glandular; rarely it is a drupe, with fleshy endocarp (e.g., *Chrysanthemoides*). Basally cypselas commonly have a carpopodium, the basal attachment area to the receptacle, whose form is a useful diagnostic character in some groups (e.g., the Eupatorieae); rarely (e.g., some Cardueae) is it replaced by an elaiosome. It often has an apical pappus (considered a modified calyx) made up of smooth, barbellate, or plumose fine hairs, bristles, scales, or awns (sometimes more or less fused together), which acts as an aid to fruit dispersal, although it is sometimes caducous or deciduous; alternatively, it may be completely lacking.

Distribution The family has a worldwide distribution, although absent from the Antarctic mainland. These flowering plants are a significant element in the floras of the semiarid regions of the tropics and subtropics, such as the Mediterranean region; Mexico; southern Africa; and the woodland, wooded grassland, grassland, and bush ecosystems of Africa, South America, and Australia. They are also abundant in arctic, arctic-alpine, temperate, and montane floras throughout the world but poorly represented in tropical rain forests. About half the species of the Asteraceae are native to the Old World and half to the New World. Generally speaking, the Barnadesieae are restricted to South America, the Liabeae to the Neotropics, the Arctotideae are mostly South African, the Heliantheae and Eupatorieae are predominantly New World, and the highest concentrations of the Cardueae are in the Old World and predominantly Eurasian.

Economic uses The importance of the Asteraceae is largely from an incalculable indirect economic value based on its contribution to the biodiversity of drier vegetation types throughout the world, especially in the temperate zones, subtropics, and tropics, where it at times approaches 10 to 15% of some floras. The direct economic importance of the family is relatively small and is based largely on a few food plants, limited sources of raw materials, medicinal and drug plants, several ornamentals and plants of horticultural interest, contrasted with the economics of often pernicious

weeds and poisonous plants. Commercially, *Lactuca sativa* (lettuce) is the most important food plant, although several others are relatively widely eaten, extracts drunk, or used as flavorings, including *Cichorium endivia* (endive), *C. intybus* (chicory), *Cynara cardunculus* (cardoon, globe artichoke), *Helianthus tuberosus* (Jerusalem artichoke), *Scorzonera hispanica*, and *Tragoponon porifolius* (salsify); *Artemisia dracunculus* (tarragon) is used as a culinary herb. Oil seed crops include *Carthamus tinctorius* (safflower), *Guizotia abyssinica* (Niger seed), and *Helianthus annuus* (Sun-

Asteraceae (Compositae).
9 *Helianthus angustifolius* flowering shoot (x⅔).
10 *Leontopodium haplophylloides* flowering shoot (x2).

flower). The family is widely used in folk medicine, and herbal remedies are common, including extracts from *Anthemis nobilis* (chamomile), *Arnica montana* (arnica), *Calendula officinalis* (calendula), *Echinacea purpurea*, *Tanacetum vulgare* (tansy), among many others. The source of natural pyrethrum is *Tanacetum cinerariifolium*, and *Artemisia annua* is the source of artemisenin, a useful antimalarial. *Artemisia absinthium* is the source of the essential oil used to flavor the liqueur absinthe. Both *Parthenium argentatum* (guayule) and *Taraxacum bicorne* have been used as minor alternative sources of latex to produce rubber.

The Asteraceae feature extensively in gardens throughout the world as ornamentals. A wide range of horticultural species is grown both under glass, or as herbaceous or shrubby garden plants throughout the world, many also important as cut flowers. These include *Achillea* (yarrow, sneezewort), *Ageratum conyzoides*, *A. houstonianum*, *Arctotis*, *Argyranthemum*, *Artemisia* (Wormwood), *Bellis* (daisy), *Bidens*, *Brachyglottis*, *Calendula officinalis* (Pot Marigold), *Callistephus* (China Aster), *Centaurea* (Cornflower, Knapweed), *Chrysanthemum*, *Coreopsis*, *Cosmos*, *Dahlia*, *Echinops* (Globe Thistle), *Eupatorium*, *Euryops*, *Felicia*, *Gaillardia*, *Gazania*, *Gerbera*, *Helenium*, *Helianthus* (Sunflower), *Helichrysum*, *Leucanthemum* (Ox-eye Daisy, Shasta Daisy), *Liatris*, *Ligularia*, *Olearia*, *Osteospermum*, *Pericallis* (Florists' Cineraria), *Ratibida*, *Rudbeckia* (cone flower), *Santolina* (Cotton Lavender), *Solidago* (Golden Rod), *Stokesia* (Stokes' Aster), *Symphiotrichum* (garden asters, Michaelmas Daisy), *Tagetes* (African and French Marigolds), *Tanacetum* (Feverfew, Tansy), *Xeranthemum*, *Xerochrysum* (Everlastings), and *Zinnia*. Thousands of cultivars can be found in *Callistephus*, *Chrysanthemum*, and *Dahlia*. Succulent plant enthusiasts grow several species of *Kleinia*, *Othonna*, and *Senecio*.

The family contains a number of weedy species, some of which are fast becoming pantropical in distribution. A number are considered pernicious or noxious, including *Ageratina riparia*, *Ageratum conyzoides*, *Ambrosia artemisiifolia*, *Bidens pilosa* (Black Jack), *Chondrilla juncea* (Skeleton Weed), *Chrysanthemoides monilifera*, *Cirsium arvense*, *C. vulgare* and *Carduus nutans* (thistles), *Chromolaena odorata* (Siam Weed), *Mikania micrantha* (Mile-a-minute Weed), *Crassocephalum crepidioides*, *Helichrysum kraussii*, various *Senecio* spp., *Silybum marianum*, *Sonchus oleraceus* (Sowthistle), *Taraxacum* spp. (dandelions), *Xanthium spinosum*, and *X. strumarium* (Cocklebur). Several *Senecio* species are poisonous and serious weeds of pasture. They are responsible for more deaths of domestic stock than all other poisonous plants together. The windborne pollen of the ragweeds *Ambrosia artemisiifolia* and *A. trifida* is one of the main causes of hay fever in the regions of North America where these species occur. It is also apparent that some New World plants are potential weeds, having relatively recently gained a foothold in Australia. These include *Praxelis clematidea* and *Synedrellopsis grisebachii*.

Asteraceae (Compositae).
11 *Argyranthemum broussonetti* flowering shoot (×2).

Begoniaceae. I *Begonia rex* (a) habit showing leaves with stipules and axillary inflorescences (x⅓); (b) young leaf with one side larger than the other—a characteristic feature (x1); (c) male flower buds (x1); (d) male flower showing 4 perianth segments and cluster of stamens each with an elongated connective (x1); (e) female flowers showing 5 perianth segments (x⅔); (f) young winged fruit with persistent styles that are fused at the base and bear twisted, papillose stigmatic surfaces (x2); (g) cross section of young winged fruit with 2 chambers and numerous seeds on branched, axile placentas (x2).

Begonia Family

A family of widely cultivated, mainly semisucculent herbs, with asymmetrical leaves. They are often grown for their attractive, fleshy leaves and waxy flowers. The Begonia family grows mainly in the tropics.

Description These flowering plants are usually semisucculent herbs up to 1 m high, sometimes acaulescent, sometimes softly woody and up to 4 m, occasionally climbing to more than 10 m, with woody stems and aerial roots.

The leaves are alternate, with conspicuous stipules. The lamina is variable in shape but is characteristically asymmetrical and is sometimes shallowly to deeply lobed or rarely with separate leaflets, the margins serrate.

The inflorescence is a compact to lax and broad (to 45 cm) cyme. The flowers are unisexual (plants monoecious), actinomorphic, or zygomorphic, and the perianth is not clearly differentiated into sepals and petals.

The male flowers have (2)4(5) tepals, usually in unequal opposite pairs, and many stamens or only 4 in sect. *Begoniella*, united into a column in sect. The female flowers have 4–5(–9) tepals or 10 in *Hillebrandia*, in sect. *Symbegonia* fused into a tube for most of their length.

The ovary is inferior or in *Hillebrandia* semi-inferior, with (2)3–8 locules, usually sharply angled and often winged. Female flowers have 2–6 styles that are free or connate and often twisted and often bifid or multifid. Placentation is axile and lobed or not, or rarely parietal (as in *Hillebrandia*), and there are many ovules.

The fruit is a capsule or berry, with regular or irregular dehiscence to release the numerous minute seeds.

Distribution With some 1,400 spp., *Begonia* is confined largely to the tropics. It is absent from the Americas north of Mexico (although 1 sp. is naturalized in Florida), from Europe and North Africa, from northern temperate Asia (extending to the Ryukyu Islands of Japan), and from Australasia. There are about 650 spp. in Asia, about 600 spp. in the Americas, and about 140 spp. in tropical and southern Africa.

The single species of *Hillebrandia* is confined to Hawaii. They are commonly in wet habitats such as forest understory and are often epiphytic or lithophytic.

Economic uses With its asymmetrical and brightly colored leaves, *Begonia* is extensively cultivated in temperate regions as a house plant or greenhouse plant or for summer bedding out of doors. It is estimated that some 10,000 cultivars have been recognized.

The leaves have been cooked as a vegetable in Malesia, and some local medicinal uses have been recorded.

1b

Alders, Birches, Hazels, and Hornbeams

A family of trees and shrubs that includes the alders (*Alnus*), birches (*Betula*), hazels (*Corylus*), and hornbeams (*Carpinus*). The birches are an important source of a range of hardwood timbers.

Description Small, anemophilous trees or shrubs, often with smooth bark exfoliating in large, thin layers. The leaves are simple, alternate, 2- to 3-ranked, deciduous and with stipules, the lamina sometimes lobed, and the margins dentate to nearly entire. The flowers are unisexual (plants dioecious), in 1- to 3-flowered clusters, adhering to their bracts. The staminate flowers are in pendulous, conspicuously bracteate, cylindrical catkins comprising 1- to 3-flowered clusters. The pistillate flowers are borne on a stiff axis, in erect to pendulous, bracteate catkins or in 2- to 3-flowered clusters subtended by a leafy involucre. The perianth, when present, is of a variable number of scale-like segments. The staminate flowers have (1–)4–6(–12) stamens, the anthers 2-celled, and without traces of vestigial carpels. The pistillate flowers are highly reduced, consisting of a single inferior ovary of 2 fused carpels and completely lacking vestigial stamens. The fruit is a single-seeded nut, which is often winged for wind-dispersal, maturing in late summer or the fall. The seeds have no endosperm and a straight embryo.

Distribution The family occurs mainly in boreal and cool temperate regions. Some species grow on tropical mountain ranges through Central America and the Andes to Argentina.

Economic uses The birches provide valuable hardwood timbers. *Betula alleghaniensis* is important in North America, and in Europe, *B. pendula* and *B. pubescens* are used for boxes, plywood, and in turnery. The bark of *B. papyrifera* is also used by Native Americans for making canoes and fancy goods. Branchlets of *Betula* spp. are used to make the besom brushes used by gardeners. *Alnus rubra* also provides a valuable timber, being a good imitation of mahogany. Both genera provide high-grade charcoal. *Ostrya* has extremely hard wood used for making mallets. Cobnuts, filberts, or hazelnuts, are produced by species of *Corylus*. Birches, hazels, and hornbeams are cultivated as ornamentals, and *Alnus* is used to aid soil nitrification.

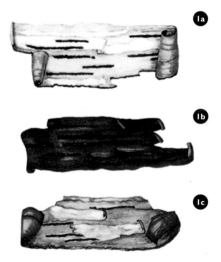

Betulaceae. 1 Barks of various birch trees (a) *Betula pendula*, (b) *B. humilis*, (c) *Betula* sp. (x⅔). **2** *Betula pendula* (a) habit showing typical drooping shoots; (b) leafy shoot with serrate, alternate entire leaves and immature male inflorescences (catkins) (x⅔); (c) pendulous mature male catkins (x⅔); (d) leaves and fruiting catkins (x⅔). **3** *Alnus glutinosa* (a) habit; (b) male catkins (x⅔); (c) shoot with (from base) old fruiting cones, immature cones and young male catkins (x⅔).

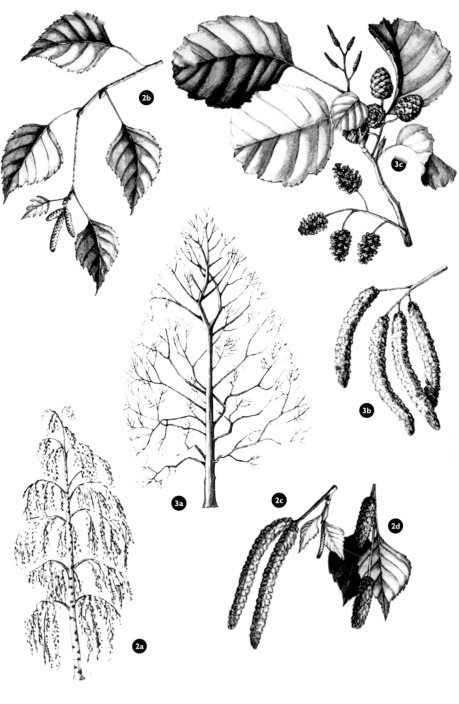

2b

3c

3b

3a

2c

2d

2a

39

Bignoniaceae. 1 *Catalpa ovata* (a) shoot bearing flowers in a terminal panicle and simple opposite leaves (x⅔); (b) half flower with fertile and infertile stamens (x1½); (c) stamen with divergent anthers (x2½); (d) part of fruit (x⅔); (e) seed bearing tufts of hair (x1½). **2** *Bignonia capreolata* flowering shoot with compound leaves in which the terminal leaflet is tendril-like (x⅔). **3** *Eccremocarpus scaber* (a) dehiscing fruit (x⅔); (b) cross section of ovary (x5). **4** *Parmentiera cereifera* base of fleshy indehiscent fruit in cross section showing numerous seeds (x⅔). **5** *Pithecoctenium aubletii* vertical section of fruit (x⅔).

Trumpet Vines, Jacarandas, and Catalpas

A family of trees, shrubs, and climbers, often with tendrils, rarely herbaceous, and mostly tropical and subtropical. They grow mainly in pantropical and subtropical regions and are often raised as ornamentals.

Description About half of all species are trees or shrubs while most of the others are woody climbers. *Incarvillea* and *Argylia* include perennial herbs, and *Tourrettia* is a herbaceous climber. Leaves are usually opposite but sometimes whorled or in a few genera alternate and compound or sometimes (e.g., *Catalpa*) simple. Compound leaves are either palmate or pinnate (often appearing 3-foliate), and in climbing South American genera the terminal leaflets of pinnate leaves are often modified to simple or branched tendrils. The flowers are solitary or in axillary or terminal racemes. The calyx is composed of 5 fused sepals, sometimes bilabiate or spathaceous to truncate or calyptrate, occasionally campanulate with a double margin. The corolla consists of 5 fused petals, usually tubular and bilabiate, or with rotate subequal lobes. Stamens are usually 5 and attached in the corolla tube, rarely 2 fertile and 3 staminodial. The ovary is bicarpellate and usually 2-locular. The fruit is a capsule dehiscing by 2 valves either loculicidally or (Oroxyleae) septicidally, or sometimes (e.g., *Kigelia*) fleshy and indehiscent. The seeds are numerous, usually flat and winged, but sometimes thicker and wingless.

Distribution The family is pantropical and subtropical with a few genera in temperate parts of North America, Asia, and the southern hemisphere. They often occupy a variety of wet forest habitats but also grow in wet or dry woodland or even subdesert conditions. The herbaceous genera *Incarvillea* and *Argylia* grow in montane grassy habitats in temperate Asia and the Andes, respectively. The tribes show interesting continental preferences: thus the Tecomeae are widespread in both Old and New World, whereas the mostly climbing Bignonieae are confined to the New World. The Coleeae grow in Africa and especially Madagascar, and the Crescentieae are present in Central and South America.

Economic uses Bignoniaceae provides many showy trees and climbers often cultivated as ornamentals. In temperate regions, *Catalpa* (Indian Bean Trees) and the climbers *Campsis radicans* (Trumpet Vine) and *Bignonia capreolata* (Trumpet Flower) from North America, *Pandorea* (Bower of Beauty) from Australia, and *Podranea* (Port St. John Creeper) and the shrub *Tecomaria* (Cape Honeysuckle) from South Africa, are often cultivated. Tropical Africa provides *Spathodea* (Flame of the Forest), *Fernandoa*, *Markhamia*, and *Stereospermum*, while *Kigelia* ("sausage trees") is well known to tourists. From Asia come other *Catalpa* spp., *Millingtonia* (Indian Cork Tree), *Radermachera*, and *Tecomanthe*, and from South America *Jacaranda mimosifolia*, *Tecoma* (Golden Bells), and *Tabebuia*, including some of the most spectacular flowering trees of the neotropics, as well as the climbing genera *Pyrostegia* (Flaming Vine), *Clytostoma* (Argentine Trumpet Vine), *Pithecoctenium* (Monkey's Hairbrush), *Crescentia* (Calabash), and *Eccremocarpus* (Glory Flower). Species of *Incarvillea* are sometimes grown as herbaceous perennials. Other useful products include timber from *Tabebuia* and ropes from some of the woody climbers. *Crescentia* fruits provide calabashes for carrying water or for use as maracas. Other genera produce condiments, red dyes for baskets, and various plant extracts used against major diseases, e.g., Pau d'arco, an extract of the bark of *Tabebuia impetiginosa* from tropical South America, commonly used as a food supplement and herbal remedy.

Borage and Forget-Me-Not Family

The Boraginaceae family ranges from large trees in tropical regions to annual herbs that grow worldwide in a wide range of habitats, usually with conspicuous stiff hairs mounted on bulbous bases.

Description Annual or perennial herbs to shrubs, occasionally woody climbers, or large forest trees. Vegetative parts characteristically bear conspicuous stiff hairs that are usually unicellular and mounted on a swollen multicellular base embedded in the epidermis, glabrous plants being rare (e.g., *Cerinthe*, some woody genera). The leaves are alternate or sometimes the lower ones opposite, or sometimes (some *Tournefortia*) all opposite, simple with entire or subentire margins, rarely serrate (some woody species), shallowly lobed (*Coldenia*) or serrate-spinulose (*Halgania*), rarely succulent (*Heliotropium curassavicum*). The inflorescence is characteristically a lax to condensed, 1-sided, terminal or axillary, cincinnate cyme, or occasionally the flowers are solitary in leaf axils. The flowers are hypogynous, gamopetalous, and actinomorphic or sometimes (*Echium*) slightly zygomorphic, usually 5-merous, sometimes unisexual (plants dioecious, *Cordia*), frequently heterostylous. The calyx lobes are free or fused and sometimes conspicuously accrescent (in *Sacellium, Auxemma, Cordia, Trichodesma*). The corolla is usually tubular to trumpet-shaped, rarely campanulate, sometimes bearing 5 appendages in the throat. The stamens are attached to the corolla tube. The ovary is bicarpellate, entire to deeply 4-lobed, with 1, 2, or 4 locules and with a terminal or gynobasic (subfamily Boraginoideae) style with 1, 2, or 4 stigmas. The ovules are usually 1 per locule and subbasal. The fruit may be a drupe with 1–4 pyrenes but is more often a schizocarp splitting into four 1-seeded nutlets, or is rarely a dehiscent capsule.

Distribution The tree genera are pantropical and subtropical, while the herbaceous genera are worldwide although particularly abundant in the Mediterranean region and warm-temperate Asia. They grow in a wide range of habitats from sea level to more than 4,000 m.

Economic uses The tropical trees of Cordioideae and Ehretioideae provide timber for construction and edible fruits, and some species are cultivated as decorative shrubs. Rhizomes of *Alkanna tinctoria*, and *Lithospermum* and *Onosma* spp. have been used for red and purple dyes. Medicinal uses are uncommon, although *Lobostemon* is used in dressings for sores in South Africa, and *Lithospermum ruderale* has been used locally as a contraceptive. *Borago* (Borage) is grown as a potherb for its edible leaves. *Symphytum* may also be eaten and is used as a forage plant. Several genera are valued by beekeepers for honey production. Many herbaceous genera are cultivated as garden ornamentals, especially *Myosotis* (Forget-Me-Not), *Symphytum* (Comfrey), *Pulmonaria, Lithospermum, Omphalodes, Onosma, Heliotropium. Echium plantagineum* (Salvation Jane or Paterson's Curse) is an aggressive weed in Australia.

Boraginaceae. 1 *Echium vulgare* (a) inflorescence of irregular flowers (x⅔); (b) flower dissected to show epipetalous stamens and 4-lobed ovary with a thin, gynobasic style which is forked at its tip (x2). **2** *Cerinthe major* (a) leafy shoot and inflorescence (x⅔); (b) corolla opened out to show 5 epipetalous stamens (x2); (c) calyx and 4-lobed gynoecium with a gynobasic style, that is, arising from the base of the ovary between the lobes (x2). **3** *Anchusa officinalis* leafy shoot and inflorescence of regular flowers (x⅔). **4** *Heliotropium* sp. flower opened out, with 5 arrow-shaped stamens and the ovary with a terminal style and an umbrella-shaped expansion below the stigma (x2).

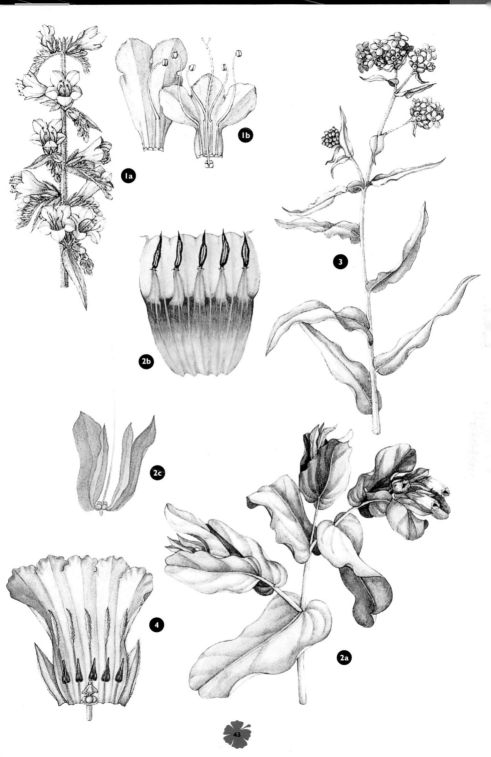

Cabbage, Mustard, Rapeseed, Turnip, and Woad

A cosmopolitan, mainly herbaceous family, often recognized by the 4-petalled cross-shaped (cruciform) flowers and the astringent mustard taste of the leaves.

Description Usually annual to perennial herbs, some geophytes (e.g., few *Cardamine*) rarely small shrubs (e.g., *Alyssum spinosum*), tall shrubs to 2 m high or small trees (e.g., *Heliophila glauca*), and rarely climbers (e.g., *Heliophila scandens*). The leaves are usually alternate, simple and entire, or variously lobed. The inflorescence is usually a raceme or corymb, usually without bracts or bracteoles. The basic floral structure is highly characteristic and constant: 4 sepals, 4 cruciform petals, 6 stamens, (4 long and 2 short), and an ovary with 2 parietal placentas.

The flowers are usually bisexual, regular, and hypogynous. Sometimes the inner sepals are swollen and convex at the base and contain nectar secreted by the nectaries at the base of the stamens.

The 4 petals are arranged in the form of a cross ("cruciform," hence Cruciferae). The stamens are typically 6, with 1 outer pair with short filaments, and 2 inner pairs with long filaments. The filaments are sometimes winged or with toothlike appendages. The nectaries appear as swellings or little cushions. The ovary is superior. The stigma is capitate to bilobed. The fruit is a 2-locular capsule with a false septum (replum), usually dehiscent. It may sometimes be indehiscent, breaking into single-seeded portions. The fruits range from linear-oblong to ovate to spherical; they may or may not be winged and stalked; the seeds may be in 1 or 2 rows. The range of variation shown in fruit types is vast. The seeds of all species are nonendospermous, and the testa often contains mucilaginous cells of various types that swell when wetted and produce a halo of mucilage. The embryo is curved with the radicle in one half of the seed, and the cotyledons in the other.

Distribution The family grows throughout the world but mainly in the north temperate region, especially around the Mediterranean basin and in southwestern and central Asia. The family grows sparingly in the southern hemisphere.

Economic uses Brassicaceae contains a considerable number and diversity of crop plants. Many crucifers are used as condiments or garnishes (e.g., mustard and cress). Many cruciferous crops have been cultivated since ancient times. The seed crops include oils and mustard condiments; forage and fodder crops; and salads and vegetables for human consumption. Rapeseed oil now ranks second in world production behind soybeans and ahead of cottonseed oil. The main oil crops are derived from *Brassica rapa* (Oilseed Rape) and *B. napus* (Oilseed Rape, Colza). Mustard is obtained from the ground seed of *Brassica juncea*, *B. nigra*, and *Sinapis alba*.

Animal feed is supplied by cruciferous crops in the form of silage, forage crops grazed in the field, and stored root fodder. Forage crops include *Brassica oleracea* (Kale, Cabbage), *B. napus* (Rape), and *Raphanus sativus* (Fodder Radish); fodder crops have swollen stems or root storage organs, such as *B. oleracea* (Kohlrabi), *B. campestris* (Turnip), and *B. napus* (Swede). The most important species of vegetables are *Brassica oleracea* (Kale, Brussels Sprouts, Kohlrabi, Cabbage, Broccoli, Calabrese, and Cauliflower) and *B. campestris* (Turnip, Chinese Cabbage, and so on). Ornamental genera include *Erysimum* (Wallflower), *Lunaria* (Honesty), *Iberis* (Candytuft), *Lobularia maritima* (Sweet Alysson), and *Matthiola* (stocks).

Brassicaceae. 1 *Iberis pinnata* leafy shoot and inflorescence with flowers having outer petals longer than the inner (×⅔). **2** *Moricandia arvensis* (a) shoot with sessile leaves, flowers, and fruit (×⅔); (b) half flower showing stamens with long and short filaments (×3). **3** *Biscutella didyma* var. *leiocarpa* shoot with leaves, flowers, and fruit (×⅔).

Frankincense and Myrrh

A tropical family of often aromatic, resinous trees and shrubs with usually imparipinnate leaves. Resin is present in all parts of the plants and has been used since ancient times for a range of purposes.

Description Large to small trees, less commonly shrubs, rarely epiphytes, often aromatic, with resin present in all parts of the plants, characteristically with flaky bark, sometimes shedding in sheets (*Bursera* spp.). The leaves are alternate, spirally arranged, usually crowded at twig-tips, imparipinnate, less frequently 1-foliate, usually exstipulate or with pseudo-stipules (*Garuga*). The flowers are small, usually greenish, cream-colored or pinkish, actinomorphic, unisexual, in axillary or terminal to subterminal, paniculate or racemose inflorescences. The sepals are 3–5(6), connate below and lobed, imbricate or valvate. The petals, when present, are 3–5, free to partly connate, imbricate or valvate. The stamens are as many as or twice as many as petals, the filaments usually free or sometimes connate at the base (e.g., *Canarium* spp.); staminodes are present in female flowers. The ovary is superior with 2–5 carpels and locules; ovules 2 per locule; style simple. The fruits show considerable diversity. They are basically compound, drupaceous, or nonfleshy, capsular (pseudocapsules), and dehiscent or remaining fused together. The dehiscent fruits in the tribes Protieae and Bursereae have as many valves as developed locules, and when fleshy, the exposed pyrenes are covered partially or almost completely by a pseudoaril. In the tribe Canarieae, the fruits are indehiscent and consist of a compound drupe with 2–3 locules, with a thin exocarp, an oily mesocarp, and a tough or bony endocarp.

Distribution The family grows in the tropics of Africa, Asia, the Americas, West Indies, and Australia, extending also into subtropical and arid areas of southern North America. They grow in a wide range of habitats, ranging from montane and lowland rain forests (such as the dipterocarp forests of central and southern Malesia) to dry forests and scrublands and desert regions. Trees and shrubs of the genus *Bursera* are particularly well represented and show great diversity in parts of Mexico (100 spp., most endemic) and, along with the genus *Protium* (c. 147 spp.), in South America such as the Amazon region. The largest genus, *Commiphora* (c.165 spp.), is common in Africa and Madagascar. *Boswellia* comprises c. 17 spp., 6 spp. of which are endemic on Socotra (Yemen), 2 spp. to India, 1 sp. to Madagascar, and the remainder mostly in the Horn of Africa.

Economic uses The aromatic resins produced by the Burseraceae have been used since ancient times for a variety of social, religious, cultural, and medicinal purposes. Frankincense is obtained from *Boswellia sacra* (Somaliland) and several other species. Myrrh, used in incense and perfumes, is obtained from *Commiphora myrryha* (True Myrrh) and other species. The wood of *Canarium littorale*, *Dacryodes costata*, *Santiria laevigata*, and *S. tomentosa* in Malesia, and *Aucoumea* and *Canarium schweinfurthii* in Africa, is used for general building construction and carpentry. Varnish is obtained from several *Bursera* spp., notably *B. glabrifolia* (whose wood is also used for carving small, painted figurines called alebrijes), in Mexico. *B. simaruba* (Gumbo-Limbo) is used as living fence posts in Central America, as well as for shade and as specimen trees.

Burseraceae. 1 *Boswellia popoviana* (a) twig with leaves crowded at tip (x⅔); (b) flower (x4); (c) cross section of ovary with 5 locules (x12). **2** *Commiphora marlothii* (a) terminal cluster of fruits (x⅔); (b) fruit (x1). **3** *Canarium hirtellum* (a) inflorescence (x⅔); (b) flower (x2); (c) flower with perianth removed to show stamens and globose stigma (x3); (d) section of 3-locular ovary (x3). **4** *Boswellia papyrifera* habit. **5** *Protium guianense* (a) inflorescence (x⅔); (b) section of ovary with 5 locules (x6); (c) shoot with imparipinnate leaf and fruits (x⅔).

Cactus Family

A large family of perennial, xerophytic trees, shrubs, climbers, and epiphytes, recognized by their more or less succulent and (except *Pereskia*) leafless appearance and many spines.

Description Perennial succulent trees, shrubs, climbers, and geophytes, mostly bearing spines. The spines, branches, and flowers arise from special sunken cushions or areoles, which may be regarded as condensed lateral branches—these are either set singly on tubercles or serially along raised ribs. Tufts of short barbed hairs (glochids) may also be present in the areoles.

Photosynthesis is undertaken by the young green shoots, but with age these shoots become corky and in the arborescent species develop into a hard, woody, unarmed trunk as in conventional trees.

The vascular system forms a hollow, cylindrical, reticulated skeleton and lacks true vessels. The roots are typically superficial and in the larger species are widely spreading and adapted for rapid absorption near the soil surface.

The flowers are solitary and sessile (*Pereskia* excepted), bisexual (with rare exceptions), and regular to oblique-limbed. Color range is from red and purple through various shades of orange and yellow to white; blue is lacking. The stamens, petals, sepals, and bracts are numerous and spirally arranged, the last 3 in transitional series without sharp boundaries between them. The ovary is inferior, borne on an areole, and is commonly covered in hairs, bristles, or spines, consisting of 2 to numerous carpels and forming 1 locule with numerous ovules on parietal placentas. The style is simple.

In *Opuntia*, the detached "fruit" (pseudocarp) grows roots and shoots, which form a new plant. The fruit is a berry, which is typically juicy, but may be dry and leathery, splitting open to release the seeds in various ways. The seeds have a straight to curved embryo and little or no endosperm.

Distribution Cacti are predominantly plants of semideserts of the warmer parts of the Americas. However, *Rhipsalis baccifera* is native to Africa, Madagascar, and Sri Lanka; and *Opuntia* is naturalized in Australia, Africa, the Mediterranean, and elsewhere.

The characteristic habitats of cacti experience erratic rainfalls, with long drought periods in between, but night dews may be heavy when the temperature falls.

Economic uses Apart from their wide appeal to specialist growers and collectors of the unusual, cacti have relatively few uses.

Cactaceae. **1** *Ariocarpus fissuratus*, a dwarf cactus with a many-ribbed, nonjointed stem bearing flowers on new areoles (x⅔). **2** *Gymnocalycium minhanovichii* (a) entire flower showing the gradual transitional series from bracts to sepals and petals (x2); (b) vertical section of flower showing inferior ovary and numerous stamens (x2) **3** *Carnegiea gigantea* showing the characteristic many-branched candelabra habit and ribbed stems (x¹/₁₂).

The fleshy fruits of many are collected locally and eaten raw or made into jams or syrups. Some are used for hedging, while those with woody skeletons are used for rustic furniture and trinkets. Opuntias (prickly pears) are grown commercially in parts of Mexico and California for their large juicy fruits and are widely consumed in Mediterranean countries where they have been introduced.

Hylocereus undatus (Dragon Fruit) is now widely seen in supermarkets in Europe. Some species, such as "peyote" (*Lophophora*

williamsii), contain hallucino-genic substances and are used locally by Native Americans. Probably all genera of cacti are represented in cultivation, collectors being un-deterred by the difficulties in growing them.

The most popular genera among collectors are those that remain dwarf and combine attractive spine colors and rib formations with freedom of flowering e.g., *Rebutia*, *Lobivia*, *Echinopsis*, *Mammillaria*, *Notocactus*, *Parodia*, and *Neoporteria*. *Astrophytum* is valued for its prominent ribs and cottony white tufts, and *Leuchtenbergia* for its extraordinarily long tubercles.

More for cacti connoisseurs are the curiously squat, tuberculate, slow-growing species of *Ariocarpus*, *Pelecyphora*, and *Strombocactus*.

Melocactus ("Turk's Cap Cactus") was one of the first cacti to reach Europe. It is unique for the large, furry inflorescence terminating the short, stumpy axis. Even more widely grown are the epiphytes. The large-flowered epicacti are products of a long line of inter-generic crossings paralleled only in the orchids and are the only group grown primarily for flowers.

Widespread collection has led all Cactaceae to be included on CITES (the Convention on International Trade in Endangered Species of Wild Fauna and Flora; an international agreement between governments), appendix 1 or 2. However, the subfamilies Pereskioideae and Maihuenioideae have been proposed for exclusion from CITES on the basis that they have little trade value.

The word *cactus* is commonly misapplied to a wide range of spiny or fleshy plants unrelated to the Cactaceae.

Cactaceae. 4 *Rhipsalis megalantha* an epiphytic cactus with many-jointed, spineless stems that are often produced in whorls (x⅔). **5** *Mammillaria zeilmanniana* a dwarf cactus with a solitary stem of spirally arranged tubercles tipped with spine-bearing areoles; flowers arise from the base of the tubercles (x⅔). **6** *Opuntia engelmannii* showing the characteristic disklike, many jointed stem-bearing numerous glochids— fine readily detached spines (x⅔).

6

Bellflower and Lobelia Family

A family of annual to perennial herbs, sometimes climbing, or occasionally secondarily woody pachycauls. They are widely cultivated as annuals and herbaceous perennials for their attractive flowers.

Description Annual to perennial herbs to herbaceous climbers (*Canarina* to 8 m high) or sometimes (giant *Lobelia* species and Hawaiian genera) pachycaul herbs to shrubs or trees several meters high. A white latex is often present.

The leaves are alternate or sometimes opposite to occasionally (*Ostrowskia*) conspicuously whorled, simple, or sometimes pinnatisect in Hawaii, sometimes 1 m or more long in pachycaul species, in South Africa sometimes ericoid (*Merciera*) or reduced to subulate scales (*Siphocodon*).

The inflorescence is racemose or cymose, sometimes a capitulum (e.g., *Jasione*). The flowers are actinomorphic to strongly zygomorphic, bisexual or rarely unisexual, usually relatively large and showy, usually 5-merous but sometimes 6-merous (*Canarina*) or up to 9-merous (*Ostrowskia*), weakly to strongly epigynous or apparently rarely (*Cyananthus*) perigynous, resupinate in Lobelioideae.

The sepals are usually elongate and acute. The corolla is regular to 2-lipped or deeply cleft down one side, cup-shaped to tubular, sometimes linear (up to 15 x 0.2 cm in *Hippobroma*). The stamens alternate with the corolla lobes and are attached to a disk or to the corolla; the filaments are free or connate.

Pollen is shed into the space between the connivent or connate anthers, and the expanding stigma pushes through it with a fringe of hairs that draw the grains into the style. The ovary is usually obviously semi-inferior but more or less superior in *Cyananthus*, with 2 or 3 or 5–9 carpels (see separate subfamilies), usually with 1 locule per carpel but these sometimes divided by intrusive placentas, or the placentation

Campanulaceae.
1 *Trachelium rumenlianum* shoots with alternate leaves and terminal inflorescences (x⅔).
2 *Canarina eminii* shoot with opposite leaves and axillary, regular flowers (x⅔). **3** *Lobelia cardinalis* "Red Flush" (x⅔).

rarely apical (*Siphocodon*) or basal (*Merciera*). The fruit is a capsule, dehiscing either by apical valves (above the calyx) or by lateral valves or pores (below the calyx), or rarely (*Parishella*) circumscissile; or (*Canarina*, *Centropogon*) a fleshy berry or (e.g., *Gunillaea*) dry and indehiscent.

Native to the Americas, *Lobelia cardinalis* (Cardinal Flower), reaching 1.2 m in height, is a perennial herbaceous plant that grows along the banks of streams and in swamps and other wet environments. Its leaves, up to 5 cm wide and 20 cm long, are lanceolate to oval and have a toothed margin. The 5-lobed, deep red flowers with a characteristic "lip" petal near the opening, are up to 4 cm wide. The flowers form racemes that can reach 70 cm in height and are pollinated by hummingbirds. The plant excretes a milky liquid.

L. cardinalis is related to *L. inflata* (Indian Tobacco) and *L. siphilitica* (Great Blue Lobelia). *L. inflata* is an annual or biennial herbaceous plant that grows from 15 to 100 cm tall. Native to eastern North America, its stems are covered in tiny hairs. The toothed, oval leaves are about 8 cm long, and the flowers are violet on the outside and yellow on the inside.

The plant contains psychoactive substances that were once widely used by certain Native Americans (the Penobscots); it is still used now. The seeds are the most powerful part of the plant because they produce the most active ingredient (lobeline), which brings about the psychoactive effects.

The Great Blue Lobelia is a perennial herbaceous plant that is native to eastern and central Canada and the United States. It grows in moist to wet soils and reaches up to 1 m in height. Its spikes of blue flowers appear in late summer and are pollinated mainly by bees.

Distribution Widespread from the Arctic to the southern hemisphere in a variety of habitats (a few species aquatic), except the major deserts. The Campanuloideae are predominantly in the north temperate Old World, with a few genera confined to South Africa and Canarina in the Canaries and tropical Africa, *Campanula* also extending across North America, and *Wahlenbergia* extending

4a

Campanulaceae. 4 *Campanula rapunculoides*
(a) leafy shoot and racemose inflorescence (x⅔);
(b) half flower showing free anthers to stamens, and
inferior ovary surmounted by a single style with a
lobed stigma (x1); (c) cross section of 3-locular ovary
with ovules on axile placentas (x3). **5** *C. rapunculus*
dehisced fruit—a capsule (x1½). **6** *Phyteuma orbiculare*
inflorescence (x⅔).

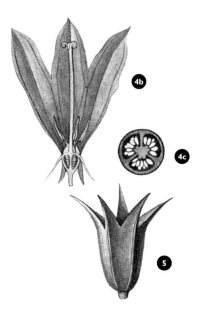

commonly into the southern hemisphere;
otherwise poorly represented in the tropics
and New World.

In contrast, the Lobelioideae grow mostly in
the tropics and southern hemisphere and are
poorly represented in the northern hemisphere
apart from *Lobelia*, which is worldwide, and
several genera endemic in Hawaii. Of the
smaller subfamilies, the Cyphioideae are
African, and the Nemacladoideae and
Cyphocarpoideae are from the New World.

Economic uses The showy flowers of the
Campanulaceae make the family attractive in
horticulture as annuals, herbaceous perennials,
and rock garden plants, especially the genera
Adenophora, *Campanula*, *Codonopsis*, *Legousia*,

Lobelia, *Michauxia*, *Phyteuma*, *Platycodon*,
and *Wahlenbergia*. The leaves are rarely eaten
as a vegetable (*Campanula rapunculus*,
Centropogon species).

Latex may contain poisonous alkaloids,
but those substances in *Lobelia* species have
been used in overcoming nicotine addiction
and respiratory disorders. Some herbalists use
L. inflata to make a substance (asthma weed)
for the treatment of asthma. Others make oint-
ments from the plant for external use.

Carnation Family

A large family of mainly temperate herbaceous plants with opposite and entire leaves. It includes the popular carnations and pinks and a number of widespread weeds.

Description Herbs, either annual or perennial, and dying back to the crown, rarely shrubby, with persistent woody stocks or small trees. The stems are often swollen at the nodes. The leaves are opposite (rarely alternate), always simple and entire, sometimes succulent, the bases of each pair often join around the stem to form a perfoliate base. Stipules are usually absent but usually scarious when present (subfamily Paronychioideae). The inflorescences are cymose, although varied in detail. Suppression of individual flowers can lead to racemelike monochasia, and, ultimately, to a single-flowered inflorescence (as in the carnation). The flowers are usually regular and bisexual, less frequently unisexual (plants then dioecious or monoecious). The calyx consists of 4 or 5 free sepals or of united sepals with a 4- or 5-lobed apex; some subtending bracts are present at the base of the calyx in some genera, notably *Dianthus*. The petals are 4 or 5 (sometimes 0), free from each other and often sharply differentiated into limb and claw, often notched or deeply cut at the apex, and sometimes with 2 small outgrowths (ligules) at the junction of the 2 parts on the inner surface. The stamens are typically twice as many as the petals but may be reduced to as many or even fewer (e.g., *Stellaria media*), and usually free from each other and attached directly to the receptacle. In some apetalous species, the stamens are attached to the sepals, making the flower perigynous. The ovary is superior, of 2–5 united carpels, usually with a single locule with free central placentation. In a few species of *Silene*

and *Lychnis*, the ovary is septate at the base. The styles are free, as many as there are carpels. The ovules are usually numerous but may be reduced to 1 when the placentation is basal. The fruit is most frequently a capsule, dehiscing by means of teeth at the apex. More rarely, in single-ovuled genera, the fruit is an achene or utricle. The seeds are usually numerous, with the embryo curved around the food-reserve material, which is usually perisperm rather than endosperm. In *Silene* and *Lychnis*, the petals, stamens, and ovary are separated from the calyx by a shortly extended internode (called an anthophore).

Distribution The family grows from the Arctic to Antarctic in all temperate regions of the world and sparingly on mountains in the tropics; several species of *Stellaria* (chickweed) and *Cerastium* (mouse-ear) have become almost cosmopolitan weeds. The center of diversity is in the Mediterranean and adjoining parts of Europe and southwestern Asia. Representation in the temperate southern hemisphere is small in terms of genera and species. All the larger genera (*Silene*, *Dianthus*, *Arenaria*) grow in the northern hemisphere, with the strongest concentrations in the Mediterranean region.

Economic uses The Caryophyllaceae provides a large number of widely cultivated garden ornamentals. The single most important species is the carnation (*Dianthus caryophyllus*), of which numerous garden forms (cultivars) exist; it is a specialized crop for the cut-flower market. Many other species of *Dianthus* (Pinks and Sweet William) are cultivated, including alpines and species of *Silene* (Catchfly, Campion), *Gypsophila* (Baby's Breath), *Agrostemma* (Corn Cockle), *Lychnis*, and *Saponaria* (Soapwort). Several species, notably *Stellaria media*, are widespread annual weeds of fields, gardens, and other disturbed habitats.

Caryophyllaceae. 1 *Telephium imperati* shoot with flowers and fruits (x⅔). **2** *Stellaria graminea* shoot with opposite leaves, swollen nodes, and cymose inflorescence (x⅔). **3** *Silene dioica* inflorescence bearing flowers with deeply cleft limb and white claw to each petal (x⅔). **4** *Dianthus deltoides* habit (x⅔). **5** *Arenaria purpurascens* habit (x⅔).

Spindle Tree Family

A family of shrubs and trees or woody climbers that grow mainly in tropical and subtropical regions, with a pronounced floral disk and often characteristic capsule and arillate seeds.

Description Shrubs, trees, and nontendrilled woody climbers, sometimes spiny. The leaves are opposite or alternate (sometimes in the same genus) or occasionally whorled, simple, usually petiolate, with entire to serrate margins. Stipules are small or absent. The inflorescence is axillary or terminal, cymose, or racemose. The flowers are actinomorphic or, rarely (*Apodostigma*), somewhat zygomorphic, bisexual, or unisexual (plants dioecious), (3)4–5-(6)-merous, with a marked cupular or occasionally lobed intrastaminal or extrastaminal disk. The sepals and petals are free, usually not particularly showy. The stamens are 3–5, inserted on or within the disk, sometimes with staminodes alternating with fertile stamens. The anthers dehisce either longitudinally or transversely or rarely apically. The ovary is superior or sometimes partly immersed in the disk, completely or incompletely 2- to 5-locular, with 1–12 or more ovules per locule, or in *Siphonodon* the locules are divided horizontally into 10 uniovulate chambers with axile placentation. The fruit is a loculicidal or sometimes (*Canotia*) also septicidal capsule, or a fleshy drupe or berry. The seeds are usually numerous and often either winged or with an aril.

Distribution Predominantly tropical and subtropical but extending sparingly into temperate regions. They grow in a wide range of habitats, including woodland, rain forest, grassland, coastal dunes, and very dry areas.

Economic uses The family has widespread uses for medicinal extracts, insecticides, oil from seeds, edible fruits and seeds, wood for timber, stems for basket weaving, and bark for arrow poisons. *Catha edulis*, known as Kat (Khat, Gat), is commonly used in tropical countries as a stimulant, the leaves being chewed or used for an infusion drunk as a tea. Numerous species of *Celastrus* and *Euonymus* are cultivated in temperate regions for their foliage, particularly for autumnal color, and brightly colored fruits and seeds. *E. europaeus* (Spindle Tree) produces a fine-grained wood, and its seeds have been used in manufacture of soap and a dye for coloring butter.

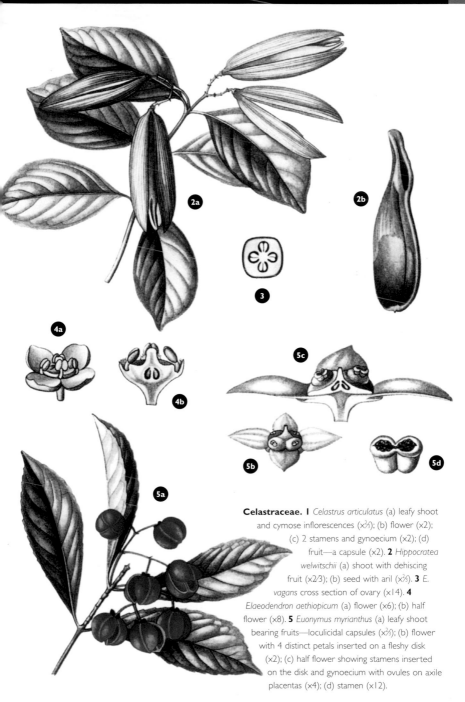

Celastraceae. 1 *Celastrus articulatus* (a) leafy shoot and cymose inflorescences (x⅔); (b) flower (x2); (c) 2 stamens and gynoecium (x2); (d) fruit—a capsule (x2). **2** *Hippocratea welwitschii* (a) shoot with dehiscing fruit (x2/3); (b) seed with aril (x⅔). **3** *E. vagans* cross section of ovary (x14). **4** *Elaeodendron aethiopicum* (a) flower (x6); (b) half flower (x8). **5** *Euonymus myrianthus* (a) leafy shoot bearing fruits—loculicidal capsules (x⅔); (b) flower with 4 distinct petals inserted on a fleshy disk (x2); (c) half flower showing stamens inserted on the disk and gynoecium with ovules on axile placentas (x4); (d) stamen (x12).

Rockroses

A family of shrubs or herbs, often with showy flowers. Rockroses grow mostly in the temperate or warm-temperate regions of southern Europe and the Mediterranean basin.

Description Mainly shrubs or subshrubs, some annual to perennial herbs. The leaves are alternate or opposite, simple, entire, with or without stipules, sometimes ericoid. The flowers are solitary or in terminal or axillary cymes, actinomorphic, often showy. The sepals are 5, the outer 2 smaller and bracetolelike. The petals are 5, 3 (*Lechea*), or absent in cleisto-gamous flowers, often crumpled in bud; ephemeral. The stamens are 3–10 or more, usually numerous, free. The ovary is superior, usually with 3 carpels (6–12 in *Cistus*), the carpels usually 1-locular but sometimes incompletely 5- to 12-locular, with parietal placentation. The fruit is a loculicidal capsule, with 3 or 5–12 valves, and few to many seeds.

Distribution Most species grow in temperate or warm-temperate regions of the northern hemisphere, notably in southern Europe and the Mediterranean basin (*Fumana* 10 spp., *Cistus* 17 spp., *Halimium* 9 spp., *Tuberaria* 10 spp., and *Helianthemum* 80 spp.) and in the eastern USA. Crocanthemum (24 spp.) occurs from North America (with a concentration of species in the southeastern part of the continent) to Mexico, with a disjunct group of 3 species in southern South America. *Hudsonia* (3 spp.) is endemic to the Atlantic coast of North America. *Lechea* (18 spp.) grows in North and Central America and the Caribbean. Only a few species of *Crocanthemum*, *Helianthemum*, and *Lechea* grow in tropical America. *Cistus* and *Halimium* are characteristic of Mediterranean shrub communities, while *Helianthemum* species are often found in base-rich grasslands or open rocky habitats of the Mediterranean region.

Economic uses Several species of *Cistus*, *Halimium,* and *Helianthemum* are cultivated widely as ornamentals for their showy flowers. *Cistus creticus* once produced the aromatic gum ladanum; the source of modern commercial ladanum used in the perfumery industry is *C. ladanifer*. Extracts of several species are used in folk medicine in some Mediterranean countries.

Cistaceae. 1 *Tuberaria guttata* habit (x⅔).
2 *Lechea mexicana* half flower with
ovary containing 2 ascending ovules
(x8). **3** *Fumana procumbens* (a) habit
showing simple opposite leaves and
solitary flowers (x⅔); (b) flower with petals
removed showing outer whorl of articulated
sterile stamens and inner whorl of fertile stamens
surrounding the elongated style with curved base
and discoid stigma (x6); (c) dehiscing capsule showing
3 valves containing seeds (x2⅔). **4** *C. symphytifolius*
cross section of ovary showing projecting placentas
bearing numerous ovules (x4). **5** *Cistus ladanifer* var.
maculatus (a) habit (x⅔); (b) dehiscing capsule with
10 valves (x2); (c) cross section of capsule showing
seed (x2⅔).

Mangosteen Family

An economically important family of trees, shrubs, and herbs that secrete latex, essential oils, or resins. Species of Mangosteens have been used to provide wood, drugs, dyes, gums, pigments, and resins.

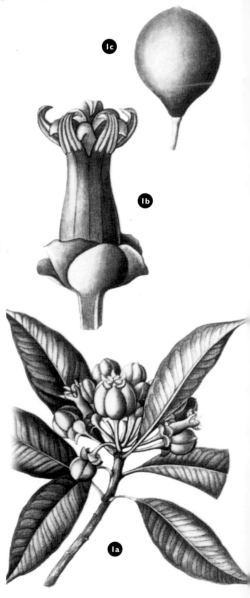

Description Trees, shrubs, or perennial to annual herbs, evergreen or deciduous, with glands or canals in most parts of the plant secreting latex, essential oils, or resins. The leaves of the Mangosteen family are simple and exstipulate, but occasionally with paired, stipuliform structures at or just below the leaf insertion point, opposite or more rarely alternate or whorled, with the margins entire or rarely fringed with glands.

The flowers are actinomorphic, hermaphrodite or unisexual (plants dioecious), terminal and often axillary, solitary or in cymose or thyrsoid inflorescences. The sepals are 2–20 but usually 4–5, free or fused, imbricate in bud, persistent or deciduous after flowering.

The petals are (3)4–5(–8) but may be absent, and free, equal, imbricate or contorted in bud, persistent or deciduous; epipetalous ligules are sometimes present in *Cratoxylum* and *Hypericum*. Essentially, the androecium consists of 2 whorls, each of 5 stamen bundles (fascicles), with filaments free almost to the base; the outer antisepalous whorl is sterile, with the members (fasciclodes) free or more or less united or absent, whereas the inner whorl is always fertile (except in female flowers) and may be modified by fusion of fascicles (most often 2+2+1) and/or stamens, or reduction to form masses or a ring of apparently free stamens. (In *Hypericum gentianoides*, each stamen fascicle is often reduced to a single stamen.)

The ovary is superior and consists of usually 2–5(–20) united carpels, each containing 1 to many ovules on axile to parietal, or more rarely apical or basal placentas. The stigmas are as many as the placentas, and the styles may be free, united, or totally lacking. Nectaries are absent; the fasciclodal bodies at the base of the ovary sometimes swell (similar to lodicules in grasses) to expand the flower.

Clusiaceae. 1 *Symphonia globulifera* (a) leafy shoot and terminal inflorescence (×⅔); (b) androecium, comprising tube of fused stamens surrounding a 5-lobed stigma (×3); (c) fruit—a berry (×1½). **2** *Hypericum calycinum* (a) shoot with decussate leaves and terminal solitary flower (×⅔); (b) half flower with stamens in bundles and numerous ovules on axile placentas (×1); (c) fruit—a capsule (×1). **3** *H. frondosum* cross section of ovary showing single locule with ovules on 3 parietal placentas (×3).

The fruit is often a capsule but may be a dry or fleshy berry or a drupe. The seeds are sometimes winged or with an aril or rarely a caruncle, and often lack endosperm at maturity, and with a usually straight embryo, and the cotyledons well developed and free or united or sometimes much reduced and replaced in function by an enlarged hypocotyl (tigellus).

The common name for *Clusia rosea* is the Autograph Tree, or *cupey* in Spanish. This slow-growing ornamental can reach 18 m in both height and diameter. It develops a huge crown with multiple trunks made up from thickened aerial roots. It has thick, large, and leathery leaves (7.5 to 15 cm long and up to 13 cm wide), which can be written on using a sharp implement. They have been used as writing paper and playing cards.

The large fruits of *Clusia rosea* contain seeds that have a sticky, red, and fleshy mesocarp. These seeds are distributed by birds to surrounding tree branches. Once germinated, the seeds develop into epiphytes that eventually produce long aerial roots that reach the ground and take root. The autograph tree slowly establishes growth on its host tree until it eventually overwhelms and kills it.

The Seashore Mangosteen (*Garcinia hombroniana*), native to Malaysia, Cambodia, Thailand, and Vietnam, is a small, attractive ornamental that reaches up to 6 m in height. Its straight trunk supports many branches, the young twigs of which are smooth and green. Older bark is dark brown and rough and produces a dark latex. *Garcinia hombroniana* has bright green opposite leaves, up to 25 cm long and 13 cm wide. The whitish flowers grow terminally, in groups up to 3. The fruits are smooth, round, and segmented, with a yellow pulp. Each segment usually contains a single flat seed. Mature trees can produce up to 500 fruits annually.

The seashore mangosteen is extremely tolerant of hostile soil and climatic conditions, growing well in sandy and rocky soils as well as in acidic clay soils. It also grows well in areas experiencing drought or high rainfall.

Another member of the mangosteen family is *Mammea americana* (common names include Mamey, Mammey Apple, and Tropical Apricot).

It is native to the West Indies and northern South America and is cultivated throughout the tropics. This large tree reaches 18 m in height and has a straight trunk and a dense, rounded crown. Bright green and smooth, the young bark gradually becomes dark brown and rough as it grows older. The leaves, branches, trunk, and roots all produce a yellow latex when cut. Glossy, bright green, opposite leaves grow up to 15 cm long and 10 cm wide. They are large, thick, and elliptical.

The flowers of *M. americana* are white and fragrant and grow singly or in clusters at the points where the leaves grow from the branches. The large, round fruit (up to 25 cm in diameter) has a brown rind covering a firm, juicy, yellow-orange pulp, which is similar to that of an apricot or peach. A mature tree can produce more than 250 fruits each year.

There are typically 1 or 2 seeds in each fruit. They are large (up to 8 cm long), brown, and have a rough surface.

Distribution The Clusiaceae are wholly pantropical and lowland except for the Hypericoideae–Hypericeae, in which *Hypericum* is widespread (especially in the northern hemisphere) and mainly lowland to upland in temperate regions but montane in tropical and warm temperate regions, *Lianthus* is a monotypic genus from montane northeastern Yunnan, *Triadenum* has a mainly temperate disjunct East Asia/eastern North America distribution, and *Thornea* occurs in the mountains of tropical Mexico to Nicaragua.

The other Hypericoidean tribes are Afro-American (Vismieae) and Madagascan–tropical eastern Asian (Cratoxyleae), respectively, and both are lowland to submontane.

Genera of the Kielmeyeroideae are either American or tropical Asian, except for *Mammea* (pantropical), *Calophyllum* (pantropical but mainly in Asia and the Pacific region), and the 2 genera of the Endodesmieae, *Endodesmia*, and *Lebrunia*, all of which are African. In the Clusioideae, the Clusieae and the genus *Clusiella* are native to the USA, the Garcineae are predominantly Old World but with some species of *Garcinia* growing in America, and the Symphonieae are pantropical.

Clusiaceae. 4 *Calophyllum inophyllum*
(a) shoot with inflorescences in axils
of terminal leaves (x⅔); (b) gynoecium
showing long, curved style (x4);
(c) stamen (x4).

Economic uses The Clusiaceae has been
used as a source of hard and/or durable wood
(species of *Mesua*, *Calophyllum*, *Cratoxylum*,
Platonia, and *Montrouziera*), easily worked
wood (species of *Calophyllum* and *Harungana*),
drugs or dyes from bark (species of *Vismiea* and
Calophyllum), gums, pigments, and resins from
stems, including species of *Garcinia* (Gamboge)
and *Clusia* (healing gums), drugs from leaves
and flowers (species of *Hypericum* and
Harungana madagascariensis), drugs and
cosmetics from flowers (*Mesua ferrea*), edible
fruits such as species of *Garcinia*, including

G. mangostana (Mangosteen), *Mammea*,
including *M. americana*, and *Platonia insignis*,
and fats and oils from seeds (species of
Calophyllum, *Mammea*, *Allanblackia*, *Garcinia*,
and *Pentadesma*).

The roots and leaves of *Garcinia hombroniana* are used medicinally to relieve itching.
The resin from the trunk of *Mammea americana* is used as an insecticide and pesticide
(to kill mites and ticks). The roots and leaves
also have insecticidal properties, while an
extract from the seeds is used to control mange
and fleas in animals.

Morning Glories and Bindweeds

A family of annual to perennial climbers, herbs, shrubs, and occasionally trees, with usually regular flowers, with an unlobed corolla with 5 conspicuous midpetaline bands.

Description Annual to perennial herbs to shrubs or often herbaceous or woody climbers up to 35 m high or more, or occasionally free-standing trees (*Humbertia*, some *Erycibe* and New World *Ipomoea* species), or leafless parasites (*Cuscuta*). The climbers twine sinistrally and have no tendrils or other climbing aids. The leaves are alternate, usually with a cordate base in the herbaceous climbers, but often coriaceous and cuneate in the woody lianes, usually simple but occasionally compound with palmate or pinnate segments (*Ipomoea* and *Merremia* species), or leaves are absent (*Cuscuta*). The inflorescence is usually an axillary cyme and may be capitate (some *Jacquemontia*, *Convolvulus*, and so on) or reduced to a single axillary flower (e.g., most *Calystegia*) but is sometimes racemose or a terminal thyrse (*Humbertia*). The flowers are actinomorphic except in *Humbertia* and *Mina lobata*, bisexual or, in *Cladostigma* and *Hildebrandtia*, functionally unisexual (plants dioecious in *Hildebrandtia*), and 5-merous except in some 4-merous *Cladostigma* and *Hildebrandtia* species. The sepals are usually free and overlapping. The corolla is campanulate to funnel- or salver-shaped and 0.2 to 9.5 cm long, or in some moth-pollinated *Ipomoea* species, the tube is narrowly cylindrical and up to 16 cm long, always characterized by conspicuous mid-petaline bands. The stamens are attached to, and usually included in, the corolla. Pollen is variable. The ovary is superior, of 2 (or rarely 3–5) carpels, with a simple or forked terminal style or 2 distinct styles; the stigma is variously divided or swollen. The ovary has 1–4 locules and usually 4 basally attached ovules. The fruit is typically a dehiscent 4-seeded capsule but may be a single-seeded utricle or a fleshy or mealy berry (*Argyreia*) or become woody and nutlike. The seeds typically have 2 flat faces and a rounded back and may bear long hairs.

When the flower is in bud, a band occupying the longitudinal middle third to fifth of each of the 5 segments of the corolla is exposed to the exterior, while the rest of the corolla is folded into the middle of the flower. These midpetaline bands are clearly seen in the opened flower. They usually differ markedly from the other areas of the corolla in color and texture and may include a clearly visible vein.

Distribution Widespread in tropical and temperate regions. In temperate and drier tropical places they are often low-growing herbs or shrubs in grassy or rocky places, sometimes on sand dunes (*Calystegia* and *Ipomoea* spp.) or salt marshes (*Cressa*, *Wils*onia), or in semi-deserts (especially *Convolvulus*), or are climbers over other vegetation. *Ipomoea aquatica* grows in still water. In wetter tropical areas they are often herbaceous climbers in thickets or at forest margins, or high-climbing, woody lianes reaching the forest canopy at 35 m or more.

Economic uses Root tubers of *Ipomoea batatas* are extensively eaten in the tropics (Sweet Potato) and are used as a source of industrial alcohol and sugar, or as livestock feed. Leaves of *I. aquatica* (Water Spinach) are eaten as a potherb (Kangkong, Ong choi) in the tropics. Minor medicinal products, mostly purgatives, are obtained from the roots of a few species of *Ipomoea* (especially *I. purga*, Jalap.), *Convolvulus* (*C. scammonia*), *Operculina*, and others produce ergoline alkaloids in their seeds and have been used in religious rituals. Species of *Ipomoea*, *Convolvulus*, *Evolvulus*, and *Poranopsis* are grown as ornamentals, and *Argyreia* and *Merremia* are used in dried flower arrangements. *Dichondra* species are sometimes used as a lawn substitute. *Cuscuta* (Dodder) may be a serious parasite of crop plants. *Convolvulus arvensis* and *Calystegia* species (Bindweeds) may be persistent aggressive weeds.

Convolvulaceae. 1 *Calystegia sepium* twining stem with solitary axillary flowers (x⅔).
2 *Ipomoea purpurea* (a) twining stem with axillary flowers (x⅔); (b) flower with corolla opened out showing stamens inserted at its base with a superior ovary surmounted by a thin style and lobed stigma (x1).
3 *Dichondra repens* (a) habit (x⅔); (b) fruit comprising 2 mericarps (x2). **4** *Erycibe paniculata* corolla opened out showing each lobe with 2 divisions at the apex and stamen filaments with broad bases (x⅔).

Gourd or Pumpkin Family

A highly specialized family of mainly climbing perennial plants, often with coarsely hairy leaves; of major importance as a food source (squashes, pumpkins, zucchini, melon, cucumber, and others).

Description Usually climbing perennial herbs with a swollen tuberous subterranean or wholly or partly superficial rootstock, formed by swelling of the hypocotyl; sometimes annual, occasionally softly woody lianas, rarely a shrub or tree (*Acanthosicyos*, *Dendrosicyos*). The stems of most are characterized by bicollateral vascular bundles with internal, as well as external, phloem. The leaves are alternate, simple or sometimes ternate, or palmately compound with 3 or more leaflets, palmately veined and usually lobed, sometimes pinnatifid (*Citrullus*), rarely absent (*Seyrigia*), usually coarsely hairy. In most species a solitary, branched or simple tendril arises at each side of the petiole base, the tip coiling around any suitable nearby object, such as a plant stem; the rest of the tendril then coils in a springlike manner, drawing the stem in close to its support; or the tip is adhesive. The inflorescences are usually axillary, of solitary flowers or in cymes, racemes, or panicles. The flowers are actinomorphic, nearly always unisexual (plants monoecious or dioecious). The sepals and petals are usually 5, borne at the top of a cup- or tubelike expanded hypanthium; the petals are often more or less united at the base. The androecium is complex, with 1–5 stamens, commonly 3, 2 of which are double with 4 pollen sacs each, and 1 single with 2 pollen sacs inserted on the lower part of the hypanthium, united in various ways, sometimes the filaments more or less completely fused into a single central column, the anthers bent to twisted or convoluted, with longitudinal dehiscence. In the pistillate flowers, the ovary is inferior, of 3 fused carpels (1 in tribe Sicyeae), 1-locular, usually with parietal placentation, or 2- to 5-locular by intrusive placentas; ovules from 1 to many in each fruit, anatropous; the seeds without endosperm, usually large and more or less flattened.

The fruit is berry, sometimes firm-walled (such as the melon), and known as pepos, or fleshy or dry capsules that may be explosively dehiscent (e.g., *Ecballium*, *Schizopepon*), or leathery and indehiscent.

Distribution The Cucurbitaceae is well represented in the moist and moderately dry tropics of both Old and New Worlds, particularly in rain forest areas of South America and woodland, grassland, and bushland areas of Africa. Some species occur in semidesert or even desert vegetation. Cucurbits are poorly represented in Australasia and all temperate regions.

Cucurbitaceae. 1 *Trichosanthes tricuspidata* leaf, tendril, and female flower (x⅔).
2 *Curcurbita moschata* (a) male flower (x⅔); (b) cross section of ovary (x⅔); (c) female flower with petals and sepals removed (x⅔). **3** *Sechium edule* (a) female flower with discoid stigma (x1½); (b) stamens partly joined in a single column (x2); (c) vertical section of ovary with single pendulous ovule (x2). **4** *Gurania speciosa* female flowers (x⅔).

Economic uses Major food crops are pro-
duced in tropical, subtropical, and temperate
regions from *Cucurbita* species (squashes,
pumpkins, and yellow-flowered gourds, veg-
etable marrows, vegetable spaghetti, zucchini),
Cucumis species (*Cucumis melo*, Melon,
Cantaloupe, honeydew, and *C. sativus*,
Cucumber), and *Citrullus lanatus*
(Watermelon). Other important crops
include *Cucumis anguria* (West Indian
Gherkin), *Lagenaria siceraria* (Calabash,
Bottle Gourd), *Benincasa hispida* (Wax
Gourd), *Sechium edule* (Chayote),
Luffa cylindrica (Loofah) and *L. acu
tangula*, *Trichosanthes cucumerina*
var. *unguina* (Snake Gourd),
Momordica charantia (Bitter Melon;
Balsam Apple), *Sicana odorifera*
(Cassa-banana), *Cyclanthera
pedata* (Achocha), *Hodgsonia
heteroclita* (Lard Fruit), *Telfairia
occidentalis* (Oyster Nuts, the
seeds yielding an edible oil),
Cucumeropsis mannii (Egussi),
and *Praecitrullus fistulosus*
(Dilpasand, Tinda).

Luffa aegyptiaca is the source of
loofah sponges (dried vascular skeleton
of the fruit), while dry fruits of *Lagenaria
siceraria* (Bottle Gourd) have medicinal
uses and have been used as containers
since ancient times. The species is one of
the earliest cultivated plants and the only
one with an archaeologically documented
prehistory in both the Old World and the
New World. Fruits of wild *Citrullus lanatus*
(Tsamma), *Acanthosicyos naudinianus*, and
A. horridus (Narras) are food and water sources
in the deserts of southern Africa.

Bitter substances, called cucurbitacins, are
widespread in the family. Many of the edible
species occur in both bitter (inedible) and non-
bitter (edible) variants.

As ornamentals, Cucurbitaceae are of minor
importance: *Cucurbita pepo* produces the ornamental gourds, and species of *Momordica*,
Kedrostis, *Corallocarpus*, *Ibervillea*, *Seyrigia*,
Gerrardanthus, *Xerosicyos*, and *Cyclantheropsis*
are sometimes cultivated by enthusiasts of
succulent plants.

Cucurbitaceae. 5 *Gynostemma penta-
phyllum* (a) leafy shoot with tendrils and
inflorescence (×⅔); (b) female flower (×6);
(c) young fruit with remains of styles (×8).
6 *Zanonia indica* (a) fruits (×2⁄3); (b) winged seed
(×¼). **7** *Kedrostis courtallensis* male flower opened out
to show 2 double and 1 single epipetalous stamen
(×4). **8** *Echinocystis lobata* fruit (×⅔). **9** *Coccinea grandis*
leaves, tendrils, female flowers, and fruit (×⅔).

Lightwood, Coachwood, and Eucryphia

A family of evergreen trees and shrubs native to the southern hemisphere, mainly in Oceania and Australasia.

Description Evergreen trees (*Eucryphia* to 25 m), shrubs, or stranglers (some *Weinmannia* spp.), with simple or complex hairs, some irritating (*Davidsonia*). The leaves are opposite or rarely whorled (spiral in *Davidsonia*), leathery, often glandular, occasionally 1-foliate, but more often compound, 3-foliate or pinnate, the margins toothed or entire. The inflorescence is variously a panicle, thyrse, raceme, capitate, or rarely a solitary flower; inflorescences are positioned at the stem apex, in axils, or rarely cauliflorous. The flowers are regular, hermaphrodite, or unisexual in a few species (plants dioecious, *Hooglandia*, *Pancheria*, *Vesselowskya*, and some species in other genera). The sepals are 3–6(–10), free or fused together at the base. The petals are alternate with the sepals and usually isomerous, free or united at the base, generally smaller than the sepals (absent in some species). The stamens are usually numerous but sometimes 4 or 5, alternating with the petals, or 8 or 10, usually inserted by their free filaments on a ringlike, nectar-secreting disk around the ovary. The ovary is superior, with 1 (*Hooglandia*) 2–5 free or fused carpels (4–14 in *Eucryphia*), usually with 2 locules. Each locule or free carpel contains numerous ovules (sometimes 1–2) set in 2 rows on recurved, axile, or apical placentas. Styles are distinct. The fruit is a woody or leathery capsule sometimes dehiscing along ventral sutures or with winglike sepals or a nut; sometimes the carpels are bladderlike (*Platylophus*), or the seeds are winged (*Eucryphia*).

Distribution The main centers of distribution are Oceania and Australasia, but there are a few genera in South Africa and tropical America. The most important genus is *Weinmannia*, with 160 spp. distributed throughout Madagascar, Malesia, the Pacific, New Zealand, Chile, Mexico, and the West Indies. *Pancheria* has 25 spp. in New Caledonia. *Geissois* has 20 spp. in Australasia, New Caledonia, and Fiji. The 20 spp. of *Spiraeanthemum* are native to New Guinea and Polynesia. *Cunonia* (15 spp.) and *Lamanonia* (10 spp.) are smaller genera. The former has a discontinuous distribution in South Africa and New Caledonia, while *Lamanonia* is native to Brazil and Paraguay. Of the 5 spp. of *Eucryphia*, 2 spp. are native to Chile, 1 sp. to New South Wales in Australia, and 2 spp. to Tasmania. Fossil evidence suggests the family once extended into the northern hemisphere.

Economic uses The wood of various genera is used in construction work. The timber (Lightwood) of *Ceratopetalum apetalum* from New South Wales is used in carpentry and cabinetmaking, and there are reports of dermatitis caused by this timber. The timber of *Eucryphia cordifolia* from Chile has been used for a variety of purposes and the bark is a source of tannin. The timber of the Tasmanian species, *E. lucida*, is used for general building and cabinetmaking. *Eucryphia* spp. and hybrids are cultivated as small ornamentals.

Cunoniaceae. I *Weinmannia hildebrandtii* (a) shoot with 3-foliate leaves and flowers in panicles (×⅔); (b) flower (×8); (c) half flower (×8). **2** *Geissois imthurnii* flower with 4 sepals, no petals, and numerous stamens inserted on a nectar-secreting disk (×2). **3** *Pancheria elegans* (a) shoot with whorls of simple leaves and flowers in compact heads (×⅔); (b) female flower showing 3 free sepals and petals and 2 free styles (×12); (c) male flower with 6 stamens (×12); (d) male flower opened out to show stamens with filaments of 2 lengths (×12); (e) bilobed fruit (×12). **4** *Davidsonia prunens* fruit (×⅔). **5** *Cunonia capensis* shoot with pinnate leaf and flowers in a panicle (×⅔).

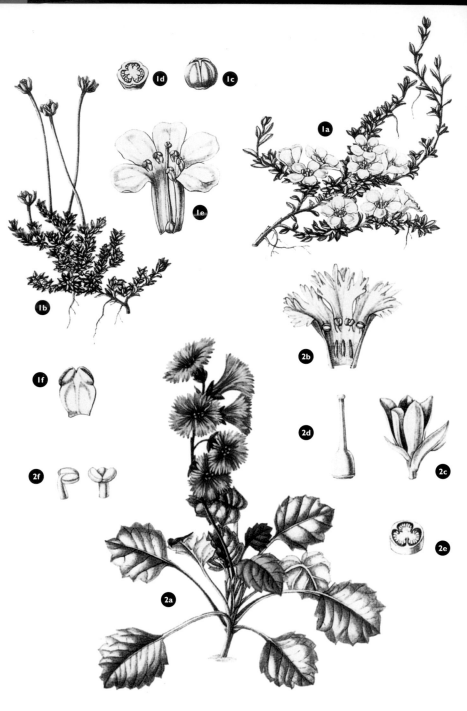

Diapensia Family

A small family of mat- or rosette-forming montane or subarctic perennial herbs with an interesting distribution, including the eastern Himalayas and Japan. Some species are popular as rock-garden plants.

Description Perennial herbs, prostrate and mat-forming, or rhizomatous and subcaulous. The leaves are alternate, simple, with entire to serrate margins; small and obovate and crowded in mat-forming genera, or long-petioled and broad with a cuneate to cordate base. The inflorescence is an elongate, many-flowered spike, or a 1- to 15-flowered raceme on a long scape, or the flowers are solitary and terminal on short branches. The flowers are actinomorphic, bisexual, 5-merous, sometimes showy. The sepals are free or shortly connate. The petals are free (*Galax*) or fused into a corolla tube with 5 lobes, which are conspicuously fringed in *Shortia*. The stamens are attached to the petals or corolla tube, sometimes alternating with 5 staminodes. In *Pyxidanthera* and *Galax*, the anthers are appendaged. The ovary is superior, of 3 fused carpels with a simple style and 3-lobed stigma. There are 3 locules, with few to many ovules on swollen axile placentas. The fruit is a loculicidal capsule.

Distribution The family has centers of diversity in the eastern Himalayas and adjacent mountains of China, in Japan to Taiwan, and in the Appalachians of North America, plus 1 circumboreal species. They grow in montane to subarctic habitats or woods or pine barrens.

Diapensiaceae. 1 *Diapensia himalaica* (a) creeping shoot bearing small, simple overlapping leaves and solitary flowers (x⅔); (b) fruiting shoot (x⅔); (c) dehiscing fruit (x3); (d) cross section of ovary (x6); (e) 5-lobed perianth opened out to reveal 5 stamens fused to corolla (x2); (f) detail of stamens (x8). **2** *Shortia soldanelloides* (a) habit (x⅔); (b) part of corolla opened out to show fertile stamens inserted on corolla tube and linear staminodes at the base (x2); (c) fruit enclosed in persistent bracts and calyx (x2); (d) gynoecium (x2); (e) cross section of ovary (x3); (f) stamens, dorsal view (left) and ventral view (right) (x6). **3** *Galax urceolata* habit (x⅔).

Economic uses In the Diapensia family, *Shortia* and *Diapensia* species are popular as rock-garden plants. *Galax* is sometimes grown on the banks of streams for its interesting architecture and has been the source of a major local industry in the Appalachians around the town of Galax in Virginia, where millions of leaves have been collected each year for use in flower arrangements.

Dilleniaceae. **1** *Tetracera masuiana* (a) flowering shoot
(x⅔); (b) vertical section of gynoecium with free carpels
(x6). **2** *Hibbertia tetrandra* (a) flowering shoot (x⅔); (b) half
flower showing lobed petals and free carpels with one basal
ovule (x3). **3** *Dillenia indica* (a) gynoecium showing ovoid
ovary and free styles and stigmas (x⅔); (b) cross section
of ovary showing numerous partly united carpels (x1).
4 *Dillenia suffruticosa* (a) shoot with winglike stipules on
leaf-stalks (x⅔); (b) cross section of ovary with united
carpels (x1); (c) gynoecium (x⅔).

Dillenia Family

Dilleniaceae is a large family of mainly tropical, medium-sized trees and shrubs that grow in lowland forests or savannas. Some species are grown as ornamentals, while others yield timber.

Description Medium-sized trees, shrubs, lianas, and perennial herbs. The leaves are alternate, simple, persistent or caducous, without stipules, the lamina serrate or dentate and often with prominent lateral veins. The inflorescences are axillary or terminal, cymose, paniculate or fasciculate. The flowers are actinomorphic, bisexual or unisexual (plants monoecious, or functionally dioecious in neotropical species of *Tetracera*), sometimes large and conspicuous. The sepals are (3–)5(–20), imbricate, persistent. The petals are 3–5, imbricate, deciduous, often crumpled in bud. The stamens are numerous (up to 500 in *Tetracera*), developing centrifugally, the anthers often with a prolonged and well-developed connective. The ovary is superior of 1–5 or more carpels, free or variously connate, sometimes compound (*Curatella* and *Pinzona*), with marginal placentation and 1–5 locules with 1 to many seeds. The styles are separate and divergent. The fruits are follicular, ventrally or dorsally dehiscent, or indehiscent and dry (nuts) or fleshy (berries). The seeds are 1 to many per carpel, with copious, oily endosperm, sometimes starchy, and often arillate.

Distribution Widespread in the tropics and warm-temperate zones, growing in lowland forests or savannas. Hibbertia (c. 115 spp.) ranges from Madagascar to Australia (to which most species are endemic) and Fiji. Tetracera is pantropical in distribution. Four genera are endemic to the *neotropics*—*Curatella*, *Davilla*, *Doliocarpus*, and *Pinzona*.

Economic uses *Hibbertia scandens* and *Dillenia indica* are occasionally grown as ornamentals. The timber of *Dillenia* spp. is used for general construction and boatbuilding. The cut

stems of *Tetracera arborescens* yield potable water. The scabrid stems of several liana species, such as *Doliocarpus dentatus* and *Davilla kunthii* (Cipó-de-fogo) have irritant hairs that cause a burning sensation if touched.

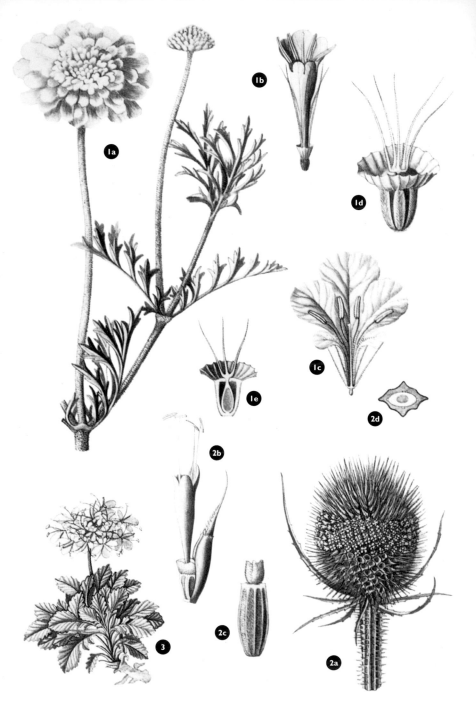

Scabious and Teasel Family

A family resembling Asteraceae (Aster, Daisy, and Sunflower family) in having flowers in a head, these Old World annual or perennial herbs to low subshrubs are related to Caprifoliaceae (Honeysuckle family).

Description Annual or perennial herbs to low subshrubs. The leaves are opposite or in a basal rosette, without stipules, and entire to deeply pinnately or bipinnately divided. The inflorescence is a terminal compact capitulum surrounded by involucral bracts, the receptacle sometimes rather elongate (*Dipsacus*). The capitulum receptacle may bear prominent scales or (*Knautia*) hairs between the flowers. Each flower is subtended by an 8-nerved involucel derived from the fusion of 2 bracteoles, except in a few species of *Cephalaria* and *Succisa*, in which it is reported to be absent. The involucel surrounds the inferior ovary and may be variously developed into a corona or setae.

The flowers are regular to slightly zygomorphic, those at the margin of the capitulum often markedly bigger than the inner ones and with enlarged outer lobes. The calyx either forms a scarious cup or is divided into 4 or 5 setae or, in *Knautia*, up to 16(–24) setae. The corolla is tubular or trumpet-shaped, with 4 or 5 lobes, and is either regular or 2-lipped. The stamens are 4, sometimes 2 long and 2 short, usually exserted. The ovary is bicarpellary, but 1 carpel aborts to leave a single locule that bears 1 ovule pendulous at its apex. The style is elongate and often exserted. The fruit is a hard, dry cypsela, often surmounted by the persistent scarious calyx, or enveloped by the involucel. The striking variation in inflorescence and calyx characters is probably related to dispersal mechanisms of the single-seeded indehiscent fruits. In *Dipsacus*, the prominent spinescent long outer bracts are members of the involucre of the capitulum, while the acute bracts separating and exceeding the flowers are scales on the capitulum receptacle, the involucel and calyx being inconspicuous. In other genera, the cup-shaped involucel surrounding the inferior ovary may be conspicuous and developed in various ways. In *Scabiosa*, the involucel has a prominent, translucent, orbicular corona persisting with the fruit. In *Pterocephalus*, the involucel may bear a corona of setae. In *Pterocephalidium*, the involucel develops on its rim one very long curved tooth far exceeding the length of the rest of the involucel. The capitulate inflorescences are superficially very similar to those of the Asteraceae, in which, however, the anthers are always connate round the style. The Dipsacaceae can be readily distinguished by their free anthers that are usually prominently exserted.

Distribution Confined to the Old World (occasionally introduced in North America), centered in the Mediterranean region but extending westward to the Canary Islands (*Pterocephalus*), southward to South Africa (*Scabiosa* and *Cephalaria*), and eastward sparingly to Japan (*Dipsacus*, *Scabiosa*). It is unusual to find a Mediterranean family with strong extensions into tropical Africa (*Dipsacus*, *Cephalaria*, *Scabiosa*, *Succisa*, *Pterocephalus*).

Economic uses The genera *Scabiosa* (Scabious), *Pterocephalus*, and *Cephalaria* are grown as ornamental herbaceous perennials or rock-garden plants. The inflorescences of *Dipsacus* species were formerly used for raising the nap on cloth (Fullers' Teasel) and although largely replaced by other means, are still used when a high-quality finish is needed.

Dipsacaceae. I *Scabiosa anthemifolia* var. *rosea* (a) leafy shoot and inflorescences (x⅔); (b) inner flower with bristlelike calyx segments (x3); large outer flower opened out (x2); (d) fruit with epicalyx (involucel) expanded into an umbrella-shaped extension and crowned by spines (x3); (e) vertical section of fruit (x2). **2** *Dipsacus fullonum* (a) dense flower head surrounded by spiny bracts (x⅔); (b) flower (x3); (c) fruit (x3); (d) cross section of fruit (x5). **3** *Pterocephalus perennis* flowering shoot (x⅔).

Dipterocarps

A pantropical family comprising some of the best-known tropical forest trees, characterizing major formations, especially in Southeast Asia, providing a main source of hardwood timber.

Description Trees, mainly evergreen, some of them reaching a height of up to 70 m, often with buttressed bases, rarely shrubs (*Pakaraimaea*). The leaves are alternate, usually coriaceous or chartaceous, simple, with margins entire. The flowers are actinomorphic, bisexual, in terminal and axillary racemes or panicles, rarely cymes. The sepals are 5, accrescent, persistent, mostly enlarged and winglike in fruit, distinct or connate at the base. The petals are 5, free or connate at the base. The stamens are 5 to numerous, the filaments free or connate below, the anthers dorsifixed or basifixed, often appendaged with the connective extended into a sterile tip. The ovary is superior to semi-inferior, with (2)3–4(5) carpels and locules, each with 1 (*Pseudomonotes*) or 2–4 ovules that are pendulous or laterally attached. The fruit is a single-seeded nut or a capsule, usually with persistent winged and membranous sepals. The seeds usually lack endosperm.

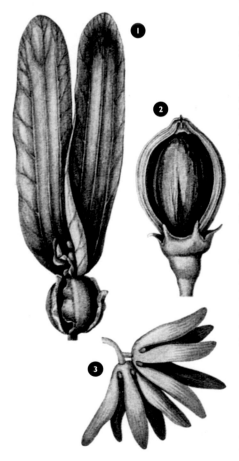

Distribution Subfamily Dipterocarpoideae is confined to the tropics of Asia (Sri Lanka, India, Myanmar, Thailand, Indo–China, southern China, Yunnan, Malaysia, Sumatra, Java, Bali, Borneo, New Guinea, the Philippines, and the Seychelles). Subfamily Monotoideae grows in Africa and Madagascar and has recently been discovered in the neotropics, in Colombia. Subfamily Pakaraimaeoideae is endemic to the Guyana highlands of South America.

Economic uses Dipterocarps, especially species of *Dipterocarpus*, *Hopea*, *Shorea*, and *Vatica* are of major importance as a source of hardwood and currently dominate the international tropical timber market. Many species are now at risk owing to overexploitation and habitat loss. Dipterocarps provide many nonwoody forest products, which are used mainly by village people, but the products from a few species have gained commercial importance in industry and trade owing to their properties and chemical constituents. Some species are a source of oleoresins (especially *Dipterocarpus*), resins (damar), "butter fat," obtained from *Shorea* spp., and camphor (*Dryobalanops aromatica* formerly a main source).

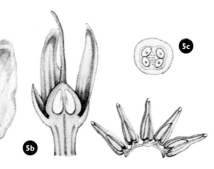

Dipterocarpaceae. The fruits are often enclosed in winged extensions of the calyx. Shown here are: **1** *Shorea ovalifolia* (×1½), **2** *Dipterocarpus oblongi-folia* vertical section of single-seeded fruit (×1), **3** *Monotes tomentellus* (×⅔), and **4** *Diptero-carpus incanus* (×⅔). **5** *Monoporandra elegans* (a) leafy twig with fruit and inflorescence (×⅔); (b) flower dissected to show sepal (left), petals, and gynoecium in vertical section (center), and stamens fused at the base and anthers with long connectives (right) (×6); (c) cross section of ovary (×6). **6** *Shorea ovalis*, tree in leaf.

Sundews, Waterwheel Plant, and Venus Flytrap

This well-known and widespread family of carnivorous plants is dominated by the diverse sundew genus, *Drosera*, which is characterized by its sticky tentacles that trap insect food.

Description Perennial or rarely annual, acaulescent or caulescent, carnivorous herbs to 3 m, evergreen or dormant by stem or root tubers in dry climates, or by apical bud in cold climates. The leaves are spirally arranged or whorled (*Aldrovanda*, some *Drosera* sect. *Stolonifera*), with or without stipules, with or without petiole, lamina attached basally or peltate, hinged in *Dionaea* and *Aldrovanda* to form a bilobed trap, upper surface of lamina bearing glandular tentacles in *Drosera*, often pubescent below.

Inflorescence is a terminal or apparently lateral cyme, usually scorpioid, 1- to many-flowered. The flowers are actinomorphic, hermaphrodite, usually 5-merous, (rarely 4-merous: *D. pygmaea*; or up to 12-merous: *D. heterophylla*), the sepals free or fused at base, the petals free, often brightly colored, alternating with the sepals. The stamens are usually 5 and free.

The ovary is superior, usually of 3 carpels, sometimes 5, fused, 1-locular. The styles are as many as the carpels, often much branched and causing confusion in number; the stigmas are often highly branched, crested, or papillate. The fruit is a dehiscent capsule containing few to many seeds.

In common with other such plants, *Drosera rotundifolia* (Common Sundew or Round-leaved Sundew) has evolved a carnivorous lifestyle in response to its nutrient-poor habitat. It is covered with red, glandular hairs or tentacles that are covered in a sticky, sugary secretion. Trapped on these tentacles, the insects are digested by plant enzymes and their nutrients are absorbed.

Dionaea muscipula (Venus Flytrap) also obtains most of its nutrients from insects. Its modified leaves are hinged to form traps that have short, stiff trigger hairs that are sensitive to touch. When anything touches these hairs, the leaves snap tightly shut in less than 1 second, trapping whatever is inside. Cilia along each edge of the trap hold the insect in place while it is digested by plant enzymes.

Distribution The family is widespread and has colonized a range of habitats, from fully aquatic (*Aldrovanda*) to seasonally dry (*Drosera* sect. *Ergaleium*), and from sea level to high altitude. The Venus Flytrap (*Dionaea*) is restricted to the Green Swamp (borders of North and South Carolina), and *Aldrovanda* is widespread but infrequent from northern temperate Old World to tropical and subtropical Australia. The type genus, *Drosera* (150–180 spp.), is cosmopolitan, with centers of diversity in southwestern Australia, South Africa, and tropical South America; absent only from Antarctica.

Economic uses The major economic use of the species is in herbal medicine, where the widespread naphthoquinones show a range of activity, including antispasmodic action, as a treatment for coughs, and anti-inflammatory properties, as well as exhibiting antibacterial action. The family is also of economic value, particularly *Dionaea muscipula*, as ornamental curiosities sold in many countries.

Droseraceae. 1 *Drosera capensis* (a) habit showing basal rosette of leaves covered in stalked glands (x⅔); (b) perianth opened out to reveal stamens (x2); (c) gynoecium (x2); (d) half section of ovary (x10). **2** *Dionaea muscipula* (a) habit showing leaves modified to form a trap (x⅔); (b) inflorescence (x⅔); (c) vertical section of base of flower showing ovary with basal ovules (x4).

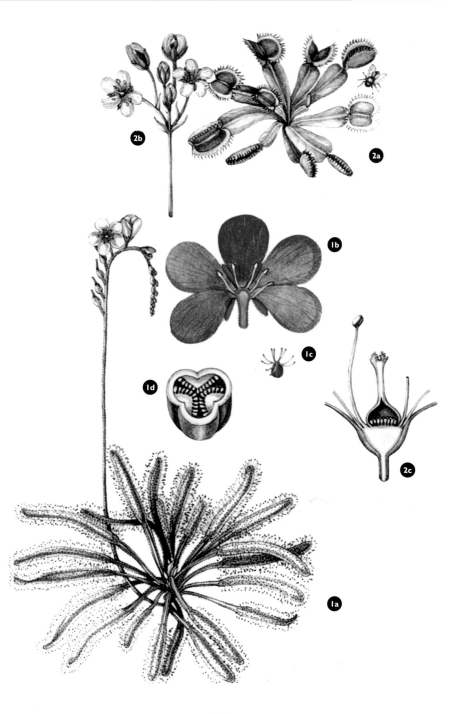

Durians

A family of tall, evergreen, tropical fruit trees that grow in Southeast Asia, and formerly included in Bombacaceae (Balsa, Baobab, Kapok, and Silk Cottons family).

Description Evergreen trees, often tall (up to 45 m), with an indumentum mainly of lepidote scales, but stellate hairs also occur. The leaves are alternate, simple, usually oblong, pinnately nerved and entire, the lower surface is densely covered in scales (sparsely in *Neesia* and also mixed with stellate hairs), the petioles pulvinate, and the stipules generally caducous and linear.

The inflorescence is usually axillary, of 1–2 flowers, but often fasciculate or subfasciculate, ramiflorous or cauliflorous. The flowers are actinomorphic, bisexual. An epicalyx is present, usually entirely enclosing the flower in bud and splitting into 2–5 lobes.

The calyx itself is shallowly to deeply divided into 5 valvate lobes. The corolla is calyptrate in *Neesia* and *Coelostegia* but otherwise is divided into 5 free linearto spathulate petals. An androgynophore is absent.

The stamens are numerous; either free, united at the base, or united into 5 phalanges that are either free or connate into a staminal tube, the filaments becoming free at various heights; the anthers are sometimes dithecal and longitudinally dehiscent, but are more usually monothecal and borne in clusters, dehiscing by terminal pores or longitudinally.

The pollen is suboblate, 3-colporate, lacking spines but with low, large, smooth verrucae. The ovary is superior or partly embedded in the receptacle (*Coelostegia*), subovoid or slightly 5-angled, clothed in peltate scales (except *Neesia*), 5-locular with 2 to numerous axile anatropous ovules in 2 ranks per locule.

Durionaceae. I *Durio zibethinus* (a) flowers arising from old wood, showing the pair of sepal-like appendages subtending the whorls of sepals and petals, and the stamens united into a tube surrounding the style (x⅔); (b) leaf (x⅔); (c) spined fruit (the evil-smelling durian) (x⅓); (d) vertical section of part of fruit showing seeds (x¼).

The style is usually well developed (± absent in *Kostermansia*), and the stigma peltate or capitate. The fruits are globose to ellipsoid, spiny to subspiny, loculicidally dehiscent capsules, each of the 5 locules with 1 to several large raphe-funicular arillate seeds. Rarely are the fruits indehiscent or the seeds exarillate.

The pollinators of durians are not recorded but it is speculated that some species are pollinated by birds. Their foul-smelling fruits are highly sought after for the sweet flesh of the seed arils that they contain. Species as varied as orangutans, tigers, hornbills, and elephants consume the fruits.

Distribution Southeast Asia, usually trees of lowland evergreen forest, with a few species in swamp forest.

Economic uses There are numerous and varied local uses attached to durians, particularly to *Durio zibethinus*, the most widespread and well known species of the family. Its roots are used to treat fever, its wood for cheap furniture, its seeds for food, the ashes for bleaching silk and to promote abortions and menstruation, while the valves are used as remedies for constipation and skin diseases.

However, it is the foul-smelling durian fruits that are highly esteemed and traded internationally within Southeast Asia, China being a major importer of these spiny comestibles. The seed arils are delicious.

Some *Durio* spp. are cultivated throughout Southeast Asia for the production of the fruits. They are distinctive for their large size (up to 30 cm long and 15 cm in diameter), unique odor, and thorny or spiny, green to brown husk. They can weigh up to 3 kg.

The fruits are banned in certain hotels and on some international airlines and other forms of transportation owing to their stench when ripening or when opened.

Oleaster and Sea Buckthorn

A smallish family of deciduous or evergreen many-branched shrubs, woody climbers, or small trees, which are often thorny and covered with silvery or golden scales.

Description Shrubs, woody climbers, or small trees, often thorny and densely covered with silver, gold, or brown peltate scales and/or stellate hairs. The leaves are deciduous or evergreen, leathery, alternate, opposite or whorled, simple, entire, without stipules. The flowers are axillary; solitary in clusters, racemes, or spikes; bisexual (*Elaeagnus*) or unisexual (plants monoecious in *Elaeagnus*, dioecious in *Shepherdia* and *Hippophaë*); strongly perigynous. The perianth is in 1 whorl, 2- to 4-lobed, rarely more, often petaloid, with a tubular hypanthium, often constricted above the level of the ovary, sometimes flat in male flowers. The stamens are inserted on the hypanthium throat, 4 in a single whorl, alternating with the perianth segments, or 8 in 2 whorls (1 alternate and 1 opposite), 2-locular, with longitudinal dehiscence. A nectary disk is often present. The ovary is superior, 1-locular, and the ovule 1, anatropous. The style is long with a basal to capitate stigma. The fruit is a single-seeded achene, drupelike. The seeds have little or no endosperm.

Distribution *Elaeagnus* (45 spp.) is widespread in temperate eastern Asia, with a single species, *E. triflora*, extending from Southeast Asia to Queensland in northeastern Australia, 1 sp. in southern Europe, and another in North America. *Hippophaë* (3 spp.) grows in temperate Eurasia, and *Shepherdia* (3 spp.) grows in North America.

Economic uses A number of species are grown as ornamental shrubs, such as *Elaeagnus angustifolia*, *E. pungens*, *E. umbellata*, and *E. macrophylla*, their hybrids and cultivars, and *Hippophaë rhamnoides* (Sea Buckthorn), whose female plants produce bright-orange berries. The fruits of some species are edible, e.g., *Shepherdia argentea* (Silver Buffalo Berry), used to make jelly, and also eaten dried with sugar in various parts of North America. The berries of *S. canadensis* (Russet Buffalo Berry) when dried or smoked are used as food by the Inuit. The wood of this species is fine-grained and is used for turnery. The fruits of the Japanese shrub *Elaeagnus multiflora* (Cherry Elaeagnus) are used as preserves and in an alcoholic beverage.

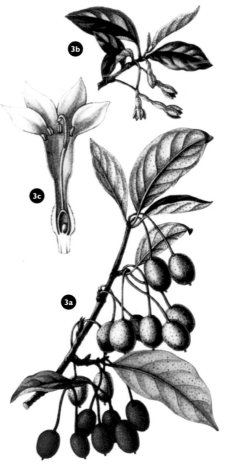

Elaeagnaceae. I *Shepherdia argentea* (a) flowering branch showing thorns and male flowers (x⅔); (b) leafy shoot with female flowers (x⅔); (c) female flower (x6); (d) male flower (x6); (e) fruit—a drupelike structure cut away here to reveal the single seed (x3). **2** *Hippophaë rhamnoides* (a) thorny, leafy, shoot bearing fruits (x⅔); (b) female flower with bilobed calyx-tube (x3); (c) gynoecium (x3); (d) fruit (x2); (e) fruit with part of fleshy calyx cut away (x2); (f) male flower (x3); (g) male flower opened out (x2). **3** *Elaeagnus multiflora* (a) shoot bearing fleshy fruits (x⅔); (b) shoot bearing bisexual flowers (x⅔); (c) flower opened out with vertical section of 1-locular ovary (x2).

Bilberries, Blueberries, Cranberries, Heathers, Heaths, Rhododendrons, and Wintergreens

This large, cosmopolitan family of evergreen or deciduous shrubs and scramblers contains many well-known ornamental plants, in particular many species of *Rhododendron*, *Erica*, *Arbutus*, and *Pieris*.

Description Evergreen or deciduous shrubs, sometimes scramblers or climbers (e.g., some *Agapetes*), herbs or trees (*Arbutus*), sometimes epiparasites without chlorophyll (*Monotropa*), with simple leaves. The leaves are alternate and spirally arranged or opposite or whorled, entire or serrate, with or without a petiole, sometimes strongly revolute and forming narrow ericoid needles, and without stipules.

The inflorescence is of terminal or axillary racemes usually with paired bracteoles (prophylls), rarely single-flowered. The flowers are regular, usually hermaphrodite, with (2–)4–5(–9) sepals fused at the base. The petals are (3–)4–5(–9), equal, and usually fused, except for pointed tips. The stamens are (2–)5(–8) or 10(–16) free or rarely adnate to the petals. The ovary is usually superior but inferior in the Vaccineae, of (1–)4–5(–14) fused carpels, containing 1 to many ovules. The style is usually as long as the corolla tube, hollow, and without lobes. The fruit is a capsule, berry, or drupe bearing small seeds.

Distribution The family is cosmopolitan, with several genera (e.g., *Empetrum*) whose species are widely disjunct. The disjunction of genera and species across major oceans is a feature of the family. *Erica*, *Rhododendron*, and *Agapetes* account for more than 50% of the species, but 50% of the genera are of 5 spp. or fewer. Notable areas of diversity are the southwestern cape of South Africa, where c. 450 *Erica* spp. grow; Southeast Asia with more than 400 *Agapetes* spp. and almost 300 spp. of *Rhododendron* sect. *Vireya*; and the area of western China, Tibet, Myanmar, and Assam, where *Rhododendron* is most diverse (c. 700 spp.). Epacrideae has a center of diversity in eastern Australia.

Economic uses The family is economically important for the many species in horticulture, *Rhododendron* particularly commanding high prices. *Erica*, *Arbutus*, *Kalmia*, and *Pieris* are all also widely grown for their bright flowers and usually glossy, evergreen foliage. The major fruit crops are Cranberry (*Vaccinium* sect. *Oxycoccus*, especially the American Cranberry, *V. macrocarpon*) and the Blueberry (*V.* sect. *Cyanococcus*, especially *V. corymbosum* and *V. angustifolium*).

Some species of Ericaceae are highly toxic, and the honey from *Rhododendron* can cause illness or even fatality thanks to the effects of a grayanotoxin (andromedotoxin). According to the Roman author Pliny the Elder, this honey was used to poison Xenophon's troops in 401 BCE, although it is now commercially available and used in recipes.

Ericaceae. I *Agapetes macrantha* part of leafy shoot with axillary inflorescence (x⅔). **2** *Arctostaphylos uva-ursi* (a) leafy shoot with terminal inflorescences (x⅔); (b) half flower (x4); (c) stamen with broad, hairy filament and anthers crowned by recurved arms and opening by terminal pores (x10); (d) cross section of ovary (x4). **3** *Erica vallis-aranearum* flowering shoot (x⅔). **4** *Cassiope selaginoides* stem covered with small clasping leaves (x⅔). **5** *Phyllothamnus erectus* flowering shoot (x⅔). **6** *Epigaea repens* (a) leafy stem and inflorescence (x1); (b) gynoecium with lobed ovary and stigma (x4). **7** *Chimaphila umbellata* shoot and inflorescence (x⅔).

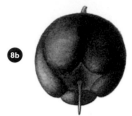

Ericaceae. 8 *Gaultheria* sp. (a) leafy shoot and berries (x⅔); (b) berry (x2⅔). 9 *Empetrum rubrum* (a) shoot with solitary flowers in leaf axils (x2); (b) cross section of ovary with 9 locules (x10); (c) male flower showing 2 whorls each of 3 perianth segments (x8); (d) gynoecium showing single, short style with 6 stigmatic branches (x12); (e) fruit—a drupe (x2). 10 *Corema conradii* (a) shoot with flowers in terminal heads (x3 mm); (b) head of flowers each with conspicuous stamens (x4). 11 *Ceratiola ericoides* (a) leafy shoot with flowers in leaf axils (x⅔); (b) male flower with 2 anthers dehiscing lengthwise (x8); (c) ovary crowned by lobed stigma (x12); (d) cross section of fruit showing 2 seeds (x6).

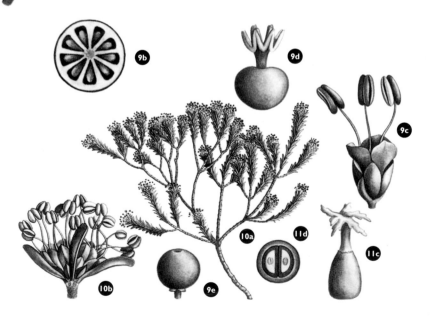

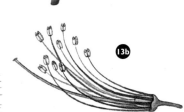

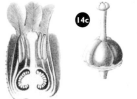

Ericaceae. 12 *Erica versicolor* var. *costata* flowering shoot. **13** *Rhododendron yunnanense* (a) flowering shoot (x⅔); (b) androecium and gynoecium (x1⅓). **14** *Sarcodes sanguinea* (a) flower (x1); (b) half flower (x2); (c) gynoecium (x2).

Euphorbiaceae. 1 *Euphorbia stapfii*
a cactuslike species (×⅔). **2** *Acalypha* sp.
leafy shoot and lateral inflorescence (×⅔)
3 *Euphorbia amygdaloides* (a) flowering
shoot showing inflorescences (cyathia)
condensed to resemble a single flower
(×⅔); (b) the cyathium consisting of an outer
cup-shaped structure bearing horseshoe-
shaped glands on the rim, within which is a ring
of male flowers each consisting of a single stamen
and in the center the female flower that consists of a
stalked ovary and branched stigmas (×6); (c) 3-lobed
fruit (×4). **4** *Croton fothergillifolius* (a) flowering shoot
(×⅔); (b) fruit (×4).

Spurge Family

A large, diverse family with unisexual flowers, superior syncarpous ovaries, and 1 ovule per locule. The family has undergone major taxonomic revision following molecular phylogenetic studies.

Description Trees, shrubs, herbs, climbers, or succulents, with hairs ranging from simple to dendritic and T-shaped to stellate and lepidote. Clear or milky latex is present in many taxa. The white milky latex of subfamily Euphorbioideae is usually caustic or toxic. Also notable is the secretion of resin from floral bracts in *Dalechampia*. The leaves are simple or palmately compound, entire to toothed or deeply lobed. Stipules are generally, but not always, present and can be minute and caducous to large and foliaceous. Leafless succulent species are often spiny, superficially resembling cacti. Inflorescences are diverse. Euphorbieae is characterized by highly specialized pseudanthial synflorescences (cyathia), consisting of bracts subtending 4–5 staminate inflorescences (reduced to a single stamen), and a terminal pistillate flower (reduced to a gynoecium). The flowers are unisexual (plants monoecious or dioecious). Sepals, petals, disks, staminodes, and pistillodes may be absent or present. The stamens range from 1–1000 (variously branched in *Ricinus*) and are free or variously fused. The ovary is superior, of (1–)2–5(–20) fused carpels, forming as many locules, each with a single ovule. The fruit is characteristically an explosive schizocarp, with typical dehiscence. In many taxa, the fruit is indehiscent, and in critical taxa (Peroideae) it is atypically nonexplosive.

Distribution Cosmopolitan, except Antarctica, with greatest diversity in the tropics; abundant in low to medium altitudes, dominant in some ecosystems.

Economic uses *Manihot esculenta* (cassava, manioc, tapioca, yuca) is the fourth most important food plant in the tropics. This starch crop of neotropical origin is known to have been in cultivation from 2000 BCE. It grows in poor, dry soils and is nearly immune to locust attack. The starchy, tuberous roots contain hydrogen cyanide (HCN), which is removed by correct preparation. Another economically important species is *Hevea brasiliensis* (Rubber Tree) originated in the Amazon Basin. In 1873, the English forester Henry Wickham brought 70,000 seeds from Brazil to England and they were shipped to Southeast Asia, now the main center of cultivation. Natural rubber has played a major role in the industrial revolution, and still accounts for around one-third of the world's consumption of tires and tire accessories. *Ricinus communis* (Castor Oil Plant) is grown as a source of oil. The seeds have been found in Egyptian tombs dating back to 4000 BCE. The seed oil is an excellent industrial lubricant. It is free of the water-soluble compound ricin, which is highly toxic to humans and animals. *Ricinus* is also grown as an ornamental, as are *Euphorbia pulcherrima* (Poinsettia), *Codiaeum variegatum* ("Croton"), *Acalypha hispida* (Cat's Tail, Chenille Plant), *A. wilkesiana* (Copper Leaf), and *Euphorbia milii* (Crown-of-thorns). Many succulent species of *Euphorbia*, mainly from Africa and Madagascar, are horticulturally desirable and threatened by illegal collecting. Many herbaceous *Euphorbia* species of temperate regions are well-known garden weeds.

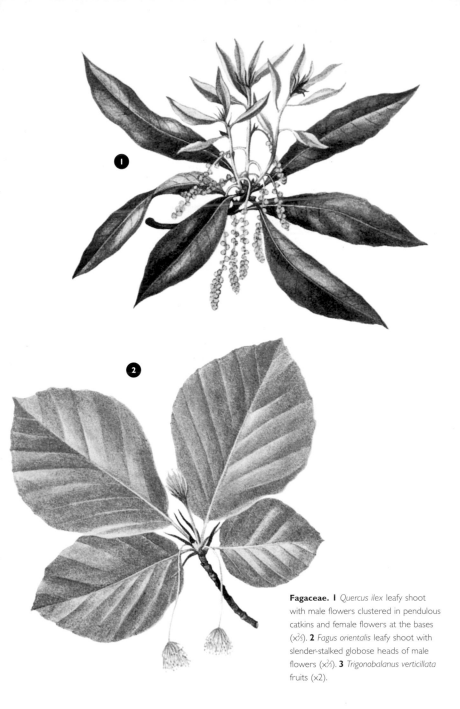

Fagaceae. 1 *Quercus ilex* leafy shoot with male flowers clustered in pendulous catkins and female flowers at the bases (x⅔). **2** *Fagus orientalis* leafy shoot with slender-stalked globose heads of male flowers (x⅔). **3** *Trigonobalanus verticillata* fruits (x2).

Beeches, Oaks, and Sweet Chestnuts

A commercially important family of deciduous or evergreen hardwood timber trees, more rarely shrubs with edible fruits, and ornamentals that grow mostly in the northern hemisphere.

Description Deciduous or evergreen trees, rarely shrubs, with alternate (rarely whorled) simple, entire to pinnately lobed leaves, and scarious, usually deciduous stipules. The flowers are unisexual (plants monoecious) and usually arranged in catkins or small spikes that may comprise only flowers of one sex, as in oaks, or may have female flowers at the base of otherwise male inflorescences, a more ancestral condition found e.g., in chestnuts. The perianth is bractlike, with 4–7 lobes. The male flowers have as many or twice as many stamens as perianth segments, occasionally up to 40, with the filaments free, with or without a pistillode. The female flowers are in groups of 1–3, each group being surrounded by a basal involucre. The ovary is inferior, with 3 or 6 styles and locules, and 2 ovules in each locule. The fruits are single-seeded nuts, in groups of 1–3(–15), surrounded or enclosed by an often hardened cupule; seed 1, filling the nut, endosperm not apparent at maturity. The fruits of the Fagaceae are animal dispersed and have a short viability. The pollen and other features, such as a strongly scented inflorescence, suggest that insect pollination is the ancestral condition in the Fagaceae, and this is retained in most members except *Fagus* and the temperate oak species.

The familiar acorn "cup" is one example of the great variety of forms shown by the cupule, surrounding 1 or more fruits, which is a unique feature of the family and the origin of which has caused controversy. Only with the discovery of *Trigonobalanus* in 1961, restricted to Sulawesi, northern Borneo, Malaysia, and northern Thailand, has it been possible to suggest firmly that the cupule is derived from a 3-lobed extension of the pedicel below each flower, which has been variously fused around single flowers or groups of flowers. It is possible that the cupule provides a link with the pteridosperm ancestors of the flowering plants. The tremendous diversity of scales and spines on the cupules appears to be derived from branched spines.

Distribution The Fagaceae grow mostly in the northern hemisphere, with a few species crossing the equator in Southeast Asia. Beeches (*Fagus*), oaks (*Quercus*), and sweet chestnuts (*Castanea*) figure prominently and are frequently the dominant members of the broad-leaved forests that cover, or used to cover, vast areas of North America and Eurasia at midlatitudes. Evergreen oaks are important in the forests around the Gulf of Mexico and in southern China and southern Japan. In

Southeast Asia, the structure of the mixed
mountain forest is determined largely
by evergreen members of the family,
particularly oaks. In total, therefore,
the Fagaceae produces a colossal
biomass, possibly exceeded only by
the conifers. The Fagaceae have a
long fossil record, suggesting an origin by at least the middle Cretaceous,
about 90 million years ago.

Economic uses The Fagaceae is
the source of some of the world's most
important temperate hardwoods, the
most notable being oak (particularly
the European and American white
oaks), beech, and chestnut.
Together with clearance for agriculture, this has resulted in the destruc-
tion of large areas dominated by the
family. Although the timber is of
good quality, the tropical members of
Castanopsis and *Lithocarpus* have as yet been
little exploited. Taken as a whole the timber of
the family exhibits a wide range of properties
and thus many uses, from floorboards and
furniture to charcoal and whisky barrels.
Commercial cork is derived from the bark of
the Mediterranean cork oak (*Quercus suber*),
and in southeastern Europe and Asia Minor
the oak galls were an important source of
tannin. Many species of chestnut, but
principally the Sweet Chestnut
(*Castanea sativa*) of southern Europe,
are grown for their large edible nuts,
from which are made purees, stuff-
ings, stews, and the French delica-
cy *marrons glacés*. The nuts of
beech (beech-mast) are rich in oil
(46%) and in many regions constitute an important food for pigs, as
also the acorns of oaks. The form
and rich autumnal coloring in many
deciduous species results in many
Fagaceae being grown as ornamentals
in parks and larger gardens, particularly oaks, chestnuts, and beech. The only
American species of Castanopsis (*C. cryso-
phylla*) and Lithocarpus (*L. densiflorus*) may
be cultivated in warmer regions.

Fagaceae. 4 *Quercus robur* (a) leafy shoot
showing fruits (nuts) surrounded at base of
the familiar cup or cupule (x⅔); (b) leafless
tree. **5** *Fagus sylvatica* leafless tree. **6** *Castanea
sativa* young fruit with closed spiny cupule
forming at the base of remains of the male
catkin (x⅔).

Gentian Family

Gentianaceae has commonly been considered to comprise only annual to perennial herbs with a few shrubs, but recent work has resulted in the inclusion of some massive tropical trees and woody lianes.

Description Mostly annual to perennial herbs (twining in *Crawfurdia* and *Tripterospermum*), but in tropical genera occasionally woody and sometimes (especially *Anthocleista* and *Fagraea*) large trees up to 35 m or woody lianes. Saprophytes without chlorophyll are rare but have evolved separately several times in different tribes (*Voyria, Voyriella, Sebaea, Bartonia, Obolaria, Cotylanthera*).

The leaves are opposite or rarely (*Saccifolium*, some *Swertia, Voyriella*) alternate or whorled, sometimes perfoliate (*Blackstonia*), usually with raised interpetiolar lines at the nodes. The lamina nearly always has an entire margin, and is rarely (*Saccifolium* from Guyana Highlands) saccate.

The inflorescence is a terminal or axillary cyme or rarely raceme, spike, or head, and flowers are rarely solitary. The flowers are bisexual except in *Veratrilla*, hypogynous, 4- or 5-merous, or rarely 3- or 6- to 16-merous, nearly always actinomorphic, occasionally heterostylous. The sepals are fused at the base, and the calyx may be zygomorphic in some *Exacum* species. The corolla is tubular to campanulate or funnel-shaped, may be slightly zygomorphic in *Chelonanthus, Symbolanthus*, and *Macrocarpaea*, and may have 4 nectariferous spurs on the outside (*Halenia*). The stamens are the same in number as the corolla lobes and inserted on the corolla tube or rarely between the corolla lobes, and may be rarely asymmetrical. The anthers open by terminal pores in *Exacum*. The ovary is superior, 2-carpellate, 1- to 2-locular, with a variety of placentation types. The fruit is a dry capsule, or a berry in the herbaceous *Chironia* and *Tripterospermum* and the woody *Anthocleista, Fagraea*, and *Potalia*.

Distribution Cosmopolitan, from arctic tundra to tropical forests, but perhaps most often associated with open grassy places, such as chalk grassland and alpine meadows.

Economic uses Many medicinal treatments are based on the unique bitter seco-iridoids and xanthones present in the family. *G. lutea* (Yellow Gentian) is the source of "gentianroot" of the Pharmacopeia and the main commercial source of the bitter tonic, gentian bitter, and used in aperitifs such as Gentiane and Suze. A number of genera are grown as ornamentals, including *Exacum* as a house plant. By far the most important commercially is *Gentiana*, many species of which are cultivated as rock-garden or herbaceous-border perennials.

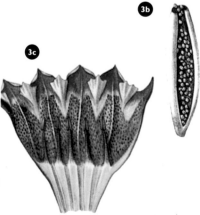

Gentianaceae. **1** *Chironia purpurascens* (a) flowering shoot (x⅔); (b) corolla opened out showing epipetalous stamens with coiled anthers (×1); (c) cross section of ovary with 2 parietal placentas (×3). **2** *Voyria primuloides* (a) habit (x⅔); (b) flower from above (x⅔); (c) half flower with epipetalous stamens and globose stigma (×3). **3** *Gentiana depressa* (a) habit (x⅔); (b) ovary with part of wall cut away (×3); (c) corolla opened out (×1). **4** *Sabatia campestris* (a) flowering shoot (x⅔); (b) section of ovary (×2); (c) corolla opened out (×1)

Geraniums and Pelargoniums

The Geraniaceae is a family of annual to perennial herbs or shrubs with usually colorful flowers, with most genera containing horticulturally valuable plants.

Description Shrubs, geophytes, and herbs, mostly perennial but some annual or biennial, usually with a pronounced taproot. Stems, when present, are sometimes woody or succulent. The leaves are alternate, with stipules and usually petiolate, the lamina simple or lobed to deeply divided and pinnate.

The inflorescences are terminal or axillary, umbellate, cymose, or of a single flower. The flowers are bisexual, radially (*Monsonia, Hypseocharis*) or bilaterally symmetrical, strongly so in *Pelargonium*, 5-merous, bracteolate, with a usually brightly colored perianth of sepals and petals, the petals clawed, highly variable in form in *Pelargonium*.

Nectaries are present (in a hypanthial tube in *Pelargonium*). The stamens are 5, 10, or 15, sometimes modified to staminodes (commonly in *Pelargonium*). The ovary is superior, of 5 fused carpels, developing into a distinctive schizocarpic fruit that separates into single-seeded mericarps, each ususally with a hygroscopic awn.

Distribution The Geraniaceae are widely distributed reaching from Arctic to sub-Antarctic regions but are commonest in temperate regions and largely absent from the wet tropics and much of Australasia. Of the major genera, *Geranium* is cosmopolitan, while *Pelargonium* has a center of diversity in the South African Cape, *Erodium* is most diverse in the Mediterranean region, and Monsonia is African in distribution. *Hypseocharis*, by contrast, is endemic to the Andes, along the western coast of South America.

Economic uses Pelargonium is of major economic importance in horticulture as a summer bedding plant and as an ornamental houseplant. *Pelargonium triste* was introduced to Europe from the Cape before 1631 and later introductions led to extensive hybridization in the eighteenth century. Oils from *Pelargonium* are used in perfume and as a flavoring. Many Geraniaceae have traditional medicinal use.

Geraniaceae. 1 *Geranium malviflorum* (a) shoot with compound leaves and inflorescences (x⅔); (b) vertical section of flower showing bilobed petals (x1⅓). **2** *G. sanguineum* fruit with persistent calyx and with 1 awn separating from the central axis to disperse a seed (x1⅓). **3** *Erodium romanum* (a) tip of leafy shoot with inflorescence and fruits (x⅔); (b) fruit before dehiscence (x1⅓). **4** *Sarcocaulon patersonii* (a) fleshy stem with thorns (remains of leaf stalks) and solitary flowers (x1); (b) flower with petals removed showing 5 pointed sepals and 15 stamens of 2 lengths and with fused filament bases (x3).

African Violets and Gloxinias

Mostly tropical herbs and shrubs, sometimes lianes or trees, often epiphytic or epilithic, related to Scrophulariaceae (Figwort and Foxglove family) and growing in pantropical regions.

Description The family varies in habit from herbs (rarely annual) to shrubs, lianes, or trees to 15 m, usually polycarpic, sometimes monocarpic. In the Old World, many genera comprise plants consisting only of 1 much enlarged cotyledon (sometimes more than 1 m long) and an inflorescence, with no normal foliage leaves. When leaves are present, they are opposite or sometimes whorled or alternate, sometimes forming a basal rosette, entire or variously toothed but rarely deeply divided, usually clothed with glandular or egandular hairs. The inflorescence is a specialized "pair-flowered" cyme found elsewhere only in a few genera of Scrophulariaceae. The 5 sepals are free or fused into a tube, sometimes 2-lipped, sometimes fleshy and colored. The corolla has a short or more often long tube (often varying greatly in 1 genus). The fertile stamens are 2 (some Old World genera) or most commonly 4 or sometimes (in regular flowers) 5. A nectary below the ovary is often well developed. The ovary consists of 2 fused carpels and may be superior or (in the New World) semi-inferior or inferior, usually 1-locular with parietal placentae, but may have an incomplete or sometimes complete septum dividing it into 2 locules with axile placenta; the ovules are many. Only 1 carpel is fertile occasionally. In the Old World, the fruit is usually a dry capsule and may be short, globose, and dehiscing in its upper part, sometimes elongate and podlike, with many small seeds. In the New World, the fruit is often fleshy and usually indehiscent.

The family shows many adaptations to specialized habitats in both vegetative and floral characters. Many epiphytic or epilithic species dry out for short periods and revive in wetter conditions. In the Old World, the cotyledons develop unequally, and in some genera the only adult vegetative structure is one much-enlarged cotyledon that lies flat against a tree trunk or rock. Floral adaptations are associated with

pollinating agents, involving often brightly colored corolla and sometimes calyx. In some species, the pollinator is attracted by extrafloral structures (colored hairs or leaves). Many New World genera have developed brightly colored fleshy fruits, which are adapted to seed dispersal by birds, bats, monkeys, or ants.

Distribution The family is pantropical, with extensions to southern temperate areas and with 6 spp. isolated in the mountains of southern Europe (Pyrenees, Balkans). It is much less represented in the Afro–Madagascan region than in the neotropics and Asia. Species grow from sea level to high alpine places in the Himalayas and Andes, most preferring a moist situation in forests, where some 25% of species are epiphytic or on wet rocks. Distributions of the major genera correspond closely with different continents. Broadly, genera that grow in one region tend to be closely related to each other. Thus, subfamily Gesnerioideae occurs in the New World, Didymocarpoideae in the Old World, and Coronantheroideae in Australasia and temperate South America. The distributions of these groups may be related to the breakup of Gondwanaland.

Economic uses The colorful flowers and comparative ease of cultivation have made many genera important in horticulture, but few are hardy in the temperate regions. The 3 European genera are occasionally grown as alpines on rock gardens. Species and hybrids of *Streptocarpus* and *Saintpaulia* are marketed extensively as house plants. Many thousands of cultivars exist. In glasshouses in temperate regions, or outside in the tropics, *Sinningia* (the florists' "Gloxinia"), *Columnea*, *Kohleria*, *Episcia*, *Nematanthus*, *Aeschynanthus*, and other genera are grown extensively; special-interest groups of gesneriad growers thrive. The family also provides many medicinal plants.

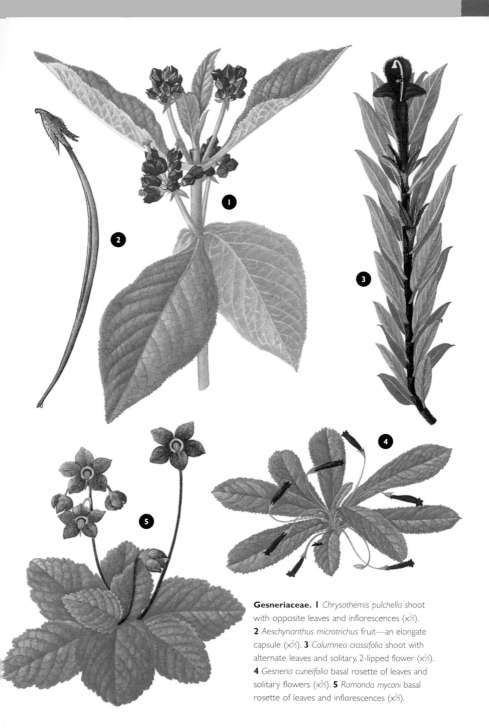

Gesneriaceae. 1 *Chrysothemis pulchella* shoot with opposite leaves and inflorescences (x⅔).
2 *Aeschynanthus microtrichus* fruit—an elongate capsule (x⅔). **3** *Columnea crassifolia* shoot with alternate leaves and solitary, 2-lipped flower (x⅔).
4 *Gesneria cuneifolia* basal rosette of leaves and solitary flowers (x⅔). **5** *Ramonda myconi* basal rosette of leaves and inflorescences (x⅔).

Hamamelidaceae. 1 *Hamamelis mollis* (a) leaf (x⅔); (b) shoot with flowers (x⅔); (c) flower with 4 hairy sepals, 4 linear petals, 4 stamens, and bilobed stigma (x3); (d) vertical section of ovary (x9); (e) fruit—a woody capsule (x2). **2** *Fothergilla major* (a) leafy shoot and inflorescence (x⅔); (b) bicarpellate gynoecium (x3); (c) dehisced fruit (x2). **3** *Rhodoleia championii* (a) shoot with many-flowered capitula surrounded by numerous bracts giving appearance of single flower (x⅔); (b) 5 gynoecia on capitulum (x1); (c) cross section of ovary (x2); (d) ripe fruits (x1).

Witch Hazel and Liquidambar Family

Temperate and tropical trees and shrubs, with petals usually linear to strap-shaped, leaves usually alternate, and inflorescences aggregated into dense spikes or heads, sometimes spherical.

Description Trees and shrubs, sometimes with stellate hairs. The leaves are alternate or rarely opposite, simple, ovate or elliptical to heart-shaped or palmately lobed, with entire to serrate margins, usually with stipules. The inflorescence is usually aggregated into a dense spike or head, sometimes spherical with many flowers, the individual flowers sessile, rarely a lax spike with shortly pedicellate flowers. The flowers are actinomorphic or (*Rhodoleia*) zygomorphic, bisexual or unisexual (plants monoecious or, in Hamamelideae, andromonoecious), hypogynous to usually epigynous. The sepals are 4–5(–10) and small, or absent. The petals are 4 or 5, or absent, usually linear or strap-shaped when present. The stamens are 4–5(–10), alternating with the petals when present, sometimes with many staminodes. The ovary is superior to inferior, of 2 fused carpels each with 1 to many ovules, with axile or rarely parietal placentation. The fruit is a capsule, usually woody, the seeds being ejected or not.

Distribution The family has a rather disjunct distribution, from eastern North America to Venezuela, eastern Mediterranean, Ethiopia to South Africa, temperate East Asia to Indo–Malesia and northern Australia, and is absent or scarce in much of South America, Africa, and Australia. In temperate regions, they usually grow in open places or woodland, but in the tropics they are more often located in rain forest.

Economic uses *Altingia*, *Liquidambar*, and *Exbucklandia* provide high-quality timber. *Liquidambar* and *Hamamelis* yield gums used in perfumery or to provide medicinal products used as expectorants, inhalants, or for the treatment of skin complaints, e.g., *H. virginica*

(Witch Hazel). Many species and cultivars of *Corylopsis*, *Fothergilla*, *Hamamelis*, *Liquidambar*, *Loropetalum*, *Parrotia*, and *Sycopsis* are grown as ornamentals (early sweet-scented flowers with an autumnal color) in temperate regions. Twigs of witch hazel have been used in water-divining ("witching").

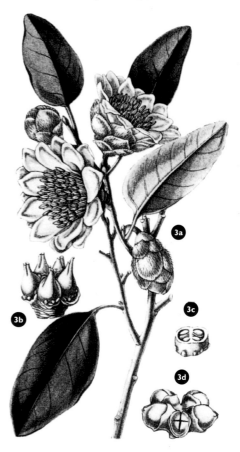

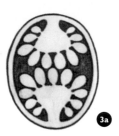

3a

3b

2

Hydrophyllaceae. 1 *Phacelia minor* shoot with leaves and flowers (x⅔). **2** *P. tanacetifolia* half flower showing appendages on bases of filaments (x4). **3** *P. franklinii* (a) cross section of ovary with ovules on parietal placentas (x18); (b) dehiscing capsule with many seeds (x1½). **4** *Hydrophyllum virginianum* (a) shoot with pinnate leaf and flowers in a headlike cyme (x⅔); (b) dehiscing capsule with 2 seeds (x4).

Phacelia Family

A New World family of annual to perennial herbs to shrubs related to Boraginaceae (Borage and Forget-me-not family) and usually resembling them in having a cincinnate inflorescence.

Description Annual to perennial herbs to shrubs, or rarely (*Wigandia*) small trees to 5 m with massive leaves. The leaves are alternate or rarely (*Draperia*) opposite, simple and entire to palmate (*Romanzoffia*, some *Hydrophyllum*), or deeply pinnately divided, sometimes 3-pinnate, in *Wigandia* sometimes broadly ovate and up to 40 cm across.

Irritant hairs are present in some genera, e.g., *Phacelia*, *Turricula*, and *Wigandia*. The inflorescences are characteristically cincinnate, the flowers opening as the coil unwinds, or sometimes flowers are solitary with long pedicels in the leaf axils. The flowers are more or less actinomorphic, bisexual, hypogynous, and 5-merous. The calyx has sepals fused at the base and is usually persistent and conspicuous and may be accrescent (especially *Tricardia*). The corolla is campanulate to funnel-shaped, with 5 usually short, rounded lobes, usually white to blue or purple, rarely yellow. The stamens are inserted on the corolla tube and may be exserted or included. The ovary is bicarpellate and 1-locular, with a single, often exserted, style and stigma (sometimes divided in *Phacelia*), and with parietal placentation and usually many ovules. The fruit is a capsule, dehiscing by 2–4 valves.

Distribution With the exclusion of *Hydrolea* and *Codon*, the family is now considered to be restricted to the New World, from Alaska to Argentina. The center of generic diversity and greatest number of species is in the southwestern USA, especially California.

Members of the family grow mostly in open, dry, sandy, or rocky habitats. A few species of *Nemophila*, *Phacelia*, and *Wigandia* are occasionally naturalized in the Old World.

Economic uses Species of *Nemophila* and *Phacelia* are grown as ornamental annuals. *Wigandia* is cultivated widely as a large-leaved, fast-growing novelty tree in the tropics.

The leaves of *Nama jamaicense* are said to be smoked as a tobacco in Argentina and are used to cure gastric ulcers in Mexico.

Icacinaceae

Small-flowered shrubs, trees, and lianes of tropical evergreen forests in the southern hemisphere, growing up to 45 m and sometimes bearing irritating hairs.

Description Shrubs or trees up to 45 m (*Platea*) or high-climbing lianes up to 40 m (*Phytocrene, Sleumeria*), sometimes with tendrils that are modified branches or inflorescences, the lower parts sometimes forming a massive rootstock above ground (*Pyrenacantha*), and sometimes (e.g., *Phytocrene*) with irritating hairs.

The leaves are alternate or, in the climbers, sometimes opposite, simple, usually entire or rarely serrulate, sometimes palmately 3- to 7-lobed, often with prominent venation beneath.

The inflorescence is racemose, sometimes compound, rarely cymose, sometimes a pendent linear spike. The flowers are actinomorphic, bisexual or unisexual (plants dioecious), (4-)5-merous, and small (mostly 3–5[7] mm).

The calyx is shallowly cup shaped, rarely absent (*Pyrenacantha*). The petals are free or fused at the base or (e.g., *Iodes*) for most of their length.

The stamens are as many as the petals or corolla lobes, free or inserted on the corolla, or with many congested antherlike chambers (*Polyporandra*).

The ovary is superior, with a simple style or sessile stigma, normally 1-locular with 2 pendent apical ovules.

The fruits are drupes, sometimes aggregated into large globose clusters (e.g., *Phytocrene*), rarely with a lateral fleshy colored appendage (*Apodytes*).

Distribution Pantropical and southern hemisphere, usually in evergreen forests.

Economic uses The wood is seldom of very good quality and is used only locally. Stems of lianes, such as *Phytocrene*, are said to hold fresh drinking water. In the New World, *Poraqueiba* has edible fruits and seeds, while starchy tubers of *Casimirella* are sold commercially. *Sarcostigma* seeds provide an oil used in India to treat rheumatism, and *Cassinopsis* leaves and bark are used to treat dysentery in Madagascar.

Icacinaceae. 1 *Iodes usambarensis* (a) leafy shoot with tendril and inflorescence (×⅔); (b) female flower (×6); (c) fruits (×1); (d) male flower (×6). **2** *Pyrenacantha volubilis* (a) leafy shoot with axillary inflorescences (×⅔); (b) female flower (×6); (c) male flower (×6); (d) vertical section of ovary (×6). **3** *Phytocrene bracteata* fruits (×⅔).

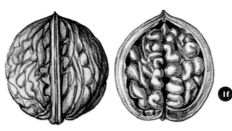

Juglandaceae. 1 *Juglans regia*
(a) imparipinnate leaf (x2/3);
(b) male, catkinlike inflorescence
borne on old wood (x²⁄₅); (c) tip
of shoot with female flower with
plumose stigmas (x²⁄₅); (d) fruit
(x2/3); (e) fruit with fleshy husk
removed to show hard, sculptured
endocarp (inner fruit wall) (x²⁄₅);
(f) fruit with endocarp removed to
show seed with contorted cotyledons (x²⁄₅); (g) habit of an old tree.

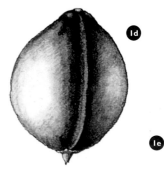

Walnuts, Hickories, and Pecan Nuts

A family of chiefly deciduous, often aromatic, trees, well known for the edible fruits (nuts) of its members and the valuable timber and nut oil of some of its species.

Description Resinous trees, usually deciduous, sometimes evergreen (*Alfaroa, Oreomunnia*). The leaves are alternate, rarely opposite (*Alfaroa, Oreomunnea*), pinnate, usually aromatic, and lacking stipules. The flowers are bracteate and unisexual (plants monoecious); male flowers usually in catkinlike, pendulous inflorescences forming on the previous year's growth, the females in smaller erect or long pendulous (*Pterocarya*) spikes on the new growth. The male flowers have 3–40 free stamens in 2 or more series, with short filaments and 2-locular anthers opening longitudinally. Pollination is by wind. The female flowers have an inferior ovary of 2 fused carpels forming a single locule containing 1 erect orthotropous ovule, lacking endosperm. The style is short with 2 stigmas. The fruit is a drupaceous nut or 3-winged and samaroid, tightly enclosed by the coriaceous or fibrous husk developed from the perianth, bracts, and bracteoles, dehiscent in most species of *Carya* and *Juglans*. The characteristic boat-shaped walnut halves, obtained on cracking open, do not correspond to the 2 carpels as the suture is along their midribs.

Distribution Temperate and subtropical regions of the northern hemisphere, and reaching the tropics of Asia and America. Most *Juglans* (21 spp.) grow in southeastern Europe, extending to East Asia and Japan, and from North America and the West Indies into northern South America. *Carya* (c. 16 spp) extends from eastern North America to southern Mexico, and from eastern China to Vietnam and eastern Pakistan. Genera that are restricted to the New World are *Alfaroa* (c. 7 spp.) from Mexico to Colombia, and *Oreomunnea* (3 spp.), from Mexico to Panama. *Cyclocarya* (1 sp.), *Engelhardia* (16 spp.), *Platycarya* (1 sp.) and *Pterocarya* (6 spp.) grow in the Far East.

Economic uses *Juglans*, and to a lesser extent *Carya*, produce valuable timber and are much prized for their fine grain and toughness; used extensively for veneers. The family is perhaps best known for its edible nuts, the walnuts (*Juglans regia* and other spp.), pecan nuts (*Carya pecan, C. illinoinensis*), and hickory nuts (*C. ovata*). The nut oil has a high percentage of oleic acid and is also regarded as a healthy oil. As a result, it is used in foods, in the manufacture of cosmetics and soap, and as a drying agent in paints. It is too expensive to use compared to commercially produced olive oil except for specialist uses. Species of walnut, hickory, and wingnut (*Pterocarya*) are also often grown for their ornamental value.

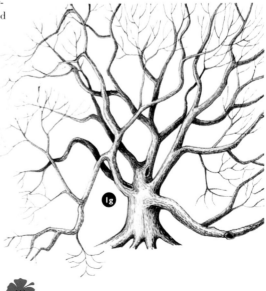

Mint Family

A large cosmopolitan family of herbs, shrubs, or trees, usually with opposite leaves and markedly zygomorphic flowers that grows from tropical forests to arctic tundra, and from sea level to high altitude.

Description Annual or perennial herbs, through shrubs to small or large trees (*Tectona grandis* to 30 m high or more) or rarely woody climbers. The stems are characteristically square in section in the more herbaceous genera. The leaves are opposite or very rarely alternate (some *Aeollanthus*) or whorled, usually simple, and often variously toothed on the margins, but sometimes deeply divided (e.g., some *Lavandula*) or 3-foliate (*Cedronella*) or digitately (*Vitex*), pinnately (*Petraeovitex*) or even bipinnately (*Perrierastrum*, now in *Plectranthus*) compound, sometimes simple and very large (*Tectona grandis* to 35 x 25 cm).

The inflorescence is cymose, usually dichasial, but sometimes monochasial, lax or often contracted into axillary verticillasters, usually with many bracts and bracteoles.

The flowers are gamopetalous and strongly zygomorphic, or occasionally secondarily actinomorphic. The calyx has a short tube, often with 10–15 conspicuous nerves, and (4)5 lobes or teeth, or 2-lipped (*Scutellaria*), rarely fleshy in fruit (*Hoslundia*).

The corolla is usually strongly 2-lipped but sometimes subactinomorphic. Stamens are usually 4 (2 long and 2 short) and characteristically exserted from the corolla tube. There is often a nectariferous disk below the ovary.

The ovary is superior, of 2 carpels, divided into 2 or 4 locules by intrusion of the carpel wall, often deeply 4-lobed and with a gynobasic style, with 4 basal or sub-basal ovules.

When the ovary is entire, the fruit may be a drupe and have 4 pyrenes, but when the ovary is 4-lobed the fruit breaks up into 4 dry nutlets.

Distribution The family is cosmopolitan, ranging from tropical forests to arctic tundra, and from sea level to high altitude, with several main centers of diversification. It is particularly characteristic of the Mediterranean region, where genera such as *Phlomis*, *Rosmarinus*, *Salvia*, *Sideritis*, *Micromeria*, and *Thymus* are common aromatic components of maquis, matorral, and garigue communities.

Economic uses The family is important economically. As expanded, it now includes important tropical timber trees, especially teak (*Tectona*), and species of *Vitex* and *Gmelina*.

G. arborea is planted widely in the tropics as a source of quick-growing fuelwood. The subfamily Nepetoideae is well known for producing aromatic oils and includes numerous culinary or aromatic herbs such as Sage (*Salvia*), Mint (*Mentha*), Marjoram or Oregano (*Origanum*), Thyme (*Thymus*), Lavender (*Lavandula*), Rosemary (*Rosmarinus*), Basil (*Ocimum*), Lemon Balm (*Melissa*), Savory (*Satureja*), Mountain Tea (*Sideritis*), and Catmint (*Nepeta*). Some of these plants are grown as commercial crops.

Decorative garden plants include species of *Salvia*, *Phlomis*, *Stachys*, *Monarda*, *Ajuga*, *Lamium*, *Physostegia*, *Rosmarinus*, *Thymus*, *Agastache*, *Caryopteris*, and *Vitex*, while *Plectranthus* (including *Coleus*) are popular house plants.

In the tropics, *Plectranthus* provides hedge plants, garden ornamentals, edible tubers, potherbs, and medicinal cures, while *Holmskioldia* is grown for its colorful accrescent calyx and *Callicarpa* for its colorful fleshy fruits.

Pogostemon provides patchouli used in the perfume industry, and the oily nutlets of *Perilla* are crushed for oil for the paint industry. *Ocimum sanctum*, a holy plant for Hindus, is frequently grown near temples in India.

Lamiaceae. 1 *Stachys sylvatica* shoot with opposite leaves and terminal inflorescence (x⅔). **2** *Scutellaria indica* flowering shoot (x⅔). **3** *Teucrium fruticans* (a) flowering shoot (x⅔); (b) detail of flower (x2).

Lamiaceae. 4 *Salvia roemeriana* flowering shoot (x⅔). **5** *Plectranthus welwitschii* (a) flowering shoot showing the square stem characteristic of herbaceous members of the family (x⅔); (b) detail of flower (x2). **6** *Salvia* sp. (a) section of flower showing stamen with much elongated connective (x2); (b) detail of stamens (x3). **7** *Rosmarinus officinalis* flower with stigma and stamens projecting from the corolla (x⅔).

Lamiaceae. 8 *Lamium maculatum* 4-lobed ovary (a) entire (x2) and (b) in vertical section (x9) showing style attached to base of ovary (i.e. gynobasic). **9** *Clerodendrum thomsoniae* (a) shoot with cymose inflorescence of flowers which have an inflated, winged calyx (x⅔); (b) fruit—a 4-lobed drupe (x1). **10** *Vitex agnus-castus* (a) shoot bearing digitate leaves and cymose inflorescences (x⅔); (b) flower (x2); (c) corolla opened out to show stamens of 2 lengths (didynamous) (x3); (d) fruit (x4); (e) cross section of fruit showing 4 locules (x4).

Peas, Beans, and Mimosa

The legumes are the third largest family of flowering plants and second only to the cereals in their economic importance—enriching nutrient-poor soils through nitrogen-fixing symbioses with *Rhizobium* bacteria.

Description Herbs, shrubs, trees, woody (e.g., *Wisteria*) or herbaceous climbers, geophytes, rarely freshwater aquatics (e.g., *Neptunia*), with usually alternate leaves. The leaves are sometimes simple (e.g., *Ulex*), sometimes absent, or present only in juveniles, then replaced by leaflike petioles (e.g., some *Acacia*) but usually 3-foliate (e.g., *Trifolium*), palmate (*Lupinus*), pinnate (e.g., *Vicia*) or bipinnate (e.g., some *Acacia*), sometimes terminating in a tendril (e.g., *Vicia*), the petioles and leaflets with pulvini, sometimes reacting to touch (e.g., *Mimosa pudica*), many allowing leaflets to fold up at night. Inflorescence terminal or axillary racemes, heads, spikes, or single flowers. The flowers are bilaterally or radially (Mimosoideae) symmetrical, hermaphrodite or unisexual (plants monoecious), the whorls of 5 sepals, 5 petals, and 2 of 5 stamens alternating. The petals are 5–4(–1) or 0, variable in size and symmetry, all free, or the lower 2 fused to form a keel (e.g., Papilionoideae). Stamens usually in 2 whorls of 5, and sometimes 50–100 or more (e.g., Acacieae). A nectary frequently surrounds the superior ovary. Carpel usually 1. The fruit is usually a 1-locular dry or fleshy, dehiscent or indehiscent, pod that is inflated, compressed, winged, or not, variously dull or brightly colored, from 4 mm to 3 m in length, with one to many seeds. The seeds usually have a tough coat and vary greatly in size and color; all have little endosperm and 2 large cotyledons. Many species form nodulating symbioses with nitrogen-fixing bacteria (usually *Rhizobium* spp.).

Distribution The family is absent only from Antarctica. Caesalpinioideae and especially Mimosoideae are predominantly tropical and warm-temperate, while Papilionoideae has major areas of diversity in temperate regions. Many genera are extremely widespread, while others are endemic to single countries. The

Leguminosae. 1 *Onobrychis radiata* inflorescence and pinnate leaf (x⅔). **2** *Piptanthus nepalensis* shooting bearing 3-foliate leaves with stipules, flowers and fruit (x⅔). **3** *Spartium junceum* inflorescence—a raceme (x⅔).

116

family has diversified in most major land biomes from arid to wet tropical, grassland, and coastal but is notably absent from marine environments (although some, e.g., some *Entada*, *Sophora*, and *Lathyrus japonicus*, have long-distance ocean dispersal of seeds) and are poorly represented in fresh water (e.g., *Neptunia oleracea* and others).

Economic uses The family is of major economic importance, especially Papilionoideae because the seeds and pods of many of the herbaceous species provide human and animal food and are rich in protein and minerals. Species such as Clover (*Trifolium repens*), Lucerne (*Medicago sativa*), and Lupin (*Lupinus polyphyllus*) can be fed to livestock or plowed into the soil as an excellent fertilizer, greatly increasing its nitrogen levels. Among the species used as human food are the Garden Pea (*Pisum sativum*); Chickpea (*Cicer arietinum*); French, Haricot, Snap, String, Green,

or Kidney Bean (*Phaseolus vulgaris*); Broad Bean (*Vicia faba*); Lima Bean (*Phaseolus. lunatus*); Mung Bean (*P. aureus*); Scarlet Runner (*P. coccineus*); Lentil (*Lens culinaris*); Soybean (*Glycine max*); and Peanut, or Groundnut, (*Arachis hypogea*). Fenugreek (*Trigonella foenum-graecum*) is a spice.

The Cowpea (*Vigna sinensis*), Clover (*Trifolium* spp.), Lucerne (*M. sativa*), and Vetch (*Vicia sativa*) are widely used as forage plants. Many genera contain species highly prized as ornamentals in temperate and tropical countries, including Lupin (*Lupinus*), Broom (*Cytisus*), Golden Rain (*Laburnum*), Sweet Pea (*Lathyrus odorata*), Wild Indigo (*Baptisia*), Locust (*Robinia*), Silk Tree (*Albizia*), *Sophora*, *Wisteria*, and *Genista*. The twigs, leaves, and flowers of *Genista tinctoria* were the source of a yellow dye used for coloring fabrics. Species of *Indigofera* yield the dye indigo. In the Mimosoideae, the Australian Black Wattle (*Acacia decurrens*) and Golden Wattle (*A. pycnantha*) provide wattle bark (used in tanning). *A. dealbata* is the "Mimosa" of florists. A number of species, including the Australian Blackwood (*A. melanoxylon*) and *A. visco*, provide useful timbers. Species including *A. stenocarpa* and *A. senegal* yield gum arabic. Some *Albizia* species are valuable timber trees. Caesalpinioideae contains a number of useful species, including *Cassia acutifolia* and *C. angustifolia* native to the Middle East, whose dried leaves are the source of the purgative senna. Several *Caesalpinia* species are sources of dyes and timber. The pods of the Tamarind (*Tamarindus indica*) are used as a fresh fruit and for medicinal purposes in India.

Leguminosae. 4 *Erythrina humeana* inflorescence (x⅔). **5** *Erythrina abyssinica* dehiscing fruit (a pod or legume) and seeds (x⅔). **6** *Phaseolus vulgaris* shoot bearing flowers and immature fruit (x⅔). **7** *Lathyrus sylvestris* shoot bearing leaves. tendrils, and inflorescence (x⅔). **8** *Ulex europaeus* half flower showing hairy sepals, upstanding standard petal, lateral wing petal, and within it the keel petal, which surrounds the stamens that have their filaments fused and ovary with numerous ovules (x2⅔). **9** (right) *Erythrostemon gilliesii* shoot with bipinnate leaf and terminal inflorescence (x⅔). **10** *Mimosa pudica* (a) shoot with sensitive, bipinnate leaves with 4 secondary stalks and axillary tight clusters of flowers (x⅔); (b) clusters of mature fruit—compressed pods (x⅔). **11** *Dichrostachys cinerea* cluster of twisted pods (x⅔).

Leguminosae. 12 *Bauhinia galpinii* shoot with simple, bilobed leaves and terminal inflorescence (x⅔). **13** *Acacia podalyriifolia* shoot with simple leaves and globose inflorescences (x⅔).

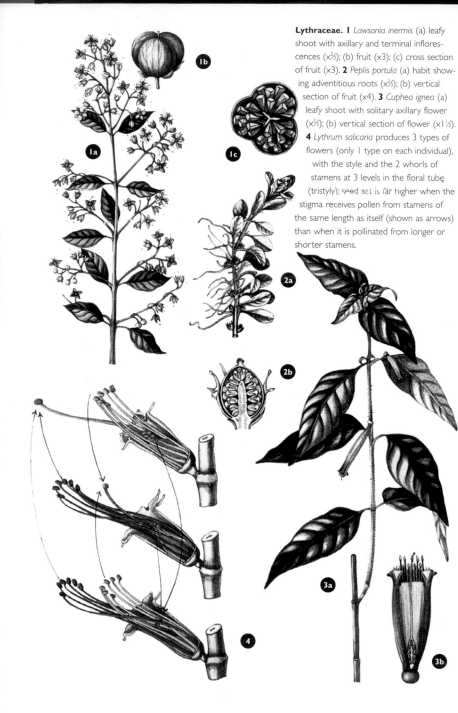

Lythraceae. 1 *Lawsonia inermis* (a) leafy shoot with axillary and terminal inflorescences (x⅔); (b) fruit (x3); (c) cross section of fruit (x3). **2** *Peplis portula* (a) habit showing adventitious roots (x⅔); (b) vertical section of fruit (x4). **3** *Cuphea ignea* (a) leafy shoot with solitary axillary flower (x⅔); (b) vertical section of flower (x1½). **4** *Lythrum salicaria* produces 3 types of flowers (only 1 type on each individual), with the style and the 2 whorls of stamens at 3 levels in the floral tube (tristyly); seed set is far higher when the stigma receives pollen from stamens of the same length as itself (shown as arrows) than when it is pollinated from longer or shorter stamens.

Loosestrife, Pomegranate, Water Chestnut, Henna, Crepe Myrtle, and Mangrove Apple

A family of trees, shrubs, and aquatics that grows primarily throughout the tropics but not in African and Arabian deserts.

Description Trees, including mangroves (*Pemphis*), some with cone-shaped pneumatophores (*Sonneratia*), shrubs, or herbs, rarely aquatic (*Trapa*), with 4-angled stems on young growth. The leaves are usually opposite, rarely whorled or alternate, simple, dimorphic in amphibious species, usually entire, rarely with swollen petioles for flotation (*Trapa*); stipules, when present, small and arising in the leaf axils. Inflorescences terminal or axillary, in racemes, panicles, cymes, or solitary. The flowers are radially symmetrical to strongly zygomorphic, usually hermaphrodite, with a distinctive campanulate to tubular hypanthium. The sepals are 4–6(–16), joined at the base, valvate, often with pronounced external ridges. The petals are 4–6(–16), crinkled in bud, often brightly colored. The stamens are usually twice as many as sepals, attached to the calyx tube in 2 whorls, free, usually alternating short and long. The ovary is usually superior, sometimes inferior, of 2–4(–many) fused carpels, each forming a locule, with 1 to many ovules per locule, the whole tipped with a simple and dry style. The fruit is variously a dry dehiscent capsule to fleshy-seeded capsule or berry. Distyly and tristyly are common in the family and appear to have arisen repeatedly as an aid to outcrossing; bat pollination occurs in *Lafoensia* and *Sonneratia*.

Distribution The family grows primarily throughout the tropics, extending into temperate regions of the world, but is generally absent from African and Arabian deserts and from high latitudes. *Cuphea* (c. 260 spp.), the largest genus, is restricted to the New World tropics; *Diplusodon* (c. 74 spp.) is restricted to Brazil; *Lagerstroemia* (c. 53 spp.) grows from tropical Asia to Australia; *Nesaea* (c. 56 spp.) through tropical and southern Africa; *Rotala* (c. 44 spp.) is temperate and pantropical; and *Lythrum* (c. 36 spp.), probably the most widespread genus, reaches from Europe to Australia and an introduced invasive in North America.

Economic uses The pomegranate (*Punica granatum*) is an ancient fruit crop of the Middle East and Mediterranean. The water chestnut (*Trapa natans*) is grown in the far east as a food crop and is a problem invasive in the USA. The dye plant Henna (*Lawsonia inermis*) is the source of the most widely used products derived from this family, and work is being conducted to improve yields; the active constituent, Lawsone, gives an orange dye used especially on skin and hair. Crepe Myrtle (*Lagerstroemia indica*, *L. speciosa*) is grown widely in warm climates as a decorative tree owing to the plentiful and colorful flowers borne in the summer. Seeds of *Cuphea* have been identified as a good source of medium-chain triglycerides (fatty acids), and work is underway to develop cultivars that can be harvested on a commercial scale. Some species provide good quality timber, particularly *Physocalymma scaberrima*, which has pink wood used in decorative products. *Cuphea* species, particularly *C. ignea* and hybrids, are grown for their ornamental flowers in warm climates, and *Lythrum salicaria* is grown as a pond-side plant in temperate regions for its decorative purple flowers, although it is replaced by *Decodon verticillatus* in North America, where *L. salicaria* has become a problem invasive.

Magnoliaceae. 1 *Magnolia stellata* leaf and flowering shoot showing bracts on flower stalks (×⅔). **2** *M. grandiflora* dehisced fruits with arillate seeds attached by silky thread (×⅔). **3** *M. denudata* half flower showing 2 whorls of perianth segments, numerous spirally arranged stamens and numerous free carpels on an elongate receptacle (×½). **4** *Liriodendron tulipifera* (a) flower and leaf (×½); (b) vertical section of carpel (×1½); (c) fruiting head (×⅔). **5** *Talauma ovata* fruit with upper portions of carpels falling away to reveal 1 or 2 seeds in each carpel locule (×⅓).

Magnolias and Tulip Tree

A family of trees and shrubs native to the Americas and Asia, usually with showy flowers, long thought to be among the earliest and least evolved of all the angiosperms.

Description Trees or shrubs, deciduous or evergreen. The leaves are alternate, simple, petiolate, entire or lobed (*Liriodendron*), often with large stipules, which at first surround the stem, but fall off as the leaf expands, leaving a conspicuous scar around the node.

The flowers are actinomorphic, hermaphrodite (rarely unisexual), terminal, usually solitary, often large and showy, with an elongate receptacle, the peduncle bearing 1 or more spathaceous bracts that enclose the young flower but fall off as it expands. The perianth is composed of 2 or more (usually 3) whorls of free tepals that are petaloid; the outer tepals may be reduced and sepal-like. The stamens are numerous, free, spirally arranged, with stout filaments; the anthers have 2 locules opening by longitudinal slits.

The ovary is superior, apocarpous, usually with numerous carpels, sometimes few (rarely single), spirally arranged, free or partly fused. Each carpel has 2 or more ventrally placed ovules. The fruit is composed of separate but coalescent woody follicles that are longitudinally dehiscent (*Magnolia*), aggregates of indehiscent samaras (*Liriodendron*), or of partially united carpels and then circumscissile or indehiscent (*Talauma*).

The seeds are large (except in *Liriodendron*), 1 or 2 in each follicle, with an arilloid testa that is free from the endocarp but attached by a silky threadlike funicle; in *Liriodendron* they adhere to the endocarp and are without an arilloid testa. The seeds have copious oily endosperm and a tiny embryo.

Distribution Approximately 75% of species in the family are distributed in temperate eastern and tropical Southeast Asia, from the Himalayas eastward to Japan and southeastward through the Malesian Archipelago to Papua New Guinea. The remainder are found in America, from temperate southeast North America to tropical and subtropical South America to Brazil, with most neotropical species occurring in Colombia. All the American species belong to the genera *Magnolia*, *Talauma*, and *Liriodendron*. *Talauma* is confined to the New World, but *Magnolia* and *Liriodendron* also grow in Asia and thus have independent discontinuous distributions. *Liriodendron* comprises 2 spp., *L. tulipifera* from eastern North America and *L. chinense* from China. Fossil records indicate that the family has a long evolutionary history of more than 100 million years and was formerly much more widely distributed in the northern hemisphere.

Economic uses The genus *Magnolia* is widely cultivated as an ornamental, with numerous species and hybrids available. *Liriodendron* is also often grown in temperate countries. The wood of the North American Tulip Tree (*Liriodendron tulipifera*) is a valuable timber product of the eastern USA. The bark and flower buds of *Magnolia officinalis* and other species yield a valuable drug or tonic exported from China for medicinal use.

Malpighiaceae

A family of tropical lianas, trees, shrubs, and some herbs, with characteristic 2-branched unicellular hairs. It grows in the tropics and subtropics in both the Old and New worlds.

Description Trees, shrubs, subshrubs or herbs, or climbers, often with unicellular and 2-branched "Malpighian hairs," rarely the hairs stellate. The leaves are simple, usually opposite, sometimes whorled, rarely alternate. Stipules are usually present.

The flowers are in axillary or terminal racemose or paniculate inflorescences or are solitary. The flowers are usually bisexual, sometimes unisexual (plants dioecious or functionally dioecious), actinomorphic to obliquely zygomorphic. The sepals are 5, united, usually imbricate, rarely valvate, with 2 (rarely 1) abaxial glands on 4 or 5 of the sepals at the base in neotropical species (much reduced or absent in Old World species).

The petals are 5, usually imbricate, clawed at the base. The stamens are 10, sometimes fewer, in a single whorl, the filaments distinct or connate at the base, the anthers 2-locular, dehiscing longitudinally. The ovary is superior, of (2)3(4) separate to united carpels, with axile placentation, and 1 pendulous anatropous ovule per locule. The fruits are diverse: dry, usually schizocarpic, splitting into 2–3 mericarps, which are often winged, or fleshy (drupe or berry). The seeds are without endosperm.

Distribution The family grows in the tropics and subtropics of both the Old and New worlds but is concentrated mainly in tropical America, where species occur in most countries, with a center of diversity in Brazil. Some genera extend into the southern USA. There are 15 Old World genera, growing in tropical and southern Africa, and from the Indian subcontinent to China to Southeast Asia and northeast Australia and the Pacific. They grow mainly in forests or savannas.

Economic uses *Malpighia emarginata*, Barbados Cherry or Acerola, is cultivated locally for its edible fruits, which are a rich source of vitamin C. Hallucinogenic compounds are obtained from species of *Banisteriopsis* and *Diplopterys*, notably *Banisteriopsis caapi*, which is widely cultivated by indigenous groups in the western Amazon, where it is used as a principal compound of a hallucinogenic beverage. Some species of *Banisteriopsis*, *Galphimia*, *Malpighia*, *Peixotoa*, and *Stigmaphyllon* are cultivated as ornamentals.

Malpighiaceae. 1 *Malpighia coccigera*
(a) flowering shoot (x⅔); (b) flower with petals
removed (x2⅔); (c) sepal dorsal view (x5½);
(d) gynoecium (x5); (e) cross section of ovary
(x6); (f) fruit (x2). **2** *Acridocarpus natalitius*
(a) inflorescence (x⅔); (b) flower with petals
removed (x2); (c) gynoecium (x2⅔);
(d) vertical section of ovary (x3); (e) cross
section of ovary (x2⅔); (f) winged fruit (x⅔).
3 *Sphedamnocarpus pruriens* (a) leafy shoot
and terminal inflorescence (x⅔); (b) flower
with filament bases united in a ring (x2);
(c) gynoecium (x3).

Cotton, Mallows, and Hollyhocks

An economically important family of mainly herbs and shrubs, rarely trees, that grows worldwide but mainly in tropical and subtropical regions. The major internationally traded economic item is cotton.

Description Subshrubs or herbs, less usually shrubs, and rarely trees; stellate hairs, often mixed with simple hairs. Most parts contain mucilage. Stem bark usually very fibrous. The leaves are alternate, simple, usually orbicular in outline. Species of drier climates often have oblong leaves. The petioles are often dilated at base and apex, especially in the shrubbier species. The inflorescences are either terminal and then often racemose, or axillary, then simple or cymose; they bear pedicellate, bisexual, usually protandrous flowers, with well developed persistent epicalyces (absent in *Abutilon* and the *Sida* group). The sepals are 5, valvate, and often nearly free. The petals are 5, convolute or imbricate, and showy, united at the base to the androecium. The androecium consists of numerous monothecal, longitudinally dehiscing, versatile stamens, their filaments united for most of their length into a cylinder around the style. The pollen is globose, long, and spiny. The ovary is superior and syncarpous, usually with 5 or more locules, each with 1 to numerous axile ovules. At anthesis, the 5 cohering styles and stigmas are concealed in the androecium. In the female phase, the stigmas emerge from the end of the androecium by extension of the styles. The fruits are many-seeded dry capsules (e.g., *Abutilon*) or break into 5 or more 1-seeded mericarps, often with awns (e.g., *Pavonia*, *Malva*, and *Lavatera*). Pollination is mainly by bees.

Distribution The Malvaceae is worldwide in distribution but primarily tropical and subtropical, extending into temperate areas. Around 75% of the species and 78 of the 115 genera grow in the New World. Estimates of species numbers vary from 1,800 to 2,300. Malvaceae are species of savanna, scrub, and forest edge and seem to be light demanders since they are absent from rain forest. A few species specialize in coastal habitats e.g., *Althaea officinalis* (saltmarshes of western Europe) and *Lavatera arborea* (cliffs of western Europe).

Economic uses Cotton is the major internationally traded commodity produced by the family, derived from the seed hairs mainly of 2 spp. of *Gossypium*. The stem fibers of *Hibiscus cannabinus* (Kenaf) also produce a fiber but of lesser importance. *Abelmoschus esculentus*

(Okra or Ladies' Fingers) is cultivated throughout the tropics and subtropics for the mucilaginous, edible, immature fruit and is also exported. *Hibiscus sabdariffa* (Roselle) is cultivated
extensively for the fleshy calyces, rich in vitamin C, consumed as an infusion. In the floricultural industry, Malvaceae are significant for
providing tropical shrubs, particularly *Hibiscus
rosasinensis*, which is common throughout
the tropics in the form of numerous cultivars
and hybrids with related species. In northern
temperate gardens, species of *Alcea* and, more
recently, *Lavatera* are also cultivated for their
flowers, while species of *Abutilon* are increasing in popularity as pot plants.

Malvaceae. 1 *Malva sylvestris* (a) flowering shoot
(x⅔); (b) gynoecium (x4); (c) androecium and base
of corolla (x4); (d) fruit and persistent calyx viewed
from above (x1½). **2** *Malope trifida* (a) flowering
shoot (x⅔); (b) young fruit with remains of styles and
stigmas removed (x2); (c) vertical section of young
fruit (x2); (d) ripe fruit enclosed in calyx and epicalyx
(x⅔); (e) flower (x1). **3** *Hibiscus schizopetalus* (a) leafy
shoot bearing flower and fruit—a capsule (x⅔); (b)
vertical section of lower part of flower showing ovary
containing ovules on axile placentas (x1); (c) cross
section of ovary showing 5 locules (x2).

Melianthaceae

This formerly entirely African family now includes Greyiaceae (South Africa) and Francoaceae (Chile) to give 5 genera diverse in habit and leaf characters but with similarities in inflorescence and flower structure.

Description *Bersama* includes shrubs and trees up to 24 m; *Greyia* comprises shrubs and small spreading trees up to 5(–7) m high, with soft wooded and sometimes almost succulent stems; *Melianthus* is a shrub or robust sub-shrub up to 2.3 m high with leaves crowded in the lower parts; *Francoa* and *Tetilla* are rhizomatous erect herbs up to 1.5 or 0.3 m high, respectively, with leaves mostly crowded near the base. The leaves are alternate, pinnate, and sometimes with a winged rhachis in *Bersama* and *Melianthus*, lyrate to pinnatisect in *Francoa* with a large terminal lobe resembling the lamina of *Greyia*, simple and suborbicular with lobed and crenate margins and distinct petioles in *Greyia* and *Tetilla*. The stipules are small to very large and sheathing. The inflorescence is a lax to dense terminal raceme or spike with pedicels spreading widely. The flowers are actinomorphic to weakly zygomorphic, resupinate at least in *Bersama* and *Melianthus*, bisexual or unisexual (plants polygamodioecious), 5-merous in *Bersama* and 4- to 5-merous in the other genera. The sepals are 4 or 5. The petals are 4 or 5, free, sometimes showy. There is a disk between the petals and stamens that is either annular with 8–10 acute lobes alternating with the stamens or unilateral and crescent- or V-shaped. The stamens are equal in number to the petals in *Bersama* and

Melianthus, twice as many (obdiplostemonous) in the other genera. The ovary is superior, longitudinally furrowed, with 4–5 carpels in *Bersama*; 4 in *Greyia*, *Melianthus*, and *Francoa*; and 2–4 in *Tetilla*. It is either completely divided into separate locules with axile placentas (*Bersama*, *Melianthus*) or is 1-locular with intrusive parietal placentas, each carpel with few (*Bersama*, *Melianthus*) to many (other genera) ovules in 2 rows. The fruit is a capsule, usually elongate and chartaceous.

Distribution *Bersama*, with 7 spp. in rain forest and woodland in tropical and South Africa, and *Melianthus*, with 6 spp. in both wet and dry habitats in South Africa, have long comprised Melianthaceae. *Greyia* has 3 spp. in eastern South Africa, growing in rocky places, on riverbanks, and at forest margins up to 1,500 m altitude. *Francoa*, with probably 1 highly polymorphic species, *F. appendiculata* (Bridal Wreath) and *Tetilla hydrocotylifolia* are both confined to Chile in woods and rocky places from sea level to 1,500 m.

Economic uses Some species are used in traditional medicine (e.g., *Bersama tysoniana* in South Africa). The root, bark, and leaves of *Melianthus comosus* are used in South Africa for treating snakebites, while a decoction of the leaves of *M. major* is used for healing wounds. *Bersama abyssinica* produces a hard, heavy wood that is used for house construction in West Africa. The soft wood of *Greyia* is used in South Africa for carving ornaments and household utensils. Species of *Melianthus* emit a strong scent, and the wood may be burned as incense. *Greyia sutherlandii* and *G. radlkoferi* are attractive showy small trees that are increasingly cultivated in tropical countries or in temperate conservatories. *Francoa appendiculata* is widely cultivated under several different species names as an herbaceous perennial.

Melianthaceae. I *Melianthus pectinatus* (a) shoot with pinnate leaves, small stipules, and inflorescence with flowers and immature fruits (x⅔); (b) half flower with irregular sepals and petals and swollen nectar-secreting disk (x1); (c) capsule (x⅔). **2** *Bersama tysoniana* (a) leafy shoot with stipules in the axils (x⅔); (b) inflorescence (x⅔); (c) mature flowers with long stamens (x3); (d) young androecium with 4 short stamens fused at the base and ovary crowned by simple style and lobed stigma (x4½); (e) cross section of ovary with 4 locules and ovules on axile placentas (x3); (f) fruits (x⅔); (g) seed with aril (x1).

Ice Plants, Living Stones, Vygies, and Mesembs

A large family of succulent annual or perennial herbs or small shrubs with usually showy, daisylike flowers, often forming brilliant sheets of color when growing en masse.

Description Annual or perennial herbs or small shrubs, usually more or less succulent. The leaves are alternate or opposite, mostly simple, entire, with or without stipules.

The flowers are solitary or in cymes, and regular, with their parts in whorls, and usually bisexual. The sepals are 4–8 (usually 5) and are imbricate or rarely valvate, more or less united below.

Petals are absent, their role fulfilled by whorls of petaloid staminodes, often brightly colored. The stamens are perigynous, usually numerous, sometimes with connate filaments.

The ovary is superior or inferior, with between 1 and 20 (usually 5) stigmas and locules and usually numerous ovules.

The fruit is a dry capsule, rarely a berry or nut. The seed has a large curved embryo surrounding a mealy endosperm.

Many of the features of the Mesembryanthemaceae are the result of adaptations to extremely dry climates (xeromorphy), and typical members are able to survive long periods of extreme insolation and drought, e.g., in the desert regions of South Africa.

The leaves are more or less succulent, and in addition some plants have succulent roots or caudices. Often the plant is reduced to a single annual pair of opposite leaves, which may be so condensed as to approach a sphere, with minimal surface in relation to volume, enabling the plant to resist desiccation.

The internal tissues also show modifications. Large watery cells rich in sugars called pentosans are characteristic of succulents. In *Muiria*, these cells may be 1 mm in diameter and can retain their moisture for weeks when separated and exposed to dry air.

The possession of 2 different leaf forms (heterophylly) is common (*Mitrophyllum*,

Monilaria), the leaf pair formed at the start of the dormant season being more united and compact than that formed when in full growth and acting as a protective sheath to the stem apex. Other genera are partly subterranean, with only the clear "window" in each leaf tip exposed above soil.

A type of optical system exists whereby a layer of apical tissue rich in calcium oxalate crystals acts as a filter to intense sunlight before it reaches the thin chlorophyllous layer below (*Fenestraria*, *Frithia*, *Conophytum* subgen. *Ophthalmophyllum*).

Other so-called mimicry plants show a striking similarity to their background rocks and are difficult to detect when not in flower. These are the pebble plants or living stones (*Lithops*); each species is associated with one particular type of rock formation and occurs nowhere else. *Titanopsis*, with a white encrustation to the leaves, is confined to limestone outcrops. This is probably a rare case of protective coloration in plants akin to examples of mimicry found in the animal kingdom.

The phenomenon of crassulacean acid metabolism occurs in members of the Mesembryanthemaceae, having evolved independently in many different families of succulent plants.

The mostly showy, diurnal flowers have a superficial resemblance to the flower heads of the Compositae. They are insect-pollinated, and most flowers require full sunlight before they will expand. Several plants have set hours for opening and closing.

Carpobrotus produces an edible berry, the Hottentot Fig, but the remainder form dry, dehiscent capsules operated by a hygroscopic mechanism that expands the valves in response to moistening, closing them again upon drying out. In desert conditions, this behavior ensures germination during the brief rainy periods. *Conicosia* and certain related genera have 3 different methods of seed dispersal. The capsule first opens hygroscopically, and some seeds are washed out by the impact of raindrops. It remains open when dry, and the remaining loose seeds are shaken out as from a pepper pot over a longer period. Finally, the whole fruit breaks up into segments, which are then dispersed by the wind, each winglike lamella containing up to 2 seeds trapped in 2 pocketlike folds.

Distribution The majority of species are endemic to southern Africa, especially the Succulent Karoo. By contrast, most *Disphyma* are native to Australasia, and some *Carpobrotus* and *Sarcozona* species are restricted to this region. A few other outlying species occur in

Mesembryanthemaceae. 1 *Lampranthus* sp. (a) shoot with opposite succulent leaves and terminal, solitary flowers (x⅔); (b) half flower with free sepals, several series of petals, numerous stamens and gynoecium with separate styles and numerous ovules (x2). **2** *Pleiospilos bolusii* a plant comprising 2 large succulent leaves with flowers produced between (x⅔).

Mesembryanthemaceae. 3 *Ruschia uncinata* flowering shoot (x⅔). **4** *Lithops pseudotruncatella* and **5** *L. lesliei* pebblelike plants (living stones) of 2 succulent leaves with flowers arising from the fissure (x⅔).

coastal regions of the Mediterranean, southwestern South America, the Near East, and North Africa.

Some species have naturalized extensively in mediterranean climate ecosystems of Europe, Australia, and America.

Economic uses The Hottentot Fig, *Carpobrotus edulis*, produces edible fruit. Shrubby members of the Ruschioideae (*Lampranthus, Oscularia, Drosanthemum, Erepsia*, and others) are half-hardy and grown for summer bedding, especially in southern Europe and California, where they flower pro-

fusely. Only 1 sp., *Ruschia uncinata*, verges on complete hardiness, although *Carpobrotus* survives most winters in coastal areas and is much planted as a sandbinder.

Several species of *Carpobrotus*, notably *C. edulis, C. acinaciformis*, and *C. chilensis*, have become naturalized and serious invasives in parts of the Mediterranean basin and California. Hybrids of the annual *Dorotheanthus* enjoy great popularity and have supplanted the original ice plant *Mesembryanthemum crystallinum*, which has glossy papillae-like water droplets covering the foliage, in popularity in gardens.

Mesembryanthemaceae. 6 *Oscularia deltoides* flowering shoot (x⅔). **7** *Faucaria tigrina* with a dense rosette of spiny leaves (x⅔). **8** *Mesembryanthemum crystallinum* (a) the ice plants, so-called for the glistening papillae that cover the whole plant (x⅔); (b) dehiscing capsule (x2); (c) capsule from above (x1½).

Monimiaceae. 1 *Monimia rotundifolia* (a) leaf and
axillary inflorescence (x⅔); (b) female flower with
hairy receptacle and many separate styles (x4);
(c) vertical section of female flower showing free
carpels (x4); (d) male flower with many stamens (x4);
(e) stamen with basal glands (x18). **2** *Hedycarya*
arborea (a) leafy shoot bearing axillary inflorescences
of male flowers (x⅔); (b) leafy shoot with female
flowers and fruits (x⅔); (c) male flower with uniform
perianth segments (x2); (d) female flower with
numerous free carpels (x2); (e) carpel (x6).
3 *Tambourissa elliptica* (a) flower (x2); (b) vertical
section of fruit showing achenes deeply embedded
in the receptacle (x2). **4** *Tambourissa* sp. fruit (x⅔).

Monimiaceae

A family of small trees, shrubs, and some lianas that grows throughout the tropics and subtropics and yields wood and aromatic oil extracts from the leaves and bark.

Description Monoecious, dioecious, or polygamous trees, shrubs, some lianas. The leaves are opposite, rarely whorled, simple, the margins entire or serrate-dentate, without stipules. The flowers are actinomorphic, usually unisexual, or with rudiments of the other sex (*Peumus boldus*), rarely hermaphrodite (*Hortonia*), usually small, in axillary cymes or cauliflorous on older wood. The perianth is sepaloid or petaloid, sometimes calyptrate, the tepals 3 to many, commonly 4–6(–8) in 2 whorls (10–20), spirally arranged in *Hortonia* and *Peumus*), free or connate. The stamens are few to numerous (up to 1,800), scattered in the hollow receptacle, filaments free. The ovary is superior, apocarpous, the carpels one to few or up to 1,000 (*Decarydendron*) or 2,000 (*Tambourissa*), often deeply embedded in the receptacular tissue. The fruit is an aggregate of stalked or sessile, juicy, dark blue or red drupelets, often embedded or enclosed in the conspicuous well-developed fleshy or woody receptacle; seeds 1 in each carpel.

Distribution The family is distributed in the tropics and subtropics. In the neotropics, it ranges from Mexico and Central America to Chile, and it occurs in southwestern and southeastern tropical Africa, Madagascar, Sri Lanka, Malesia, tropical and eastern Australia, Polynesia, and New Zealand. The largest genus, *Tambourissa* (50 spp.), grows in Madagascar, the Mascarenes, and the Comores. *Mollinedia* (20 spp.) grows in lowland moist forest from Mexico down to the Amazon, and in gallery forests of Argentina, Brazil, and Paraguay. *Monimia* (3 spp.) is endemic to the Mascarenes (Mauritius and Réunion), while *Hortonia* (1–3 spp.) is endemic to Sri Lanka.

Economic uses The wood of several species is used locally, and aromatic oil extracts from the leaves and bark may be used medicinally and as perfumes. A tonic or herbal tea is obtained from *Peumus boldus* (Boldo) and is a traditional remedy used by the Araucanian Native Americans of Chile.

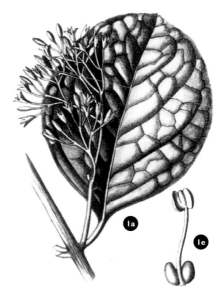

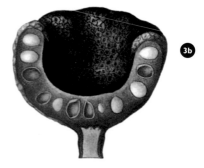

Myoporaceae. 1 *Myoporum petiolatum* (a) shoot with flowers in leaf axils (x⅔); (b) flower comprising a 5-lobed fused calyx and corolla, 4 stamens and a simple style (x1½); (c) corolla opened out showing epipetalous stamens alternating with the corolla lobes (x2); (d) calyx and gynoecium (x2⅔); (e) fruit—a drupe (x2); (f) cross section of fruit (x2). **2** *Eremophila bignoniiflora* (a) shoot bearing linear leaves, flower with irregular 2-lipped corolla, and fruits (x⅔); (b) corolla opened out showing stamens of 2 lengths (x⅔); (c) stamen with divergent anthers and longitudinal dehiscence (x2); (d) fruit (x⅔); (e) vertical section of fruit (x⅔). **3** *Eremophila glabra* leafy shoot with flowers and fruits (x⅔).

Myoporaceae

A family of herbs or woody plants mostly of the southern hemisphere, often resembling Scrophulariaceae (Figwort and Foxglove family) but with characteristic resin cavities and different ovary and fruit structure.

Description Tall shrubs or small trees, or rarely up to 10 m. Vegetative parts are characterized by unique secretory resin cavities, which often protrude through the epidermis as raised tubercles. The leaves are alternate or rarely opposite or whorled, entire or toothed, without stipules, often glandular, scaly or woolly. The flowers are solitary or in cymose clusters in leaf axils, and are usually zygomorphic, but in *Myoporum* often almost regular. The calyx comprises (4)5 sepals that are free or fused into a tube, and is often accrescent. The corolla has 5 lobes and may be strongly 2-lipped or, in *Myoporum*, shortly tubular with 5 subequal rotate lobes. The stamens are 4(5), fused to the corolla tube, and alternating with the lobes. The anther locules run into one another. The ovary is superior, of 2 fused carpels with 2 locules, each cell with a single pendulous ovule (rarely up to 4 in *Eremophila*). The fruit is dry or fleshy, indehiscent or dividing toward the apex and semidehiscent, rarely (*Pentacoelium*) with 5 subapical pores, or rarely (*Eremophila tetraptera*) splitting into 4 single-seeded segments, with a thick woody endocarp and sometimes a fleshy mesocarp, with 1–4 locules, each with 1–3 seeds.

Distribution *Eremophila*, with about 215 spp., is confined to Australia, but with 1 sp. in New Zealand. *Myoporum* (c. 30 spp.) ranges from Timor to Australia and New Zealand and the Pacific islands with a single species in Mauritius and Rodrigues. *Pentacoelium* has 1 sp. from the coasts of northern Vietnam, China, Taiwan, and Japan, often in mangrove communities. The monotypic genus *Bontia* grows in the Caribbean, markedly disjunct from the main center of distribution. Three further endemic Australian genera, widely recognized in herbaria have not yet been formally described.

Economic uses A number of *Myoporum* spp., often known as Boobialla in Australia, are cultivated as ornamentals, hedges, or windbreaks.

M. sandwicense from Hawaii provides useful timber. *Eremophila* spp. are grown extensively as ornamentals in Australia and increasingly elsewhere. The purplish fleshy fruits of many species are important food for birds.

Nutmeg and Mace

A pantropical family of mainly trees, usually evergreen, that grow mostly in lowland rain forests. The best-known member is the Nutmeg Tree, which provides the spices nutmeg and mace.

Description Trees, some shrubs, usually evergreen, the wood exuding a reddish sap when wounded. The leaves are alternate, entire, without stipules, often with glandular dots containing aromatic oil.

The flowers are unisexual (plants dioecious, sometimes monoecious—*Doyleanthus*), small and inconspicuous, actinomorphic, borne in terminal racemose or corymbose inflorescences, sometimes cauliflorous. The perianth is in one series consisting of (2)3(–5) partly connate, sepal-like tepals.

In the male flowers, the stamens are fused into a synandrium, which consists of a sterile column and a collection of 2–60 anthers fused to various degrees to this column, exceptionally with short filaments (*Mauloutchia*); the anthers shed their pollen through 2 longitudinal slits. The female flowers have a 1-locular superior ovary containing 1 basal ovule.

The fruit becomes fleshy, and on maturity it splits into 2 or 4 valves (a dehiscent berry), disclosing the large seed, or is rarely leathery and indehiscent.

The seed contains a small embryo and much endosperm, rich in oil, ruminate in cross section, and enveloped by an aril consisting of a usually brightly colored network of tissue.

Myristicaceae. 1 *Virola glaziovii* (a) leaf and male inflorescence (x⅔); (b) male flower (x4); (c) half female flower (x4); (d) vertical section of fruit (x⅔). **2** *Knema pectinata* shoot with male flowers (x⅔). **3** *Myristica fragrans* (a) shoot with flowers and fruit (nutmeg) split open to show seed covered by the red aril (x⅔); (b) fruit cut open (x⅔); (c) vertical section of seed (x⅔); (d) half male flower (x2); (e) androecium with stamens in a column (x4); (f) vertical section of column (x4); (g) half female flower (x2); (h) female flower opened out (x2). **4** *Horsfieldia macrocoma* (a) male inflorescence (x⅔); (b) female and (c) male flowers with one sepal removed (x4); (d) fruit cut open (x⅔); (e) cross section of seed (x⅔).

Distribution The family is exclusively tropical, mainly in lowland rain forests, occurring in the Indo-Malesian region, especially in New Guinea and the Phillipines, in tropical America, especially the Amazon basin, and in Africa and Madagascar. Most members inhabit lowland rain forests.

The largest genus is *Myristica*, with about 175 spp. centered in New Guinea. Other large Asian genera are *Horsfieldia* (105 spp.), which grows in south Asia from India to Papua New Guinea, and *Knema* (85–90 spp.) in south Asia from India to the Philippines and Papua New Guinea. *Virola* (45 spp.) is confined to tropical Central and South America, where it is an important constituent of the Amazon forests.

Recent phylogenetic analyses of the family, based on morphology and several plastid regions, reinforce the view that the ancestral area was Africa-Madagascar and that Asian taxa are derived.

Economic uses *Myristica fragrans* is the Nutmeg Tree from which the spices nutmeg (the seed) and mace (the aril) are obtained. They also have powerful narcotic properties. Although nutmeg originated in the Moluccas, it is now widely cultivated, especially in the West Indies. The pericarp of the fruit is also used to make a jelly preserve, and inferior seeds are pressed to make "nutmeg butter" used in perfumery and making candles, as are the Asian *Gymnacranthera farquhariana* and the Brazilian *Virola surinamensis* (ucuúba), whose waxy seeds are also used as a source of "butter" and for making candles.

The wood of the family Myristicaceae makes poor-quality lumber with a high moisture content, and is little used with the exception of *Virola surinamensis*, which is widely used in carpentry and as plywood and is also the source of an indigenous hallucinogenic snuff throughout Amazonia.

Tropical Pitcher Plants

The family consists of the genus *Nepenthes* only, well known because of their brightly colored pitchers—distinctive cuplike vessels with lids, which develop from the end of tendrils and attract the plant's insect food.

Description Perennial, dioecious, insectivorous climbers (to 40 m), scramblers or epiphytes, with alternate leaves. Young plants form a basal rosette from which 1 to many climbing stems develop.

The leaves lack stipules and are often without distinct petioles. The lamina forms wings along an often prominent midrib, the basal portion often clasping the stem.

The plant climbs by means of tendrils that are prolongations of the leaf midrib. The end of the tendril generally develops into a pitcher, with a lid projecting over the mouth, which opens as the pitcher matures. The distinctive pitcher usually consists of an elongated cuplike structure, with a pronounced rim of hard tissue, the upper opening capped by a lid, with basal spur that prevents entry of rainwater. Pitchers vary from 5 cm to as much as 40 cm in length, and some in Borneo are large enough to hold 2 liters of water. In some species, the young pitchers are clothed in tight, rusty, branched hairs. At the entrance of the pitcher there are secretory glands, below which the interior is slippery with fine wax scales. Insects are attracted to the pitcher by smell or bright color, which may be red or green and is often blotched. Animals entering the pitcher are unable to climb out because of the slippery surface and eventually drown in the liquid secretions in the base of the pitcher. The plant absorbs the products of decay.

Many members of the Nepenthaceae are epiphytic and have climbing stems up to 3 cm in diameter. The small red, yellow, or green flowers often smell strongly of stale sweat and are 4-merous, regular, and unisexual (plants dioecious) and are borne in a spikelike inflorescence. The perianth consists of 3 or 4 tepals. In the male flower, the filaments of the 4–24 stamens are united into a column, and the anthers crowded into a mass. The female flower has a discoid stigma.

The style is short or totally absent. The ovary is superior, of 4 fused carpels, and has 4 locules bearing numerous ovules on central placentas.

The fruit is a leathery capsule, and the light seeds have hairlike projections on the end. The seeds have a minute embryo and fleshy endosperm.

Distribution The family is largely endemic to the Malesian region, with a center of diversity in Borneo and outlying species around the Indian Ocean in Madagascar, Seychelles, Sri Lanka, northern India, and northern Australia.

Species grow from sea level (*N. mirabilis*) to >2,500 m (*N. villosa*) in nutrient-poor soils, often in open or disturbed sites at the edge of woodland, although some species grow in open grassland (for example, *N. pervillei* and *N. distillatoria*).

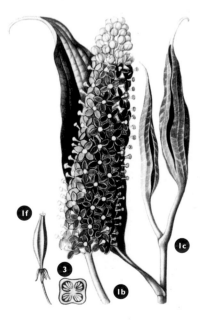

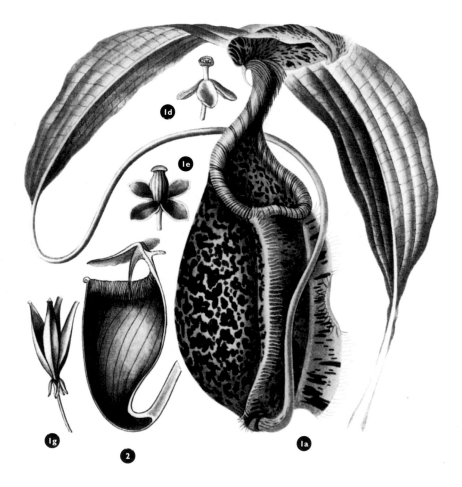

Economic uses The family are grown as ornamental plants by specialist horticulturists.

All species are listed by CITES (Convention on International Trade in Endangered Species of Wild Fauna and Flora); some species are on Appendix 1.

The stems of some species (for example, *N. distillatoria* in Sri Lanka and *N. reinwardtiana* in Malesia) are used locally for basket-making and as a type of cordage.

Nepenthaceae. **1** *Nepenthes rafflesiana* (a) leaf, the tip of which is modified to form a pitcher (x⅔); (b) male inflorescence (x⅔); (c) leaves with apical tendrils (x⅔); (d) male flower with filaments united into a column (x1½); (e) female flower with sessile stigma (x1½); (f) fruit—a capsule (x⅔); (g) fruit dehiscing by 4 valves (x⅔). **2** *N. bicalcarata* vertical section of pitcher (x½). **3** *N. fimbriata* cross section of ovary with 4 locules and numerous ovules on axile placentas (x2⅔).

Bougainvilleas and Four-O'Clocks

A family of trees, shrubs, climbers, and herbs that is best known for Bougainvillea, which is widely cultivated in the tropics and warm-temperate regions as an ornamental.

Description Trees, shrubs, climbers, and herbs, with swollen nodes and sometimes fleshy roots. The leaves are alternate, opposite or whorled, petiolate, simple, often dark grey, and without stipules. The flowers are bisexual or sometimes unisexual (plants dioecious), and sometimes surrounded by colored bracts that resemble a calyx, in usually cymose or paniculate inflorescences. The perianth is usually petal-like and tubular. There are no petals and the 1 to many stamens, usually 5, alternate with the 5 perianth lobes; the filaments are free or fused at the base, or sometimes branched above. The ovary is superior, comprising a single carpel with a single basal erect ovule, usually surmounted by a long style. The fruit is an indehiscent achene, sometimes enclosed by the persistent base of the calyx, which may assist fruit dispersal. The seeds have endosperm, perisperm, and a straight or curved embryo.

Distribution Grows throughout the tropics and warm-temperate zones but is more strongly represented in the Americas. Species most commonly grow at low altitudes, but habitats include beaches, forest understory, and hillsides.

Economic uses Bougainvilleas are often grown as defensive and decorative hedges in warmer climates and as greenhouse plants farther north. The 2 most commonly grown species are *Bougainvillea glabra* and *B. spectabilis*. From these, and from *B. peruviana* and *B.* x *buttiana*, many cultivars have been produced. *Mirabilis jalapa* and *M. coccinea* are among many species of *Mirabilis* cultivated for their ornamental value. The flowers of *Mirabilis jalapa* open in the evening, which gives rise to one of the common names—"Four O'clock." Another common name, Marvel of Peru, relates

to the polychromic flowers, which are white, yellow, or red. The tuberous roots of *M. jalapa* are the source of a purgative drug used as a substitute for jalap. The leaves of the Brown Cabbage Tree (*Pisonia grandis*) and the Lettuce Tree (*P. alba*) can be used as a vegetable. Decoctions of the leaves of *P. aculeata* and of the fruits of *P. capitata* are used medicinally to treat a range of complaints. Several species have become pantropical weeds, e.g., *Pisonia*.

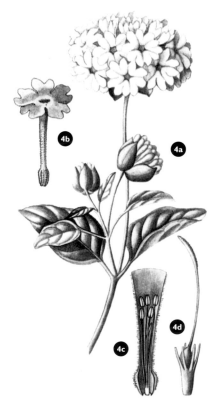

Nyctaginaceae. **I** *Bougainvillea spectabilis* (a) leafy shoot with flowers subtended by conspicuous bracts (x⅔); (b) bract and half flower showing petaloid tubular calyx and no petals (x2). **2** *Mirabilis jalapa* (a) leafy shoot with each flower enclosed by a calyxlike involucre of bracts (x⅔); (b) indehiscent fruit (x3½); (c) vertical section of fruit showing single seed (x3½).

3 *Pisonia aculeata* glandular fruit that is dispersed by birds (x1). **4** *Abronia fragrans* (a) shoot bearing dense clusters of flowers (x⅔); (b) flower (x1); (c) section of base of perianth-tube showing stamens and style (x2); (d) gynoecium with elongate, hairy stigma (x4).

143

Water Lilies

A cosmopolitan family of large-flowered water plants, the water lilies, which grow in a variety of freshwater habitats in both temperate and tropical regions.

Description Freshwater aquatic herbs, normally perennial with long horizontal rhizomes, sometimes tuberous, or short and erect. The leaves are submerged, floating or emergent, simple, peltate, cordate or sagittate, with or without stipules; the lamina is ovate to orbicular, entire or dentate. In *Victoria amazonica*, the leaves may attain 2 m in diameter, with spines on the surface and petioles, and upturned rims. They are able to support a weight of 40–75 kg due to the network of tubular veins on their undersides. The flowers are often large and showy, actinomorphic, hermaphrodite, solitary, borne above the water surface on stout peduncles. The sepals are 4–9, green or colored, and petaloid (*Nuphar*). The petals are 3 to many (absent in *Ondinea*), white, yellow, pink, red, blue, or purplish, grading in some genera into the numerous stamens. The ovary is inferior or semi-inferior (*Barclaya*, *Euryale*, *Nymphaea*, *Victoria*) or superior (*Nuphar*, *Ondinea*). The carpels are 3–40, united or partly free. The fruit is a spongy berrylike capsule, dehiscing by the swelling of mucilage within or indehiscent. The seeds often have an aril (*Nymphaea*, *Ondinea*). The flowers are pollinated by insects, especially beetles.

Distribution The water lily family occurs worldwide in freshwater habitats (lakes and ponds, rivers and streams, springs, marshes, ditches, canals, and tidal waters) in both temperate and tropical regions. The largest genus *Nymphaea* (c. 40 spp.) is also the most widespread, occurring in both temperate and tropical regions. *Nuphar* (c. 14 spp.) grows in north-temperate regions of North America, Europe, and Asia, with 1 sp. (*N. advena*) extending into the neotropics (Mexico and Cuba). *Victoria* (2 spp.) is endemic to tropical and subtropical South America, *Barclaya* (3–4 spp.) is tropical Indo-Malesian, *Euryale* (1 sp.) occurs in eastern Asia, and *Ondinea* (1 sp.) is endemic to western Australia.

Economic uses Many species from the family are cultivated as ornamentals, especially *Nymphaea* (water lilies), *Nuphar* (yellow water lilies), *Euryale*, and *Victoria*. The seeds and rhizomes of *Nymphaea* spp. are sometimes eaten, as are the roasted seeds of *Victoria*. *Euryale* seeds yield arrowroot.

Nymphaeaceae. 1 *Nymphaea micrantha* (a) habit, showing floating leaves and aerial flowers (x⅓); (b) half flower with greenish sepals, many petals grading into numerous stamens and ovary sunk in receptacle (x1). **2** *Barclaya motleyi* (sometimes placed in the Barclayaceae) (a) habit (x⅔); (b) cross section of fruit containing many seeds (x⅔). **3** *Victoria amazonica* vertical section of flower (x⅔).

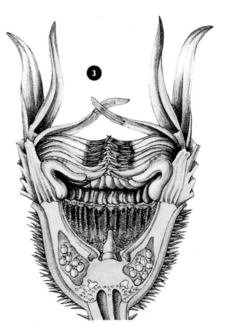

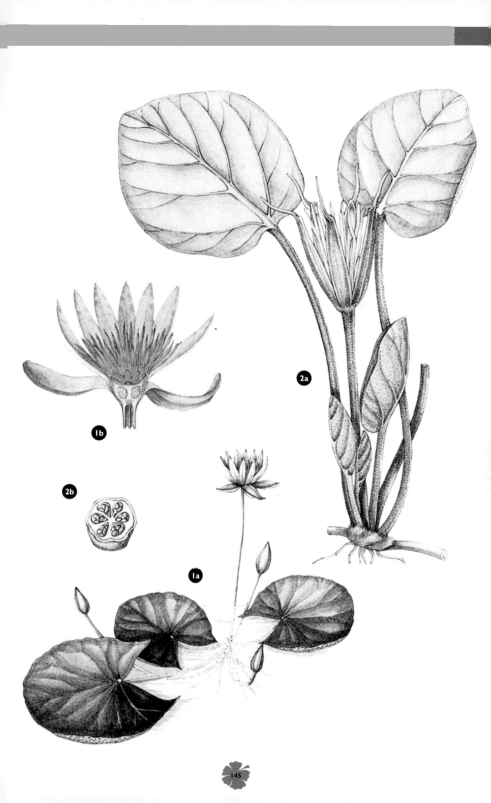

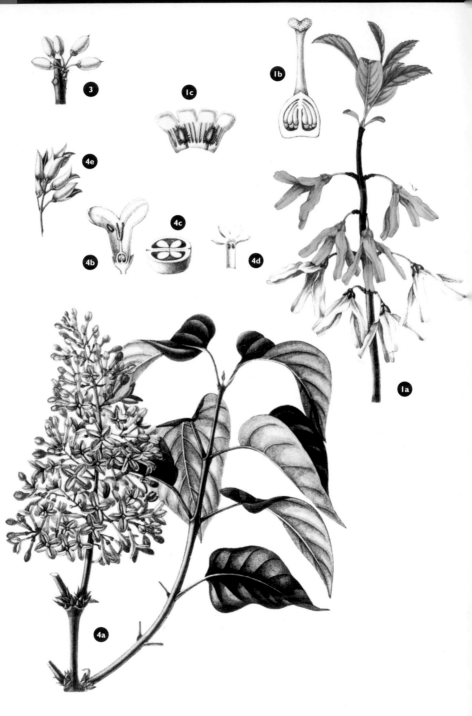

Olive Family

A widespread family of shrubs, trees, and woody climbers that grows well in temperate and tropical regions. The olive has been cultivated by humans for thousands of years.

Description The family comprises mostly trees and shrubs, but *Jasminum* and *Myxopyrum* include woody climbers to 12 m or more, and *Menodora* and *Dimetra* may be herbs with a woody rootstock. The leaves are opposite except in *Jasminum* sect. *Alternifolia* and simple to imparipinnate. The inflorescence is a compound cyme and is usually terminal. The flowers are actinomorphic, occasionally unisexual or the plants dioecious, usually sweetly scented. The calyx is 4-lobed, or in *Jasmineae* 5- to 15-lobed, or sometimes absent. The corolla is usually gamopetalous and actinomorphic but is absent in *Forestiera* and most *Fraxinus* and *Nestegis*, and usually 4-lobed but 5- to 12-lobed in Jasmineae.

The stamens are characteristically 2 but rarely 4 in *Fraxinus*, *Chionanthus*, *Nestegis*, and *Priogymnanthus*. The ovary is 2-carpellate and 2-locular, each locule bearing 1, 2, 4, or (*Forsythia*) more ovules. The fruit is a capsule, samara, berry, or drupe.

Distribution Widespread in temperate and tropical regions. Several genera show an unusual disjunction between southern Europe and the Far East. Most tropical genera have relatively narrow distributions in either the New World or Old World, but *Schrebera* and *Chionanthus* span both hemispheres. *Menodora* is in the New World, apart from 3 spp. in South Africa (one of which has its closest relatives in the USA and Mexico), and *Nestegis* is confined to New Zealand and Norfolk Island, except for 1 sp. in Hawaii. *Hesperelaea* was confined to Guadalupe Island off the Pacific coast of Mexico but is now extinct. *Fraxinus* is an important woodland genus in the temperate northern hemisphere but also extends to the tropics in Costa Rica and to the mountains of Malaysia.

Economic uses *Olea europaea* subsp. *europaea* (Olive) has been cultivated by humans for thousands of years for its edible fruits and the oil extracted from them for multiple purposes. The genus *Fraxinus* (Ash) yields valuable timber. *Ligustrum ovalifolium*, native of Japan, is extensively planted as an urban hedge plant (Privet). Many other plants are cultivated as ornamental (often strongly scented) garden plants, especially *Jasminum* (jasmines), *Syringa* (lilacs), *Forsythia*, *Osmanthus*, and *Abeliophyllum*.

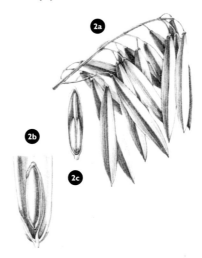

Oleaceae. I *Forsythia viridissima* (a) shoot with flowers borne on previous year's side shoots (x⅔); (b) vertical section of ovary (x4); (c) part of corolla opened out to show epipetalous stamens (x1). **2** *Fraxinus platypoda* (a) winged fruit—samaras (x⅔); (b) vertical section of samara base (x2); (c) vertical section of seed (x2). **3** *Phillyrea vilmoriniana* fleshy fruits (x⅔). **4** *Syringa vulgaris* (a) leaves and inflorescence (x⅔); (b) half flower (x1½); (c) cross section of ovary (x6); (d) corolla opened out to show epipetalous stamens (x⅔); (e) dehisced fruits—2-locular capsules (x⅔).

Wood Sorrel, Bermuda Buttercup, Oca, and Starfruit

This family of small trees, shrubs, climbers, and perennial herbs is dominated by the weedy genus *Oxalis* but is also known for the Starfruit (*Averrhoa carambola*).

Description Small trees, shrubs, climbers, or usually perennial herbs (rarely annual), with alternate leaves, often with underground storage bulbs, tubers, or fleshy roots. Plants are often clump-forming or spreading by stolons. The leaves are sometimes simple but often pinnately or palmately compound from a well-defined petiole, the leaflets articulate, and in many *Oxalis* species, folding downward at night and in cold weather. In some *Biophytum* species, the leaflets bend when touched.

In a few *Oxalis* species (e.g., *O. bupleurifolia*), the ordinary leaves are replaced by phyllodes (leaflike petioles). The petioles are sometimes woody and persistent or rarely succulent (*Oxalis herrerae*). The inflorescence is thyrso-paniculate, racemose in *Dapania*, forming an umbel, spike, or head. The flowers are frequently bright and showy, rarely without petals and cleistogamous, actinomorphic, hermaphrodite, but unisexual (plant androdioecious) in *Dapania*. The sepals are 5, persistent and overlapping. The petals are 5, usually twisted together in bud, and free or fused at the base, clawed at the base, often brightly colored. The stamens are 10, arranged in 2 whorls and connate at the base, the outer whorl of 5 lying opposite the petals. Sometimes the outer stamens are sterile (some *Averrhoa* species).

The ovary is superior, consisting of 5 free (e.g., *Biophytum*) or fused (e.g., *Oxalis*) carpels with 5 free styles and capitate stigmas, and with 5 locules, each with 1 or 2 rows of ovules on axile placentas. Many *Oxalis* species display trimorphic heterostyly, i.e., flowers with long styles and medium and short stamens, medium styles and long and short stamens, and short styles and long and medium stamens. Fertile crosses are possible only between different types of flowers. The Eurasian species *Oxalis acetosella* (Wood Sorrel) has flowers that exhibit cleistogamy in cold conditions. The fruit is a capsule. The seeds of some *Biophytum* and *Oxalis* species may have a fleshy aril at the base. The turgid inner cell layers of the aril turn inside out rapidly, separate from the testa, and the seed is explosively flung out.

Distribution Most of the family is native to the tropics, with many species at high altitudes, the remainder subtropical or sometimes temperate. The full extent of the natural distribution is blurred by the presence of several widespread and weedy species. The origin of *O. corniculata* is unknown, because it has become so widespread and established around the tropics.

Economic uses Some Andean *Oxalis* species have tubers that are boiled and eaten as a vegetable (Oca), and the leaves may be used in salads. The leaves of *O. acetosella* are sometimes used in salads instead of sorrel, and the bulbous stems of *O. pescaprae* (Bermuda Buttercup) are sometimes used as a vegetable in southern France and North Africa. The tubers of the Mexican species *O. deppei* are also used as food and are cultivated in France and Belgium. A number of *Oxalis* species are cultivated as ornamentals, and some are troublesome weeds. The Starfruit (*Averrhoa carambola*) is eaten but also used as a bleaching agent, and *A. bilimbi* (Cucumber Tree) produces somewhat sour fruit used in pickles and jams.

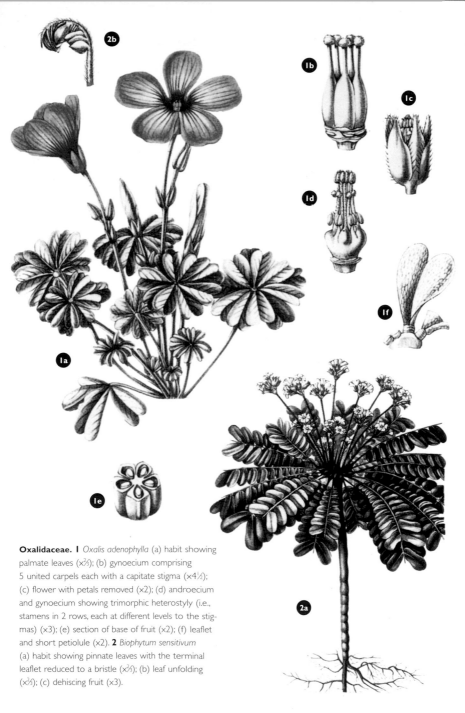

Oxalidaceae. 1 *Oxalis adenophylla* (a) habit showing palmate leaves (x⅔); (b) gynoecium comprising 5 united carpels each with a capitate stigma (x4½); (c) flower with petals removed (x2); (d) androecium and gynoecium showing trimorphic heterostyly (i.e., stamens in 2 rows, each at different levels to the stigmas) (x3); (e) section of base of fruit (x2); (f) leaflet and short petiolule (x2). **2** *Biophytum sensitivum* (a) habit showing pinnate leaves with the terminal leaflet reduced to a bristle (x⅔); (b) leaf unfolding (x⅔); (c) dehiscing fruit (x3).

Peonies

A family comprising a single genus (*Paeonia*) of perennial, rhizomatous herbs or shrubs, with large showy flowers that is native to northern-temperate regions.

Description Perennial herbs with fleshy roots to soft-wooded shrubs. The leaves are alternate, compound, without stipules, variously divided once or twice into 3 to many (*P. tenuifolia*) leaflets, segments, and lobes, the leaflets linear to broadly elliptical, entire, or lobed.

The flowers are bisexual, actinomorphic, large, conspicuous, white, pink, red, purple, or yellow, solitary, and mostly terminal. Leafy floral bracts are present below the calyx. The sepals are (3–)5(–7), free, persistent, unequal. The petals are 5–9 or more.

The stamens are numerous, arranged centrifugally. The ovary consists of (1)2–5(–8) free carpels borne on a conspicuous fleshy disk; ovules numerous and in 2 rows.

The fruit consist of 1–5 large leathery divergent follicles. The seeds are large, fleshy, arillate, red initially, and turning black when mature.

Distribution Native to northern-temperate regions, chiefly southern Europe, northern and east Asia, and western North America. Fifteen spp., 10 spp. of which are endemic, grow in China. One species, *P. coriacea*, grows in northwestern Africa.

Economic uses
Species of *Paeonia* have long been the source of medicinally active compounds. The European *P. officinalis* has been cultivated and used

in traditional herbal healing since the Middle Ages as an antispasmodic or a sedative.

Radix Paeoniae is the dried root of *Paeonia lactiflora* from Siberia, Mongolia, and China. It has been cultivated in China for more than 2,500 years. It and 3 other Chinese species are

used in Chinese herbal medicine. Many species, hybrids, and cultivars are grown as garden flowers, making attractive border plants. More than 20 spp. are grown in European gardens alone.

The "tree peonies," soft-woody shrubs such as *P. suffruticosa* (*P. moutan*), *P. delavayi*, *P. lutea*, and *P. potaninii*, which grow in some cases to 2.5 m, are also popular.

Paeoniaceae. 1 *Paeonia peregrina* (a) shoot with upper leaves and solitary terminal flower (x⅔); (b) young fruit comprising 3 follicles (x⅔); (c) dehisced fruit (x⅔); (d) vertical section of seed with copious endosperm and a small embryo (x2); (e) young leafy shoots (x1/2). **2** *P. wittmanniana* (a) cross section of carpel (x⅔); (b) vertical section of carpel (x2/3); (c) young fruit (x⅔). **3** *P. mascula* fruit of 5 follicles (x⅔). **4** *P. emodi* fruit (x⅔). **5** *P. tenuifolia* flower (x⅔).

Poppies and Fumitories

A family of mainly herbaceous annuals or perennials, but with some shrubs, most of which produce latex. Current circumscriptions of the family now usually include Fumariaceae and Pteridophyllaceae.

Description Annual or perennial herbs, rarely shrubs (e.g., *Dendromecon*, *Hunnemannia*, *Romneya*), geophytes (e.g., some *Corydalis*), or scramblers and climbers (e.g., *Dactylicapnos*) with alternate leaves. The stems, leaves, and other parts of many species contain a well-developed system of secretory canals that produce yellow, milky, or watery latex. All contain alkaloids.

The leaves are entire but often lobed or deeply dissected (Papaveroideae), or usually pinnately or palmately compound (Fumarioideae, *Pteridophyllum*), without stipules. The inflorescence is usually racemose or cymose, sometimes a thyrse or solitary.

The flowers are generally large and conspicuous, regular or disymmetric, bisexual and hypogynous (perigynous in *Eschscholzia*); in Fumarioideae, the flowers are of complex and unusual structure, whose derivation from the simpler papaveraceous type is, however, demonstrated by some of the smaller genera.

In Papaveroideae and *Pteridophyllum*, the sepals are 2, free, falling off before the flower opens, and the petals are usually in 2 whorls of 2, free, showy (absent in *Macleaya*) and often crumpled in the bud. The stamens are usually numerous, in several whorls, few in *Pteridophyllum*. The filaments are sometimes petaloid, while the anthers have 2 locules and dehisce longitudinally. The gynoecium consists of 2 to numerous fused carpels (separate except at the base in *Platystemon*).

The ovary is superior and contains usually a single locule with intruding parietal placentas, as many as the number of carpels, and each bearing numerous ovules.

The stigmas are as many as the carpels and are opposite to, or alternate with, the placentas. The fruit is a capsule, opening by valves or pores (follicular in *Platystemon*), and containing seeds with a small embryo and copious mealy or oily endosperm.

In Fumarioideae, a more complex situation is found in *Hypecoum*, in which the 2 inner petals are prominently 3-lobed, with the middle lobe stalked and with an expanded, cuplike apex; the apices of the middle lobes wrap around the anthers and form a chamber into which the pollen falls. Here again, the stamens are 4, with nectar secreted at the filament bases. In *Dicentra*, there is further elaboration: all 4 petals are variably fused, particularly toward the apex; the outer petals are spurred at the base, and the apices of the inner petals are fused around the anthers. The stamens are arranged in 2 bundles opposite the inner petals; each bundle has a single filament that divides into 3 parts at the apex; the central division of each bears a complete anther, while the lateral divisions each bear half an anther. This complex structure appears to have evolved from the 4-staminate condition by the splitting of the stamens opposite the outer petals. The base of each compound filament is prolonged into the petal spur and secretes nectar there. In the other genera, only 1 of the outer petals is spurred, producing an unusual irregular flower; all have similar staminal arrangements to *Dicentra*, and all have a 2-carpellate ovary, which is usually many-ovuled, though with 1 ovule in *Fumaria* and related genera.

The fruit is usually a capsule, sometimes swollen and bladderlike; more rarely it is indehiscent, either a single-seeded nutlet, or many-seeded and breaking up into single-seeded indehiscent segments. *Ceratocapnos heterocarpa* has dimorphic fruits. The seed has a small embryo and fleshy endosperm.

Distribution The family grows throughout northern temperate regions. Only a few are found south of the Equator: *Bocconia* occurs in Central and South America; a few species of *Corydalis* on mountains in East Africa; and *Papaver aculeatum* and the small genera

Phacocapnos, *Cysticapnos*, *Trigonocapnos*, and *Discocapnos* in southern Africa. They often grow in open areas, mountain screes, and disturbed ground.

Economic uses Economically, the most important species in this family is *Papaver somniferum* (Opium Poppy), which yields opium. The seeds do not contain opium and are used in baking. They also yield an important drying oil. The seeds of *Glaucium flavum* and *Argemone mexicana* yield oils that are important in the manufacture of soaps. Many species are cultivated as garden ornamental plants, e.g., *Dendromecon rigida* (Californian Bushy Poppy). *Eschscholzia californica* (Californian

Poppy), *Papaver alpinum* (Alpine Poppy), *P. nudicaule* (Iceland Poppy), *P. orientalis* (Oriental Poppy), *Macleaya cordata* (Plume Poppy), and a few species of *Corydalis* and *Dicentra* (Bleeding Heart). Some species of *Fumaria* are agricultural weeds, e.g., *Fumaria officinalis* (fumitory).

Papaveraceae. 1 *Eschscholzia californica* (a) leafy shoot and flower with 4 petals (x1); (b) flower bud with calyx forming cap (x1½); (c) fruit—a capsule dehiscing by 2 valves (x1); (d) cross section of fruit (x7). **2** *Glaucium flavum* (a) capsule (x⅔); (b) tip of opened capsule showing seeds and apical valve (x1½). **3** *Platystemon californicus* fruit—a group of follicles (x1½). **4** *Macleaya cordata* inflorescence (x⅓).

Papaveraceae. 5 *Argemone mexicana* dehisced spiny capsule with seeds exposed (x⅔). **6** *Papaver dubium* (a) shoot with dissected leaves and solitary flowers (x⅔); (b) capsule dehiscing by apical pores (x1½); (c) vertical section of a capsule (x1½); (d) cross section of capsule (x1½).

Papaveraceae. 7 *Corydalis lutea* (a) shoot with much divided leaves and irregular flowers in a racemose inflorescence (x⅔); (b) half flower showing spurred petal and elongate ovary (x4); (c) vertical section of fruit (x2). **8** *Pteridophyllum racemosum* (a) habit showing fernlike leaves (x⅔); (b) flower—the simplest form in this family (x2); (c) vertical section of ovary (x4). **9** *Fumaria muralis* (a) flowering shoot (x⅔); (b) half flower with spurred petal and stamens in 2 bundles (x3); (c) vertical section of bladderlike fruit (x6). **10** *Dicentra spectabilis* (a) leaf and inflorescence (x1); (b) flower dissected to show varied form of petals and stamens arranged in 2 bundles (x2).

Passion Flower and Granadillo

The many climbers in this family are famous for their extraordinary flowers and edible fruit. The poisonous leaves of *Passiflora* are also well known as a foodstuff for *Heliconius* butterflies.

Description Trees or shrubs (e.g., *Androsiphonia, Barteria, Paropsia, Viridivia,* some *Adenia*), woody or herbaceous climbers (e.g., *Passiflora*, some *Adenia*), annual or perennial herbs (e.g., *Basananthe*), sometimes with a swollen tuber or large swollen trunk (e.g., some *Adenia*), sometimes spiny, with alternate leaves.

Tendrils derived from modified axillary inflorescences are present on climbing species. The leaves are simple or lobed, rarely compound, strongly 2-lobed in some *Passiflora*, petiolate and with small to large and foliose stipules present.

Extrafloral nectaries are often present on the petiole or stem. The inflorescence is usually axillary, rarely terminal or cauliflorous, a 1- to many-flowered cyme, rarely a raceme or fascicle. The flowers are actinomorphic, hermaphrodite, varying in size and shape.

The sepals are (3–)5(–8), petals equalling the sepals or rarely absent. A distinctive extrastaminal ring of filaments, the corona, usually forms a bright and showy structure between the petals and stamens.

The stamens are (4)5 or 8(–10), on the hypanthium or androgynophore (*Passiflora*). The ovary is superior, of (2)3(–5) carpels, usually forming a many-seeded berry.

Passifloraceae. 1 *Passiflora caerulea* (a) twining stem with coiled tendrils, solitary flower with conspicuous filamentous corona and 5-lobed leaves subtended by leafy bracts (x⅔); (b) vertical section of flower with, from the base upward, subtending bracts, hollowed-out receptacle bearing spurred sepals, petals and filaments (the latter forming the corona) and a central stalk (androgynophore) with at the apex the ovary bearing long styles with capitate stigmas and at the base downward curving stamens (x1½); (c) fruit (x⅔); (d) cross section of fruit containing numerous seeds (x1½); (e) seed (x6).

Distribution The family grows throughout the tropics and subtropics, with some species reaching temperate regions. *Passiflora* (c. 525 spp.) has its center of diversity in wet tropical South America with only c. 20 spp. reaching southern Asia to New Zealand and with none native to Africa. By contrast, *Adenia* (c. 95 spp.) is most diverse in semiarid regions of Africa but extends to tropical Australia. *Basananthe* (25 spp.) occurs in tropical and southern Africa. *Paropsia* (11 spp.) grows in tropical Africa, Madagascar, and eastern Malesia. Other genera are small: 8 occur in Africa and Madagascar, 3 in tropical America, and *Paropsiopsis* in Malesia and Papuasia.

Economic uses Many *Passiflora* species are grown for their edible fruit, especially *P. edulis* (including var. *flavicarpa*), the basis of industrially produced juice, and *P. quadrangularis*, the Giant Granadilla, grown for its exceptionally large fruit. Other species grown for their fruit are the Banana Passion Fruit (*P. mollissima*), Fragrant Granadilla (*P. alata*), Red Granadilla (*P. coccinea*), Maypop (*P. incarnata*), Sweet Calabash (*P. maliformis*), Sweet Granadilla (*P. ligularis*), and Yellow Granadilla (*P. laurifolia*), although even more are utilized locally.

Many species of *Passiflora* are also grown as ornamentals, *P. caerulea* being popular in Europe due to its frost hardiness, showy flowers, and colorful fruit. Some species of *Adenia* are grown as ornamental curiosities for their swollen stem (caudiciform) habit.

Passiflora has a close interrelationship with *Heliconius* butterflies, whose larvae feed on the leaves and are resistant to the numerous toxins the plants produce. Some *Passiflora* deter the butterflies owing to outgrowths on the leaves that look like *Heliconius* eggs.

Barteria from Africa has a mutualistic association with *Pachysima* ants that keep insect predators away.

Pepper Family

Small trees, shrubs, lianas, and herbs, with spicate inflorescences that grow in tropical and subtropical regions worldwide. They are the source of culinary peppers and some ornamental plants.

Description Small trees or shrubs, lianas (climbing by means of adventitious roots), and herbs, sometimes epiphytic.

The leaves are entire, membranous or succulent, alternate, opposite, spirally arranged or basal, from 2 mm to 70 cm.

In many *Piper* species, a stipulelike structure called the prophyll is present. The inflorescences are spicate, erect, arched or pendulous, axillary, terminal or leaf-opposed, and composed of minute asepalous apetalous flowers, stalked or sessile, each subtended by a tiny bract.

The flowers are actinomorphic, unisexual (plants dioecious or monoecious), or bisexual.

The stamens are 2–6, free. The ovary is superior, 1-locular, with a single ovule.

The fruits are drupaceous or berrylike, with glochidiate hairs (*Zippelia*), fleshy and coalescent (*Sarcorhachis* and *Macropiper*), beaked with pennicillate stigmas (*Peperomia*), and obovoid or flask-shaped, often with prominent styles (*Piper*). The seeds are starchy. The larger fleshy infructescences are often eaten by bats or birds.

Distribution Tropical and subtropical regions of the world, often colonizing forest clearings. *Macropiper* is confined to the South Pacific; *Zippelia* to Southeast Asia.

Economic uses *Piper nigrum* (Black Pepper) is the source of commercial peppercorns, which are the dried fruits of this flowering vine. They are used as a spice and for seasoning, either whole or powdered.

P. longum is the "Long Pepper" of India; it is a close relative of *P. nigrum* but has a hotter taste. *P. betle* leaves are used to wrap betel nuts (*Areca catechu*); species of *Piper* and *Macropiper* are used in local medicine or as infusions; some species of *Peperomia* are grown as ornamental plants.

Piperaceae. **1** *Peperomia fraseri* (a) shoot with opposite entire leaves and flowers in a terminal spike (x⅔); (b) ovary entire and half section with basal ovule (x6); (c) anthers (x6); (d) succulent bract (x6); (e) part of fruiting head (x2). **2** *Peperomia brasiliensis* (a) creeping stem with adventitious roots (x⅔); (b) inflorescence (x3); (c) flower (x9). **3** *Peperomia ovalifolia* (a) habit (x⅔); (b) flower with 2 stamens (x3); (c) fruit (x3); (d) vertical section of fruit with minute embryo (x3). **4** *P. marmorata* (a) shoot with leaves and flower spikes (x⅔); (b) part of spike with flowers (x1½); (c) flower with mushroomlike fleshy bract, 2 stamens and a single ovary crowned by a dissected stigma (x6); (d) flower (x6).

Leadwort, Sea Lavender, and Thrift

A family of annual and perennial herbs, shrubs, and climbers, many of which are halophytes or psammophytes, which grow worldwide (except in Antarctica), especially in dry or saline habitats.

Description Shrubs, lianes, or annual and perennial herbs with spirally arranged leaves, often in a basal rosette. The leaves are simple and entire, sometimes with basal auricles but without stipules, often with secretory glands exuding water, calcium salts, or mucilage. The flowers are actinomorphic, hermaphrodite, in cymose or racemose (e.g., *Limonium*), spicate (e.g., *Acantholimon*) inflorescences or in dense, capitulate clusters (e.g., *Armeria*). The bracts are scarious and sometimes form an involucre. The sepals are 5, persistent, fused to form a 5-toothed or 5-lobed tube. The petals are 5, free or fused into a long tube. The stamens are 5, opposite the petals, free or inserted at the base of the corolla. The anthers are 2-locular and split open longitudinally. The ovary is superior, of 5 fused carpels, and with a single locule containing a single basal ovule; 5 styles or 5 sessile stigmas surmount the ovary. The fruit is usually enclosed by the calyx and indehiscent. The seed contains a straight embryo surrounded by mealy endosperm.

Distribution The family is cosmopolitan, although absent from Antarctica, but especially frequent in dry or saline habitats, e.g., sea coasts and salt steppes. Subfamily Plumbaginoideae is predominantly tropical and warm temperate, while subfamily Staticoideae is largely coastal and north-temperate Old World. *Aegialitis* (2 sp.) is restricted to mangroves of Indo-Malesia and Australia. *Limonium* (c. 350 spp.), by far the largest genus in the family, has many narrow endemics.

Economic uses A number of species yield extracts that are used in medicine, e.g., those from *Plumbago europaea* and *P. scandens* are used to treat dental ailments; those from tropical *P. zeylanica* are used to treat skin diseases; and those from the roots of *Limonium vulgare* are used to treat bronchial hemorrhages. Many members of the family are grown in gardens, such as *Armeria* spp. (Sea Pink or Thrift) and *Limonium* spp. (Sea Lavender) whose cut flowers may be dried and used as everlastings. The climbers *Plumbago auriculata* (pale blue flowers) and *P. rosea* (red flowers) are widely grown. *Ceratostigma willmottianum* is a popular ornamental garden shrub.

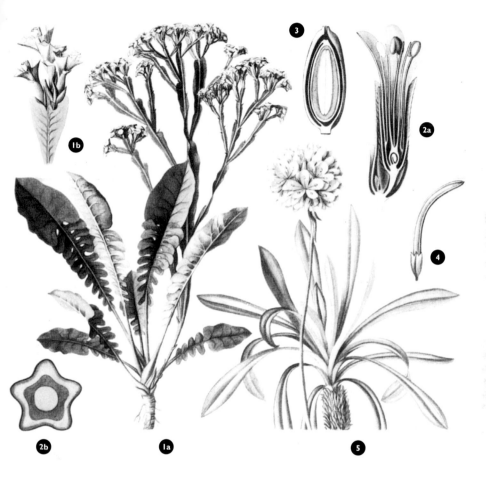

Plumbaginaceae. 1 *Limonium imbricatum* (a) habit showing part of tap root, rosette of leaves and flowers in branched panicles (x⅓); (b) part of inflorescence (x2). **2** *L. tunetanum* (a) half flower showing stamens inserted at base of corolla tube (x8); (b) cross section of ovary with a single ovule (x40). **3** *L. thouini* vertical section of fruit (x⅔). **4** *Aegialitis annulata* indehiscent fruit with persistent calyx (x1). **5** *Armeria pseudarmeria* habit showing radical leaves and flowers in dense capitulate clusters (x⅔). **6** *A. maritima* half flower with lobed petals, epipetalous stamens and gynoecium with simple hairy styles and a single basal ovule (x4). **7** *Plumbago auriculata* shoot bearing simple leaves and inflorescences (x⅔).

Phlox Family

Small annual to perennial temperate herbs centered in western North America, and woody plants and climbers centered in Mexico and the Andes, often with showy flowers.

Description Small annual to perennial herbs to shrubs (spiny in *Acanthogilia*) or trees up to 8 m (*Cantua*) or herbaceous to woody tendrilled climbers up to 25 m (*Cobaea*).

The leaves are alternate or opposite (*Phlox*, *Leptodactylon*, and *Linanthus*) or in a whorl below the inflorescence (*Gymnosteris*), varying from simple (often linear in herbaceous species but broad and coriaceous in woody species) to linear-pinnatisect or with linear palmate leaflets (tribe Leptodactyloneae), or pinnate with distinct leaflets.

In *Cobaea* the leaves usually have about 3 pairs of fairly large distinct leaflets and the rhachis is terminated by branched tendrils that each end in a pair of clawlike hooks, which are important in the climbing habit. These hooks closely resemble the apex of the leaflets, suggesting that each tendril branch is a modified leaflet.

Stipules are absent (in some *Cobaea* species, the basal pair of leaflets may resemble stipules). The inflorescence is a usually terminal cyme, often aggregated and more or less capitate, in *Cobaea* leaf-opposed and long-peduncled, with 2 opposite bracteoles closely resembling leaves in being pinnate and tendrilled.

The flowers are actinomorphic or sometimes bilateral, bisexual, 5-merous, or occasionally 4- to 6-merous in *Linanthus*, often showy. The sepals are 5, usually fused into a tube but in *Cobaea* free and sometimes broad and overlapping. The corolla is usually narrowly tubular, up to 8 cm in *Cantua*, but broadly campanulate in *Cobaea*.

The stamens are as many as the corolla lobes and alternating with them. There is usually an annular nectariferous disk surrounding the ovary base.

The ovary is superior of (2)3(4) fused carpels, each with a separate locule bearing 1 to many ovules.

The fruit is a capsule, dehiscing loculicidally or septicidally (*Cobaea*), with 1 to many seeds, which may be winged.

Distribution The family is predominantly in the New World, but *Polemonium* is widespread in northern temperate regions, and *Phlox* has 1 sp. in Siberia.

The herbaceous genera grow mostly in drier habitats in North America, especially western USA and Mexico, but extend to Chile and Argentina.

The trees and climbers are predominantly in Mexico and the Andes, and sometimes reach cloud forest at up to 3,000 m.

Economic uses Numerous species of *Phlox*, *Gilia* (Gilias), and *Polemonium* (e.g., Jacob's Ladder) are grown in temperate gardens as ornamentals. *Phlox* cultivars are available in purple, pink, blue, white, and yellow. They are renowned for attracting butterflies. *Phlox paniculata* (Garden Phlox) and *P. maculata* (Meadow Phlox) are among the more commonly grown herbaceous perennials. *P. drummondii* is an annual often used as a bedding plant.

Cobaea scandens is a spectacular climbing plant and may be grown as an annual in temperate regions but is widely naturalized in tropical countries.

Polemoniaceae. 1 *Loeselia cordifolia* (a) shoot with toothed, opposite leaves and small cymose clusters of flowers (x⅔); (b) flower (x4); (c) vertical section of ovary showing basal disk and ovules on axile placentas (x12). **2** *Linanthus androsaceus* (a) flowering shoot (x⅔); (b) flower opened to show anthers inserted at apex of long corolla tube (x1). **3** *Phlox paniculata* (a) corolla opened to show irregular insertion of stamens (x1½); (b) part of calyx and entire gynoecium (x1½); (c) cross section of ovary (x14). **4** *Gilia achilleifolia* (a) flowering shoot (x⅔); (b) flower opened out showing insertion of stamens between corolla lobes (x4); (c) cross section of fruit (x6).

Polygalaceae. 1 *Xanthophyllum scortechinii* (a) leafy shoot and irregular flowers (x⅔); (b) flower with petals removed showing free stamens (x1½); (c) petal (x1½); (d) gynoecium (x2); (e) cross section of ovary (x2); (f) globose fruit (x⅔). **2** *Polygala apopetala* (a) inflorescence (x⅔); (b) flower with lateral sepals removed (x2); (c) androecium with filaments united in a split sheath (x3); (d) stamens (x4); (e) gynoecium (x3); (f) vertical section of ovary (x8). **3** *Carpolobia lutea* (a) leaves and fruit—a drupe (x⅔); (b) fruit entire and in cross section (x⅔). **4** *Bredemeyera colletioides* flowering shoot (x⅔). **5** *Securidaca longipedunculata* winged fruits—samaras (x⅔).

Milkwort Family

Herbs, shrubs, small trees, climbers, and even saprophytes, remarkable for the superficial resemblance of the flowers to the well-known papilionaceous flower of the Leguminosae (Pea and Bean family).

Description Perennial or annual herbs and shrubs, occasionally trees or lianas, rarely saprophytes (*Epirhizanthes*), with usually alternate leaves.

The leaves are simple, without stipules, but sometimes with extrafloral nectaries at the junction of the petiole and stem.

The inflorescence is axillary or terminal spikes, racemes, solitary or paniculate (*Monnina hirta*). The flowers are hermaphrodite, usually zygomorphic, each subtended by a bract and 2 bracteoles.

The calyx of 5 (rarely 4–7) sepals is variously modified, most commonly either with the 2 lowermost united or with the 2 inner (lateral) enlarged and often petaloid.

The corolla is usually of 3 petals, with the lowest (median) petal often saucer-shaped and sometimes with a fringed crest.

The stamens are usually 8, generally joined to the base of the corolla, with their united filaments forming a split sheath; the anthers are basifixed, usually dehiscing by an apical pore; the pollen grains have a distinctive pattern on their outer wall. A ring-shaped disk is sometimes present inside the base of the staminal whorl.

The ovary is superior, of (1)2(5) united carpels, with a single pendulous ovule on an axile placenta in each of the 2 locules, although there are various exceptions to this general structure.

The style is simple. The fruit is usually a loculicidal capsule (e.g., *Polygala*, *Muraltia*), septicidal in *Salomonia*, a drupe (e.g., *Nylandtia*, *Monnina*), samara-like with 1 (*Securidaca*) or 2 (*Ancylotropis*, *Pteromonnina*) wings, or a nut (*Atroximia*). The seeds, sometimes hairy, generally have an aril and contain a straight embryo and fleshy endosperm (sometimes absent).

Distribution The Polygalaceae is almost cosmopolitan, being absent only from New Zealand and many of the southern Pacific Islands and the extreme northern parts of the northern hemisphere.

Economic uses Local medicines are extracted from several species, for example, snakeroot from *Polygala senega* of eastern North America. The constituent glucoside seregin is used by Native Americans to cure snakebites.

Buckwheat, Rhubarb, and Dock Family

A large cosmopolitan family of annual or perennial herbs, some shrubs, a few trees, scramblers, or climbers, often with swollen nodes, and most growing in temperate northern regions.

Description Annual or perennial herbs, shrubs, trees, scramblers, or climbers. The leaves are usually basal or alternate, opposite, or occasionally whorled (some *Eriogonum*), simple (highly reduced in *Calligonum* and *Muehlenbeckia*), and, in subfamily Polygonoideaei, with a characteristic ochrea, or membranous sheath, around the stem and uniting the stipules. The inflorescence is terminal or axillary, simple or a branched thyrse, appearing paniculate, racemose, spikelike, or umbel-like (*Eriogonum heracleioides*). The flowers are usually hermaphrodite, occasionally unisexual, small, white, greenish, or pinkish. The tepals are 3–6, usually in 2 whorls of 3 or 1 whorl of 5 (by fusion of 2 tepals), often becoming enlarged and membranous in fruit. The stamens are (2–)6–9, with 2-locular anthers opening lengthwise. The ovary is superior, of (2)3(4) fused carpels, with a single locule containing a single basal ovule. The styles are 2–4. The fruit is a triangular achene or nut that is sometimes attached to, or enclosed in, a fleshy expanded perianth (e.g., *Antigonon* and *Muehlenbeckia*).

Distribution Most genera inhabit the temperate northern regions. A few are tropical or subtropical, notably *Antigonon* (Mexico and Central America), *Coccoloba* (tropical America and Jamaica), and *Muehlenbeckia* (Australasia and South America).

Economic uses Cultivated ornamentals include *Antigonon leptopus* (Coral Vine or Rosa de Montaña), *Muehlenbeckia axillaris*, *Atraphaxis frutescens*, the rock-garden species of *Eriogonum* (grown for their gray and white foliage), the waterside *Rheum palmatum* and *Rumex hydrolapathum*, and fast-growing border, ground cover, and rock-garden species of *Persicaria*. The purple berries of the West Indian Seaside Grape, *Coccoloba unifera*, are eaten, as are the leaves of the Common Sorrel, *Rumex acetosa* (a salad and potherb), and the petioles of the Common Rhubarb, *Rheum* x *hybridum*. *Fagopyrum esculentum* (Common Buckwheat) is cultivated for its seeds and as a manure and cover crop. Similar uses are made of *F. tataricum* (Tartary Buckwheat), although the seeds are not eaten by humans.

la

Polygonaceae. 1 *Rumex hymenosepalus* (a) leafy shoot with flowers and winged fruit (x⅔); (b) mature fruits showing persistent perianth (x⅔); (c) cross section of fruit (x1); (d) flower (x2). **2** *Oxyria digyna* (a) habit (x⅔); (b) winged fruit (x4); (c) cross section of fruit (x4). **3** *Polygonum amplexicaule* (a) flowering spike showing sheathing stipules or ochreas clasping the stem above the leaf bases (x⅔); (b) perianth opened out to show 8 stamens (x2); (c) vertical section of ovary (x4). **4** *Homalocladium platycladum* (a) flowering shoot (x⅔); (b) flower buds and young fruits (x4); (c) mature fruit (x4); (d) seed (x4); (e) cross section of seed (x4); (f) flower viewed from above (x7).

Purslane and Lewisia

This nearly cosmopolitan family of trees, shrubs, scramblers, and herbs is related to Cactaceae (Cactus family) and other succulent plants. Many genera grow in arid or semiarid regions.

Description Trees (*Calyptrotheca*), shrubs, scramblers (*Grahamia*), and herbs, sometimes with a woody base, succulent or tuberous.

The leaves are spirally arranged or apparently opposite, usually simple with entire margins, usually glabrous but sometimes with hairs or glandular barbs, often fleshy, the petioles short or almost absent and poorly defined; stipules are lacking but basal scales, spines, or bristles are sometimes present.

The flowers are hermaphrodite (unisexual in *Ceraria*; plants dioecious), actinomorphic, rarely slightly zygomorphic, in terminal cymes or panicles, sometimes condensed into a dense head or flowers solitary.

The sepals are 2(3)–5 or more in *Lewisia*, and often unequal in size when 2, persistent or deciduous.

The petals are (2–)5(–12 or more), sometimes brightly colored, free or connate. The stamens are usually 5, or 1 (in *Monocosmia*), sometimes many, free or connate to the base of the petals. The ovary is superior or inferior (*Portulaca*) of 2–5 fused carpels, 1-locular, with free central placentation at maturity. The style is usually divided.

The fruit is capsular, usually dehiscing through terminal valves, or circumscissile, or the fruit is a nut. Seeds with or without an aril.

Distribution The family is nearly cosmopolitan with the major diversity in the southern hemisphere, with centers of diversity in the Andes and South Africa, but species also grow in North America and Eurasia. *Portulaca* is pantropical. Many genera occur in arid or semiarid conditions (e.g., *Anacampseros, Calandrinia, Portulaca, Talinum*).

Economic uses Purslane (*Portulaca oleracea*) is a widely eaten, but not commercialized, vegetable. Several genera are grown as ornamentals because of their bright flowers or as curiosities (*Anacampseros* spp., *Portulaca grandiflora, Lewisia tweedyi*, and hybrids). *Portulaca oleracea* is used medicinally.

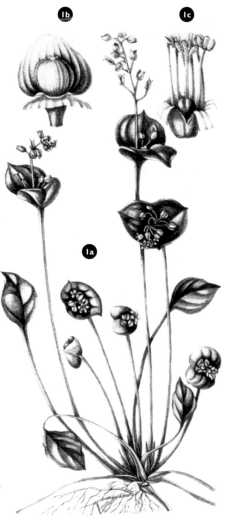

Portulacaceae. I *Claytonia perfoliata* (a) habit showing flower stalks erect before, and curved downward after, pollination, and erect when bearing fruit (x⅔); (b) mature capsule with 1 of 2 persistent sepals removed (x6); (c) flower with petals partly removed (x12). **2** *Lewisia cotyledon* (a) habit showing basal rosette of leaves and inflorescence (x⅔); (b) vertical section of ovary with basal ovules (x3). **3** *Portulaca grandiflora* (a) flowering shoot showing hairy stipules (x⅔); (b) cross section of 1-locular ovary (x4); (c) half flower showing overlapping petals (x4). **4** *Montia fontana* (a) habit (x⅔); (b) fruit—a capsule dehiscing by 3 valves (x6); (c) flower (x6).

Primula Family

A predominantly north-temperate family of herbs with often showy tubular flowers and stamens opposite the corolla lobes. Many species are of major horticultural importance.

Description Annual to perennial herbs, sometimes caespitose or mat-forming. The leaves are alternate or opposite to whorled, often forming a basal rosette, simple and linear (*Asterolinon*, *Pelletiera*) to orbicular, with an entire to serrate margin, except in the aquatic genus *Hottonia*, in which they are finely dissected into linear segments and in *Potamosace*, in which they are pinnatisect. Occasionally (some *Lysimachia*) the leaves are glandular-punctate.

The inflorescence may be scapose with a solitary terminal flower, a terminal umbel of several whorls, a terminal raceme, an axillary cluster, or solitary axillary flower. The flowers are actinomorphic, bisexual, and often heterostylous, and usually 5-merous except in *Trientalis*, which is 7-merous, and in *Pelletiera* in which the corolla is 3-merous. The sepals are free or fused into a tubular to campanulate calyx. The corolla is tubular to campanulate, with the tube sometimes very short and the lobes free almost to the base; in *Glaux* the corolla is absent. The stamens are 5, attached to the corolla opposite the lobes. The ovary is superior, of 5 fused carpels, and has a single locule. Placentation is free central, with usually many (up to 400) ovules that are often embedded in the placenta. The fruit is usually a characteristically subspherical capsule, but in some genera of Primuleae it is elongate, especially in *Bryocarpum*, where it is linear and c. 5 cm long.

The capsule either dehisces by apical valves or by a circumscissile split (*Anagallis*, *Potamosace*, some *Primula*), or the upper part lifts off irregularly (*Soldanella*, *Bryocarpum*, some *Primula*), or the whole capsule breaks up irregularly to release the seeds. Seeds are angular, and there are few in *Asterolinon* and *Pelletiera* but many in the other genera.

Distribution Most genera are in the northern-temperate region, including the Himalayas and China. *Lysimachia* is in all the major regions

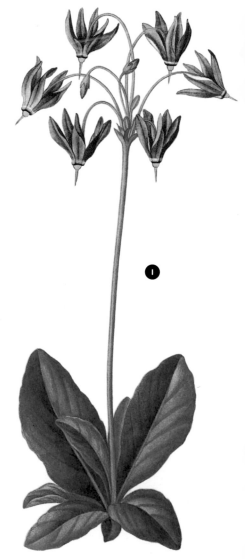

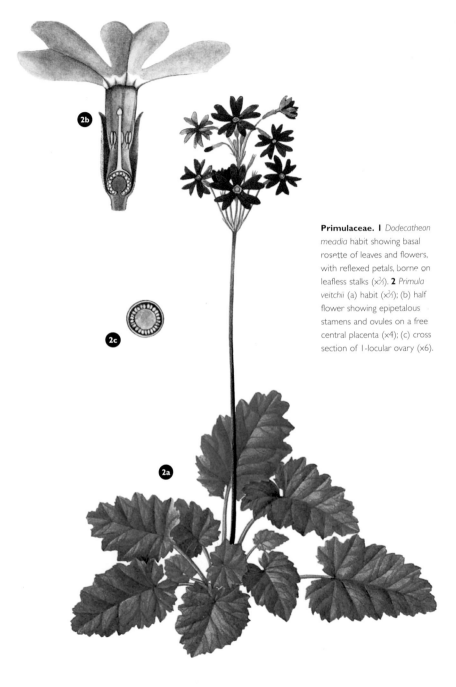

Primulaceae. 1 *Dodecatheon meadia* habit showing basal rosette of leaves and flowers, with reflexed petals, borne on leafless stalks (x⅔). **2** *Primula veitchii* (a) habit (x⅔); (b) half flower showing epipetalous stamens and ovules on a free central placenta (x4); (c) cross section of 1-locular ovary (x6).

but is very restricted in Australasia and South America. *Anagallis* is widespread but is not native in most of Malesia and Australasia. *Ardisiandra* is confined to African mountains, from Bioko to Ethiopia and south to Zimbabwe. *Cyclamen* extends from the Mediterranean to Ethiopia. *Asterolinon* extends from the Mediterranean to Tanzania, while the closely related *Pelletiera* grows in temperate South America (and is introduced in the Canary Islands). *Primula* has perhaps 400 northern temperate species, 1 in eastern tropical Africa, 2 in Malesia to New Guinea, 2–3 in Mexico, and 1–2 in temperate South America, including the Falkland Islands. *Androsace* has more than 150 northern temperate species and 1 in temperate South America.

Economic uses *Primula*, *Lysimachia*, and *Cyclamen* are all of major horticultural importance, and *Androsace*, *Dionysia*, *Cortusa*, *Dodecatheon*, and *Soldanella* are all also widely cultivated. Otherwise there is little economic use of the family. Poisonous glycosides are produced in *Cyclamen* and *Anagallis*.

Primulaceae. 3 *Soldanella alpina* habit showing flowers with deeply divided petals (×⅔). **4** *Primula veris* dehisced fruit (a capsule) with part of persistent calyx removed (×3). **5** *Cyclamen hederifolium* (a) habit showing basal tuber (×⅔); (b) dehisced fruit (×4). **6** *Lysimachia punctata* leafy terminal inflorescence with yellow flowers (×⅔).

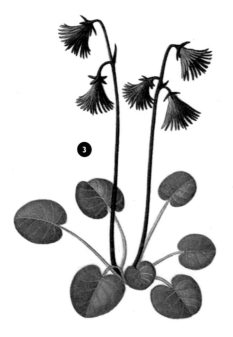

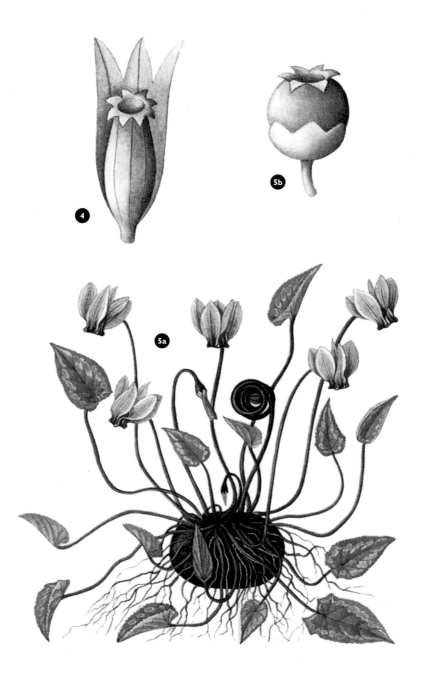

Protea Family

Perennial trees and shrubs, including macadamias, characterized mostly by flowers with a single whorl of 4 tepals, fused to the inside of which are 4 stamens, and growing mainly in the southern hemisphere.

Description Perennial subshrubs, shrubs, or trees to 40 m. Clusters of short, lateral roots ("proteoid roots") are often produced. The leaves are highly variable but mostly leathery, with pinnate venation. They are compound, deeply dissected or lobed, up to a fourth order of dissection, toothed, lobed and toothed, or simple and entire. The degree to which leaf shape varies between different stages in development is a striking feature of some species, especially many rain-forest taxa.

The inflorescence varies spectacularly but can be interpreted as variation on 2 basic "structural plans": simple or branching racemes of flower pairs in the subfamily Grevilleoideae, and racemose, simple, or compound inflorescences in the other subfamilies. These have been modified in some taxa by reduction, elaboration, compaction, and thickening to yield conelike, headlike, leafy, and 1-flowered inflorescences.

The flowers are usually completely bisexual but sometimes unisexual (plants dioecious or monoecious), usually either radially or bilaterally symmetrical, with a perianth of 4 (rarely 3 or 5) free or variously united tepals.

The stamens are 4 (rarely 3 or 5), opposite the tepals, with their filaments partly or wholly fused to them or rarely free, usually all fertile but sometimes 1 or more are sterile, usually with 2-locular anthers, but occasionally the lateral anthers are 1-locular.

One to 4 hypogynous nectary glands are usually present, free or fused into a crescentic or annular nectary.

The ovary is superior, sessile or stipitate, with a single carpel (rarely 2, free) containing 1 to many ovules inserted on marginal placentae. The style is usually distinct, often with its apex functioning as a pollen presenter. The fruits are dehiscent or indehiscent, dry or succulent, containing 1 to many, sometimes winged, seeds.

Distribution Mainly in the southern hemisphere (but extending into southern and eastern Asia, Central America, and western and northeastern tropical Africa), where the family is almost completely restricted to Gondwanic continental blocks and fragments.

They grow in a variety of habitats, ranging from open shrubland or grassland to rain forests, from alpine meadows to tropical lowlands, usually on acidic, well-drained, nutrient-poor soils.

Economic uses Proteaceae have long been used by various indigenous peoples as sources of food, medicine, tannins and other dyes, firewood, and timber.

Many arborescent species have been logged commercially for timber, but this use is declining with the gradual cessation of rain-forest logging in the southern hemisphere.

The commercial significance of the Proteaceae is now dominated by trade in macadamia nuts (*Macadamia integrifolia*, *M. tetraphylla*, and their hybrids) and, to a much lesser extent, the sale of ornamentals. Important ornamental genera include *Protea*, *Leucadendron*, *Leucospermum*, *Serruria*, *Banksia*, *Grevillea*, *Telopea*, and *Persoonia*.

Proteaceae. 1 *Leucospermum conocarpodendron* (a) leafy shoot with terminal conelike inflorescence, each flower with a conspicuous arrow-shaped pollen presenter (x⅔); (b) flower with stamens fused to perianth segments and long style with arrow-shaped pollen presenter (x1½); (c) perianth opened out to show fruit (x10); (d) hairy bract (x4). **2** *Grevillea robusta* (a) deeply divided leaf (x⅔); (b) inflorescence each flower with a projecting style (x⅔); (c) young flower with pollen presenter retained in bud (x2); (d) tepal with anthers directly attached (x5½); (e) mature flower with extended style and stigma (x2); (f) fruits (x⅔); (g) winged seed (x⅔).

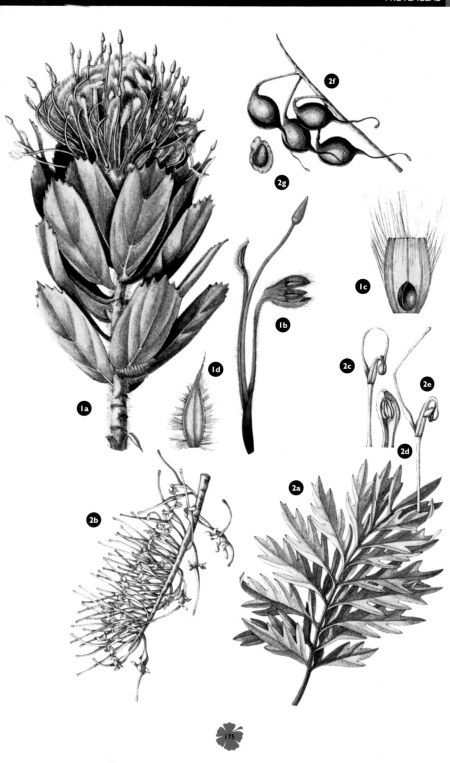

Rafflesiaceae. 1 *Rafflesia manillana* (a)
male flower (x⅓); (b) flower buds (x⅓).
2 *R. patma* half male flower bud showing
"mycelia" ramifying through host tissue
(x¼). **3** *R. rochussenii* vertical section of
fruit (x⅓).

Rafflesiaceae

A tropical and subtropical family of stem and root parasites that grows in parts of southern and southeastern Asia and into areas of China. At 1 m across, *Rafflesia arnoldii* is reputed to be the largest flower in the world.

Description Endoparasitic, achlorophyllous (and hence nonphotosynthesizing) herbs, with a vegetative body similar to a mycelium, residing completely in the roots and stems of the vine *Tetrastigma* (Vitaceae).

Rafflesia species do not typically kill their host plants despite the drain on resources that these parasites cause.

There are no stems, and the leaves are represented by a variable number of bracts subtending the flowers. The only parts of the plant that can be seen outside the host vine are the petals and other structures that make up the flowers.

The flowers are solitary or in inflorescences and arise from within the host; they are usually unisexual (plants monoecious or dioecious), occasionally also with bisexual flowers (*Rhizanthes*) and actinomorphic. Each flower ranges in size from 8 cm (*Rhizanthes*) to more than 1 m across and weighing up to 7 kg (*Rafflesia*). Each flower has a lifespan of between 5 and 7 days.

The flower color varies from pure white to brown (*Rhizanthes*), orange, brick red, with white spots or yellow and black (*Rafflesia*). The flowers are often malodorous, smelling of rotten flesh (*Rafflesia*; hence its nicknames of "corpse flower" or "meat flower") or rotting apples (*Rhizanthes*).

The malodorous smell that the flowers of *Rafflesia arnoldii* give off attracts insects such as flies and carrion beetles, which carry pollen from male to female flowers.

The perianth is uniseriate with 5 (*Rafflesia*), 10 (*Sapria*), or 16 (*Rhizanthes*) tepals, connate below and fused to the ovary, forming a perigone tube, the lobes imbricate or valvate (*Rhizanthes*). The perianth is fused distally to the ovary into a perigone tube that forms a centrally located aperture called the diaphragm in *Sapria* and *Rafflesia* (but not *Rhizanthes*). In the staminate flowers, the androecium consists of a ring of 12–40 extrorse anthers with 2 (*Rhizanthes, Sapria*) to several (*Rafflesia*) pores, the connectives fused and adnate to a central column (gynostemium).

In the pistillate flowers, the ovary is inferior of 4–8 fused carpels, 1-locular (*Rhizanthes*) or with numerous locules forming a honeycomb-like structure due to intrusive placentas (*Rafflesia, Sapria*).

The fruit is baccate, indehiscent, or irregularly dehiscent, with many small seeds.

Nickrent's Parasitic Plant Connection (based at Southern Illinois University, USA) is a valuable source of information and illustrations.

Distribution *Rafflesia* (c. 15 spp.) grows in western Malaysia, as does *Rhizanthes* (2 spp.), while *Sapria* (2 spp.) extends from Assam and Bhutan to Myanmar, Cambodia, Vietnam, China, and Thailand.

Economic uses *Rafflesia* is an official state flower of Indonesia, of Sabah state in Malaysia, and of Surat Thani Province in Thailand.

R. arnoldii and other species of the genus are an attraction to ecotourists.

Buttercup, Monkshood, Cohosh, and Columbine

One of the few truly cosmopolitan families of perennial or sometimes annual herbs or lianas, spreading across all continents except Antarctica and from sea level to high altitude.

Description Perennial, or sometimes annual, herbs, rarely shrubby, or lianas (many *Clematis*). The perennial herbaceous species usually persist by means of a condensed sympodial rootstock or rhizome, swelling into storage tubers in *Aconitum* and some *Ranunculus*. The leaves are opposite or spirally arranged, simple (e.g., *Caltha*), palmately lobed (e.g., *Ranunculus*) or compound, sometimes highly so (e.g., *Thalictrum*), usually with a petiole and without stipules. The aquatic species of *Ranunculus* (*R.* subg. *Batrachium*) usually have submerged, much-dissected leaves. In *Clematis*, the petiole is sensitive to touch and supports the stem as a tendril. In *Clematis aphylla*, the whole of the leaf becomes a tendril, photosynthesis being carried out by the stem cortex. The petioles are broadened into a sheathing base. Stipules are absent, except in *Thalictrum*, *Caltha*, *Trollius*, and *Ranunculus*. The inflorescence is terminal. In *Eranthis* and some species of *Anemone*, the flowers are solitary; more usually they are in racemes or cymes. In *Anemone*, (including *Pulsatilla*), and *Nigella* there is a protective involucre of leaves beneath the flower, alternate with the calyx segments. The flowers are usually hermaphrodite and regular but irregular in *Aconitum* and *Delphinium*. The flower has its parts typically arranged in spirals along a more or less elongated receptacle, but often the perianth segments are in whorls. The sepals vary from 3 to many, although most commonly 5, rarely persistent (*Helleborus*), and often petaloid. Rarely is a true calyx and corolla present, the exception being the genus *Ranunculus*. The numerous and spirally arranged stamens have extrorse anthers. The carpels range from 1 (*Actaea*) to many (*Myosurus*). The fruit is an achene or a many-seeded follicle. In *Actaea* sect. *Actaea*, the achene is fleshy and thus a berry. The seeds have a small straight embryo and copious endosperm.

The family shows a wide variation in flower structures and pollination methods. The family is insect-pollinated in the main, but some *Thalictrum* species are wind-pollinated and

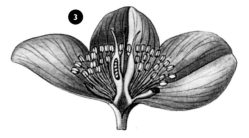

some *Aquilegia* are bird-pollinated. Many of the annual species are self-pollinated. The remaining insect-pollinated types are visited for their pollen or nectar. The genera *Anemone* (including *Pulsatilla*), and *Clematis* do not produce nectar and are visited only for their pollen. Nectar flowers with well-developed nectaries are present in *Ranunculus*, *Aquilegia*, *Delphinium*, and *Helleborus*. In *Anemone* and *Clematis*, insects are attracted by brightly colored sepals, in *Ranunculus* by showy petals (with prominent nectar pouches, or honeyleaves); in *Aconitum* by showy sepals and petals; and in some *Thalictrum* species by attractive stamen filaments or anthers. The family is generally protandrous, the stamens shedding their pollen before the ovaries mature, but protogyny (ovary maturing before the stamens) also occurs. However, some anthers may not have shed their pollen before the ovaries start to mature. These processes

Ranunculaceae.
1 *Trollius europeaus* flowering shoot (x⅔).
2 *Helleborus cyclophyllus* flowering shoot (x⅔).
3 *H. niger* (Christmas Rose) half flower showing large sepals, small tubular nectaries (modified petals), numerous stamens, and carpels slightly fused at base, each containing numerous ovules (x⅔).

favor cross-pollination and outbreeding. Seed dispersal is by a variety of agencies. *Clematis* and *Anemone* sect. *Pulsatilla* have styles that lengthen into long feathery structures adapted for wind distribution after pollination. Some species of *Ranunculus* (e.g., *R. arvensis*) have tubercules or hooked spines on the surface for animal dispersal. *Helleborus* species have an elaiosome or oil-containing swelling on the raphe, which attracts ants that then disperse the seeds (myrmecochory).

Distribution The family is distributed throughout the world but is centered in temperate and cold regions of the northern and southern hemispheres, with few tropical species. At least 75% of the genera grow in East Asia, and many are endemic; about 45% of genera occur in North America, of which 5 are endemic; and a similar number of genera in Europe but none are endemic. Most species grow in mesic or wet environments, some are aquatic (*Ranunculus* subg. *Batrachium*).

Economic uses Many genera have species that provide excellent plants for the garden. Most of the generic names are familiar to nursery workers and gardeners as showy herbaceous border plants (in the case of *Clematis*, climbers): *Trollius* (Globeflower), *Aconitum* (Monkshood and Aconites), *Helleborus* (Christmas rose, Lenten Lily, and other Hellebores). Other genera that include ornamental species (many with cultivated varieties) are *Actaea* (Baneberries, Herb Christopher), *Anemone*, *Aquilegia* (columbines), *Ranunculus* (buttercups, Spearwort, and crowfoots), *Caltha* (Marsh Marigold), *Delphinium* (including larkspurs), *Eranthis* (Winter Aconite), *Hepatica*, *Nigella* (Love-in-a-Mist, Fennel Flower), *Thalictrum*, and *Ficaria*. A number of genera are highly poisonous and have caused deaths. Victorian medical books give lurid details of the symptoms and deaths of gardeners who have inadvertently eaten *Aconitum* tubers, having confused them with Jerusalem artichokes. Many species have traditional medicinal uses, several having been researched for their active constituents, although this has led some species close to extinction through overharvesting.

Ranunculaceae. **4** *Eranthis hyemalis* (Winter Aconite) (a) habit (x⅔); (b) fruit—a group of follicles (x1½); (c) seed (x4). **5** *Aquilegia caerulea* shoot bearing regular flowers with spurred perianth segments (x⅔). **6** *Nigella damescena* fruit—a capsule surrounded by feathery bracts (x⅔). **7** *Aconitum napellus* (a) shoot bearing irregular flowers (x⅔); (b) half flower with large hooded upper sepal (x1½). **8** *Anemone coronaria* leaf and flower (x⅔).

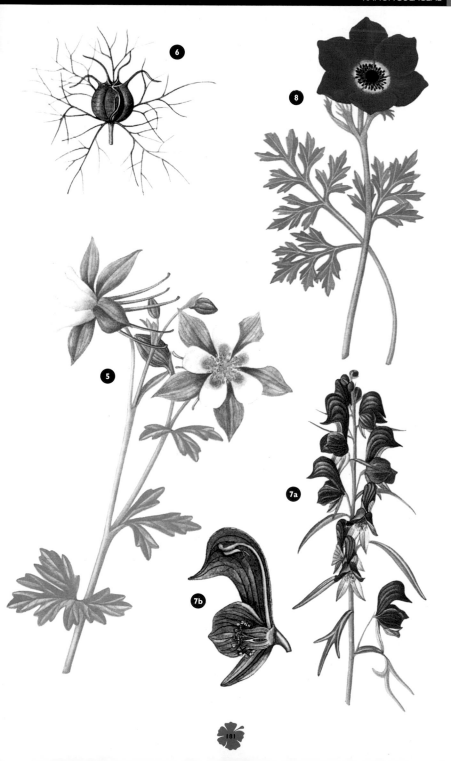

Ranunculaceae. 9 *Thalictrum minus* (a) leaf and flowers in a terminal inflorescence (x⅔); (b) flower with inconspicuous perianth and numerous large stamens (x4). **10** *Clematis alpina* (a) shoot with opposite leaves with long petioles that aid climbing and axillary flowers (x⅔); (b) fruit—a group of achenes, each with a persistent hairy style (x2⅔). **11** *Ranunculus* sp. half flower with free sepals and petals, numerous stamens and carpels, the latter with single ovules (x2). **12** *Myosurus minimus* (a) habit (x⅔); (b) flower with long receptacle bearing numerous carpels (x2⅔). **13** *Ficaria verna* habit showing tuberous roots (x⅔).

Rose Family

A large family of woody trees, shrubs, climbers, and herbaceous plants. The family is valued both for its genera of bush and tree fruits and for many popular horticultural ornamentals.

Description Deciduous or evergreen trees, shrubs, shrublets, or mostly perennial herbs; few climbers but no aquatics. Branch thorns occur in *Crataegus*, *Prunus*, and other genera, with emergences (surface prickles) in *Rosa* and *Rubus*. The leaves are alternate (rarely opposite), simple, or compound (pinnate or palmate); stipules are present on twigs or at the petiole base (but not always obvious), absent in a few genera (*Exochorda*, *Spiraea* and allies), persistent or caducous; glands are commonly present, often paired at the top of the petiole. The inflorescences are terminal or axillary, racemose, cymose, paniculate, or flowers solitary. The flowers are actinomorphic, usually bisexual, rarely unisexual (plants dioecious), frequently large and showy (insect-pollinated, rarely small and wind-pollinated), usually (4-)5-merous, the carpels appearing as if swallowed up by the hypanthium. *Rosa* is unique in retaining free carpels, and although the flower appears epigynous, it is perigynous. An epicalyx is usually present as a second, smaller whorl of 5 sepal-like organs below and alternating with the calyx lobes. The sepals and petals are (3–)5(–10), rarely absent (*Acaena*), although petal multiplication is common in cultivars developed for ornament (*Kerria*, *Prunus*, *Rosa*, and others) by replacement of the numerous stamens (sometimes also styles) by petaloid organs. The range of petal color is wide but blue is almost completely absent. The stamens are numerous, whorled, 2, 3, or more times as many as the petals; anthers are 2-locular, dehiscing longitudinally. The ovary is superior, semi-inferior to inferior, the carpels are normally numerous, free, with varying degrees of fusion; in Prunoideae reduced to 1, with 2 usually anatropous ovules. The fruits are diverse: fleshy drupes (*Prunus*), pomes (*Malus*), drupelets (*Rubus*), or dry capsules or follicles, dehiscent or not; seeds 1 to several, testa firm; endosperm usually absent; cotyledons flat.

Woody members of Rosaceae may propagate vegetatively by suckers, as in *Rubus*, which also tip-roots in the brambles. Runners (stolons) are a characteristic of some herbaceous genera (*Fragaria*).

The flowers of the Rosaceae are mostly among the simplest and least specialized for pollination, relying on a large and wasteful production of pollen that attracts a wide range of insects, large and small.

Some genera, such as *Rosa*, produce pollen only, but most also secrete nectar from a disk surrounding the carpels. This disk may be freely exposed (*Rubus*) or more or less screened by the filaments (*Geum*). The latter flowers are regarded as more highly evolved, eliminating short-tongued visitors and attracting only the longer-tongued flies and bees.

Protandry is the general rule, and self-compatibility is exceptional. Several genera are characterized by agamospermy, combined with polyploidy and hybridization. The dog roses (*Rosa* section *Caninae*) are said to be "subsexual" because half or more of the chromosomes remain unpaired and are lost prior to gamete formation. *Alchemilla*, *Sorbus*, and the brambles (*Rubus*) are more or less completely apomictic.

A marked departure from insect pollination is found in the Sanguisorbeae, notably in the genera *Acaena* and *Poterium*, which rely on wind pollination. The flowers are much reduced, in part unisexual, lacking petals and nectar, and are massed together in capitate or spicate heads.

Distribution The family is worldwide but with maximum development in the temperate to subtropical zones of the northern hemisphere.

Economic uses Most of the important bush and tree fruits of temperate regions are found in the Rosaceae. By far the most important

Rosaceae. I *Rubus ulmifolius* (a) flowering shoot (x⅔); (b) fleshy fruits (x⅔). **2** *Rubus occidentalis* half flower showing hypogynous arrangement of parts (x2). **3** *Fragaria* sp. vertical section of false fruit—a fleshy receptacle with the true fruits embedded in it (x1). **4** *Sanguisorba minor* leafy shoot and fruit (x⅔).

economically is the apple (*Malus*), now grown in numerous hybrid cultivars of complex origin. They are grown mainly for dessert, but are also used for making cider. The next most important genus is *Prunus*, which produces almonds, apricots, cherries, damsons, nectarines, peaches, and plums, all of which are grown extensively for consumption as fresh fruit and for canning and making into jams, conserves, and liqueurs. Other major rosaceous fruits are blackberries, loganberries, and raspberries (*Rubus*); loquats (*Eriobotrya*); medlars (*Mespilus*); pears (*Pyrus*); quinces (*Cydonia*); and strawberries (*Fragaria*).

Many Prunus species are also cultivated as ornamentals, notably the Japanese flowering cherries. However, it is the rose, the "queen of flowers," that overshadows all the other ornamentals, being probably the most popular and widely cultivated garden flower in the world and valued since ancient times for its beauty and fragrance. Modern roses are complex hybrids descended from about 9 of the wild species. Rose-growing is now a large industry, with some 5,000 named cultivars estimated to be in cultivation.

Among other popular cultivated genera are herbaceous perennials such as *Alchemilla* (Lady's Mantle), *Geum* (Avens), *Filipendula* (Meadowsweet), and *Potentilla* (Cinquefoil); and trees and shrubs such as *Amelanchier*, *Chaenomeles* (flowering quinces, including *C. lagenaria*, better known as the Japonica), *Cotoneaster*, *Exochorda* (Pearl Bush), *Sorbus* (Rowan, Mountain Ash), *Photinia*, and *Pyracantha* (Fire Thorn).

Attar or Otto of roses, a volatile fragrant oil, is extracted or distilled from fresh flowers of *Rosa damascena*, *R. gallica*, *R. centifolia*, and other species; its production is a major industry in Bulgaria and parts of western Asia.

Rosaceae. 5 *Agrimonia odorata* fruit comprising a receptacle covered with hooks enclosing the achenes (not visible) (x4). **6** *Rosa* sp. vertical section of hip showing urn-shaped receptacle enclosing the achenes (x1⅓). **7** *Potentilla agyrophylla* var. *atrosanguinea* flowering shoot (x⅔). **8** *Rosa pendulina* flowering shoot clearly showing the stipules at the base of the leaf stalks (x⅔). **9** *Kerria japonica* flowering shoot (x⅔). **10** *Chaenomeles speciosa* (a) flowering shoot (x⅔); (b) vertical section of fruit comprising swollen receptacle and calyx enclosing the true fruits (x⅔); (c) cross section of ovary (x6); (d) vertical section of flower showing epigynous arrangement of parts (x2). **11** *Cotoneaster salicifolius* (a) leafy shoot with fruit (x⅔); (b) vertical section of fruit (x2⅔). **12** *Sorbus aria* flowering shoot (x⅔). **13** *Prunus insititia* leafy shoot and fruits—drupes (x⅔). **14** *Prunus* sp. vertical section of fruit (x1⅓). **15** *Spiraea cantoniensis* vertical section of flower (x4).

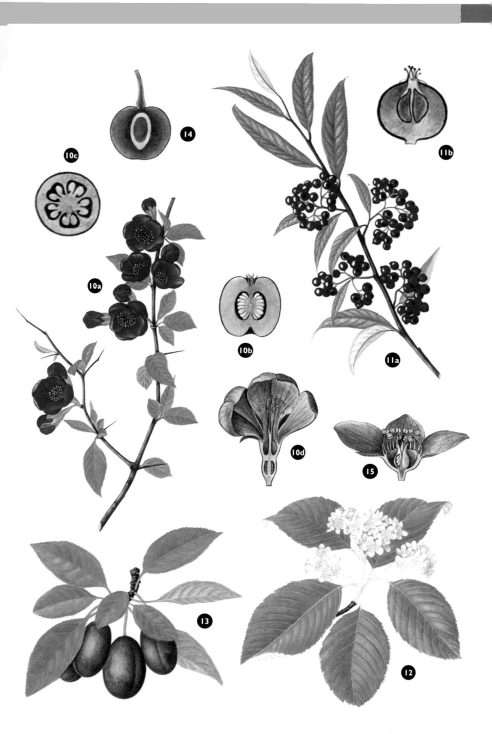

Coffee or Madder Family

The fourth largest flowering plant family after Orchidaceae, Asteraceae, and Fabaceae, usually recognized by the presence of simple, opposite, or whorled, entire leaves, interpetiolar stipules, and an inferior ovary.

Description Mostly small trees or shrubs (sometimes armed), but nearly all life-forms are found, including large trees, annual and perennial herbaceous plants, woody monocaul dwarfs, lianas, epiphytes, geofrutices (± herbaceous stems from a woody rootstock), and rarely succulent or aquatic; occasionally associated with ants (hollow stems or special chambered tubers e.g., *Myrmecodia*). The leaves are opposite or sometimes whorled, simple and nearly always entire, a few genera with bacterial nodules; domatia (pits or hairy tufts in the axils) often present. Colleters, which are modified hairs secreting exudate, are found on the inside surface of the stipule or otherwise associated with the stipule and sometimes on inflorescence and floral parts. Stipules are always present, most commonly interpetiolar, often fused above axils, sometimes forming a sheath or less often entirely free, or exactly leaflike (e.g., *Galium*), rarely intrapetiolar. The inflorescence is highly variable. The flowers are usually bisexual but also unisexual (plants usually dioecious), often heterostylous or with pollen presentation, and commonly 4- or 5-merous. The calyx is adnate to the ovary, extending to a free limb-tube and/or lobes, occasionally reduced to a rim, sometimes with calycophylls (or semaphylls: large, leaflike, white or colored calyx lobes) present. The corolla is always tubular (gamopetalous, although in a few taxa the tube is almost obsolete or rarely absent [*Dialypetalanthus*]), with radial symmetry (actinomorphic), although some species are secondarily zygomorphic. The stamens are usually as many as the corolla lobes, alternate to them and fixed to the internal surface of the corolla tube (epipetalous), occasionally the filaments are free to the base, sometimes fused in a ring (monadelphous, e.g., *Chiococceae*); the anthers are usually dorsifixed, but occasionally basifixed; dehiscence is commonly introrse or infrequently porate. A disk usually functioning as a nectary is positioned above the ovary inside the calyx limb, most commonly cushion-like or annular. The ovary is inferior, except for the genera *Gaertnera* and *Pagamea*, which have secondarily derived superior ovaries, the carpels usually 2, sometimes 5 or more, with axile placentation, or sometimes parietal, or a mixture of axile and parietal (some members of tribe Gardenieae), and ovules are 1 to numerous per locule, anatropous. The style is simple, and the stigma lobed or capitate. Morphologically elaborate stigmas are present in those groups with distinct secondary pollen presentation mechanisms, e.g., in the tribe Vanguerieae.

The fruit is small or quite large, indehiscent (berries or drupes with usually 2 or more single-seeded pyrenes, less frequently a multi-seeded stone) or dehiscent (capsules, mericarps), sometimes united into syncarps.

The seeds may be small or large, sometimes winged. Endosperm is present and usually conspicuous, sometimes ruminate; absent in the tribe Guettardeae.

Distribution The Rubiaceae has a cosmopolitan distribution, but species diversity and biomass is distinctly concentrated in the tropics and the subtropics. In humid tropical forests, the Rubiaceae is often the most species abundant woody plant family. The family is less frequent and less diverse, but still widespread, in the temperate regions. It is also found in the subpolar regions of the Arctic and Antarctic.

Economic uses Coffee (*Coffea*) is by far the most important economic product of the Rubiaceae, with some 100 million people worldwide depending on it for their livelihood. Indeed, it has become one of the world's most important commodities. Two main species are used in the production of coffee: *C. arabica* (Arabica coffee) and *C. canephora* (robusta coffee), with a small amount of production for

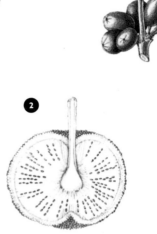

Rubiaceae. **1** *Ixora chinensis* (a) flowering shoot showing stipules between the petioles (x⅔); (b) tubular corolla opened out to show epipetalous stamens and simple style with a lobed stigma and vertical section of ovary (x1½). **2** *Sarcocephalus pobeguinii* vertical section of fruit (x½). **3** *Coffea arabica* fruits (x⅔).

C. liberica (Liberian or Liberica coffee, and excelsa coffee). *Coffea arabica* is by far the most important commercial species, making up more than 95% of the total marketable crop. Quinine (*Cinchona* spp.) was an historically important malarial prophylaxis and curative. Modern synthetic counterparts and alternatives are far more widely used, although quinine is still used as a food and drink flavoring, e.g., in tonic water.

Other economically important Rubiaceae include Ipecacuanha (*Carapichea ipecacuanha*), an amoebicide, emetic, and expectorant; and Gambir or White Cutch (*Uncaria* spp.), which is used as a tanning agent for leather and to a lesser extent as a dyestuff and in medicine. Of lesser importance are the timber species (e.g., *Adina* spp., *Anthocephalus* spp.) and the dye commonly known as madder, which is derived from the root of *Rubia tincto-*

rum. Numerous other taxa have ethnic use as red or black dyes. The alkaloid Yohimbine (*Paucinystalia johimbe*) is used as an aphrodisiac both for humans and in veterinary practice. The Rubiaceae are rich in alkaloids and other chemicals, and numerous taxa have local medicinal uses; a few taxa are poisonous to cattle; *Catunaregam* spp. are used as a fish poison. *Gardenia* is used in the perfume industry. *Galium verum* has been used in cheesemaking as "vegetarian rennet." Dried plants of *Galium odoratum* and *G. verum* were historically placed among linen to give it a pleasant freshly mown hay scent (coumarin). A number of species are used as ornamentals in the tropics, such as *Bouvardia*, *Gardenia*, *Hamelia*, *Ixora*, *Manettia*, *Mussaenda*, *Rondeletia*, and *Warszewicia*. There are a few garden plants of the temperate zones, including *Asperula*, *Galium*, *Houstonia*, and *Leptodermis*. House plants include *Gardenia*, *Nertera*, *Pentas*, and *Serissa* (as a bonsai).

Rue and Citrus Family

A variable family of trees, shrubs, or woody climbers with usually pinnately compound leaves, characterized by secretory cavities with aromatic oils and superficial pellucid gland dots.

Description Trees (usually rather small and evergreen), shrubs, or woody climbers, occasionally herbs, sometimes with prickles or spines. Most species are aromatic and have secretory cavities in most tissues and superficial gland dots. The leaves are usually alternate, rarely opposite or whorled, usually compound with pinnate, 3-foliate or 1-foliate (with a joint and pulvinus at base of lamina, e.g., *Citrus*), or perhaps rarely simple and then entire to bipinnatisect (perhaps *Calodendrum*, *Thamnosma*, *Ruta*, and others), characteristically showing pellucid gland dots on their surface or at least at their margins. The inflorescence is variable, terminal, or axillary. The flowers are usually bisexual, rarely unisexual (plants occasionally dioecious), actinomorphic or occasionally somewhat zygomorphic with unequal petals or some stamens sterile, usually 5-merous but sometimes (2–3)4-merous. The sepals are usually 5, free or united. The petals are usually 5, free or united at the base. The stamens are as many as the petals or, more commonly, twice as many in 2 whorls, occasionally up to 4 times as many, and inserted at the base of a disk or gynophore.

The ovary is superior, with (1–2–)4–5(–10) carpels, which are fully united or free and united only by their connate styles, each carpel with a separate locule or sometimes the partitions are incomplete, each carpel with usually 2 ovules on an axile placenta. The fruit is a capsule, schizocarp, drupe, or berry, in *Citrus* and in related genera a hesperidium with the locules filled by many juicy hairs.

Distribution Tropical and southern hemisphere, with proliferation of many endemic genera in Australia and South Africa. Rather few genera extend into the northern temperate regions, but *Phellodendron*, *Skimmia*, and *Dictamnus* can be found in the Russian Far East, *Haplophyllum* has more than 30 spp. from the Mediterranean to Mongolia, and *Zanthoxylum* and *Ptelea* reach southern Canada. In the tropics, many species are in the understory of evergreen forest, but in more temperate regions they are often in dry country.

Economic uses The genus *Citrus* is of major economic importance. The fruits of its species, hybrids, and backcrosses include the lemon, citron, sweet orange, Seville orange, tangerine, satsuma, mandarin, clementine, lime, grapefruit, and kumquat. Other species are cultivated for their essential oils, such as bergamot oil. Among many cultivated ornamentals are *Choisya ternata* and *Skimmia japonica*.

Rutaceae. 1 *Ruta graveolens* (a) shoot with bipinnate leaves and cymose inflorescences (x⅔); (b) flower with 4 sepals, 4 petals, 8 stamens, and a superior, lobed ovary with a basal disk and crowned by a single style (x2⅔); (c) vertical section of ovary (x6); (d) cross section of ovary showing 4 locules and ovules on axile placentas (x4). **2** *Citrus aurantium* (sweet orange) (a) half flower with numerous stamens and prominent disk at the base of the ovary (x2); (b) fruit—a hesperidium (x⅔). **3** *Ptelea trifoliata* winged fruit—an unusual feature for the family (x1½). **4** *Citrus limon* (lemon) flowering shoot (x⅔). **5** *Crowea saligna* flowering shoot (x⅔).

Willow and Poplar Family

Trees and shrubs, sometimes dwarf, with catkins of flowers lacking a normal perianth. *Salix* and *Populus* species are both widespread in the northern hemisphere but not in the southern hemisphere.

Description Dwarf prostrate subshrubs (almost herbaceous in *S. herbacea*) to shrubs and trees up to 30 m tall. The leaves are simple, linear to suborbicular, entire to serrate, or in *Populus* sometimes somewhat lobed, and usually deciduous. The stipules are usually conspicuous but often caducous.

The flowers are unisexual (plants dioecious), reduced, borne in compact spikes (catkins) up to several centimeters long, which are held upright in nearly all *Salix* but are pendent in *Populus*, these often appearing before the leaves develop. Each flower is subtended by a bract that is small and entire in *Salix* but obtriangular and toothed to fimbriate in *Populus*. In *Salix*, the perianth is replaced by 1–3 small nectariferous glands, while in *Populus* it is represented by a raised cuplike glandular rim, and normal sepals and petals are lacking. The male flowers in *Salix* consist of (1)2(–5) stamens, and in *Populus* of 5–60 stamens. The female flowers consist of a superior ovary derived from 2(–4) carpels with a single locule with 2–4 parietal placentas, each with numerous ovules and narrowed above to a short style with 2 often bifid stigmas. The fruit is a 2- to 4-valved capsule dehiscing from the top.

The seeds are small and enveloped by a plume of long hairs arising from their base. Dehiscence of all the capsules of a catkin of a female plant releases a mass of wind-borne plumose seeds, or the whole dehisced catkin may fall to the ground.

Distribution *Salix* has c. 350 spp. widespread in the northern hemisphere from the Arctic to subtropics, especially in China, but few in the southern hemisphere (1 each in South America, Africa, and tropical Asia, but absent from New Guinea and Australasia). There are about 30–40 spp. of *Populus* in the northern hemisphere but the genus is absent from the southern hemisphere apart from 1 sp.

in East Africa. The species occupy a wide range of habitats, from arctic tundra to riverbanks, other wet places, and mountains.

Economic uses The wood is fast-growing but is usually of poor quality as timber and is often used for making small objects. A specialist use of *Salix* is in making cricket bats, for which female plants of *S. alba* var. *caerulea* are the most prized. The Osier, *S. viminalis*, is harvested in juvenile growth for its pliant stems, which have long been woven into baskets or used for hedging. Many species are planted for ornamental or achitectural effect, especially the Weeping Willow, aptly named as *S.* x *sepulcralis* (*S. alba* x *babylonica*). The fastigiate Lombardy Poplar, *P. nigra* var. *italica*, is widely planted as an avenue tree or windbreak and is a conspicuous feature of many French roadsides. The bark has been used for tanning leather. Aspirin was originally derived from the bark of *Salix* but is now made synthetically.

Salicaceae. 1 *Populus sieboldii* (a) leafy shoot and pendulous fruiting catkins (x⅔); (b) young female catkin (x⅔); (c) female flower with cuplike disk (x6); (d) ovary (x6); (e) stigmas (x6); (f) shoot with young male catkin (x⅔); (g) male flower (x6); (h) mature male catkins together with remains of 1 from the previous year (x⅔). **2** *P. nigra* "Italica" (Lombardy Poplar) habit. **3** *Salix caprea* (a) leaves (x⅔); (b) young female catkins (x⅔); (c) female flower and bract (x6); (d) vertical section of female flower (x6); (e) cross section of ovary (x8); (f) mature female catkins (x⅔); (g) male catkin; (h) male flower (x6).

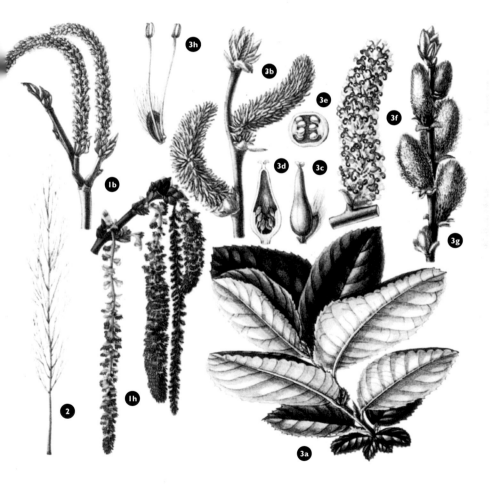

Sarraceniaceae. I *Heliamphora nutans* (a) pitchers (leaves) and flowers on leafless stalks (x⅔); (b) stamens, ovary, and style (x2); (c) section of 3-locular ovary with ovules on axile placentas (x3). **2** *Sarracenia purpurea* (a) pitchers and flower stalk (x2); (b) flower with green sepals and reddish petals (x1); style and stigma (x1); (d) cross section of ovary with ovules on inrolled carpel walls (x2). **3** *Darlingtonia californica* (a) pitchers and atypical flowers (x⅔); (b) vertical section of gynoecium with stamens attached at the base (x3).

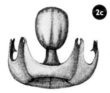

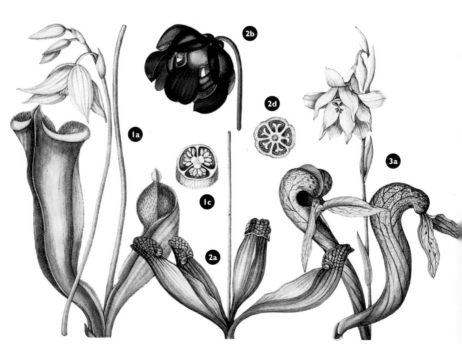

North American Pitcher Plant, Cobra Lily, and Marsh-Pitcher

An American family of carnivorous rhizomatous or, rarely, woody perennial pitcher plants where each trap is formed from a single rolled and modified leaf.

Description Rhizomatous or rarely woody (*Heliamphora tatei*) perennials with distinctive rolled leaves forming insect-trapping pitchers.

Each leaf is rolled into a tube with a ventral wing, variously with a flat or expanded, swollen-globose or small cup-shaped lid, sometimes water-filled (*Heliamphora* and *S. purpurea* agg.), sometimes green but often with bright red markings and sometimes clear windows (*S. minor*, *S. psittacina*, and *D. californica*).

S. psittacina, also called the Parrot Pitcher Plant, has a small entrance in the pitcher mouth. Insects are attracted through this entrance by nectar on the rim of the mouth of the pitcher. Once inside, the insects are drawn into the pitcher toward the light shining through clear windows in the structure. Dense, downward-growing hairs lining the inside of the pitcher act to guide and trap the insects, forcing them toward the base, where there are digestive juices. Water arthropods and tadpoles are also trapped when the pitchers are submerged in their watery habitat.

Sometimes heterophyllous (*Sarracenia*) with noncarnivorous laterally flattened leaves produced in winter (*S. flava* and *S. oreophila*). The inflorescence is terminal from the rhizome on an erect scape, of 1 flower (*Sarracenia* and *Darlingtonia*) or a few-flowered raceme (*Heliamphora*).

The flowers are actinomorphic, hermaphrodite, 5-merous, with distinct calyx and corolla (*Sarracenia* and *Darlingtonia*) or with overlapping petaloid segments (*Heliamphora*).

The sepals, where present, are in 1 whorl of 5 overlapping (*Sarracenia*) or nonoverlapping (*Darlingtonia*) segments, sometimes dark red, usually green; the petals are 5, hanging below sepals and bending outward, red or yellow (*Sarracenia*) or translucent with red veining and adpressed to form a chamber (*Darlingtonia*). The petal-like structures of *Heliamphora* are 4–6 overlapping, usually white, sometimes red or pink tinged

The stamens are 10–20 (*Heliamphora*) or many (*Darlingtonia* and *Sarracenia*). The ovary is superior, 1-locular formed from 3 (*Heliamphora*) or 5 (*Darlingtonia* and *Sarracenia*) fused carpels.

The style in *Sarracenia* is distinctive, forming an umbrella-like outgrowth from the tip of the ovary, curving out to project between the petals.

The fruit is a longitudinally splitting globose capsule containing many seeds.

Distribution *Sarracenia* (8–11 spp.) has its center of diversity in southeastern USA and occurs predominantly on wet sandy coastal plains but extends north around the Great Lakes and into Canada.

In common with its genus, *S. purpurea* (the Purple Pitcher Plant or Side-Saddle Flower) ranges along the entire eastern seaboard of the USA, the Great Lakes, and southeastern Canada. It is the most common and widely distributed pitcher plant, and the only member of the genus to grow in cold temperate climates.

Darlingtonia (1 sp.) is restricted to the mountains of California and Oregon in wet flushes and by streams. *Heliamphora* (8–11 spp.) grows in marshes on sandstone outcrops among the tepuis of the Guyana Highlands.

Economic uses There is amateur interest in the family as an ornamental curiosity. Many species are listed by CITES (Convention on International Trade in Endangered Species of Wild Fauna and Flora).

Lizard's Tail Family

A small family of rhizomatous or stoloniferous, usually aromatic, perennial herbs with cordate leaves and axillary spicate inflorescences that grows in parts of North America and eastern Asia.

Description Rhizomatous or stoloniferous, usually aromatic, perennial herbs, procumbent or up to 1.2 m high. The leaves are alternate, simple, cordate at the base, with entire margins, the petioles with membranous stipules along their lower margin, these connate and encircling the stem at their base.

The inflorescence is an axillary dense spike or narrow raceme of 10–350 flowers, sometimes (*Anemopsis, Houttuynia, Gymnotheca involucrata*) with an involucre of petaloid bracts at its base and so superficially resembling a single flower. The flowers lack a perianth and are actinomorphic and bisexual.

The stamens are 3 in *Houttuynia*, and (3–)6(–8) in other genera, free in *Saururus* but elsewhere adnate to the base of the ovary. The ovary is superior in *Saururus* with (1–)4(–7) carpels, free or basally connate, and in *Anemopsis* with 1–3 fused carpels. The ovary is semi-inferior in *Houttuynia* and *Gymnotheca*, with 3 or 4 carpels, respectively, and 1-locular. Placentation is parietal, with 6–13 ovules per locule.

The fruit in *Saururus* is a schizocarp with 4 single-seeded mericarps, but a capsule with 8–40 seeds in other genera.

Distribution The family is disjunct between North America and eastern Asia: *Saururus cernuus* extends from southeastern Canada to Texas and Florida, while *S. chinensis* ranges across China, Korea, Japan, and the Philippines. *Gymnotheca* has 2 spp. in China, with *G. chinensis* extending into northern Vietnam.

Anemopsis californica ranges from Washington State to Texas and southwestern

Mexico, while *Houttuynia cordata* extends from central Himalaya to Korea, Japan, and western Java and is cultivated and perhaps naturalized elsewhere (Madagascar, New Caledonia, and so on).

Economic uses Several species are used medicinally, for example, the rhizomes of *Saururus chinensis* are boiled and eaten in India, and the leaves and shoots of *Houttuynia* are eaten as a vegetable.

Houttuynia is also grown as an ornamental or curiosity ground-cover plant, with several variegated cultivars.

Saururaceae. 1 *Anemopsis californica* (a) shoot with upper leaves and inflorescence surrounded by petal-like involucre of bracts (x⅔); (b) shoot with fruiting head (x⅔); (c) leaf (x⅔); (d) flower lacking a perianth and with an ovary that is sunk into the receptacle (x4); (e) cross section of inflorescence (x1½). **2** *Gymnotheca chinensis* (a) flowering shoot with cordate leaves (x⅔); (b) flowers (x2); (c) gynoecium (x4); (d) ovary opened out to show ovules on parietal placentas (x6). **3** *Saururus cernuus* (a) flower and bract (x2); (b) half flower with free carpels (x3). **4** *Houttuynia cordata* (a) flowering shoot (x⅔); (b) flower (x4); (c) fruit dehiscing from apex (x4); (d) fruit opened out to show seeds (x4).

Scrophulariaceae. 3 *Verbascum betonicifolium* shoot with alternate leaves and inflorescence of irregular flowers (x⅔). **4** *Linaria vulgaris* (a) shoot with linear leaves and inflorescence (x⅔); (b) half flower with spurred corolla and stamens of 2 lengths (x3). **5** *Digitalis obscura* leafy shoot and inflorescence (x⅔). **6** *Veronica fruticans* leafy shoot and inflorescence (x⅔). **7** *Scrophularia macrantha* (a) lower lip of corolla opened out showing 4 stamens with anthers linked in pairs and a central, small staminode (x4⅔); (b) cross section of ovary showing 2 locules and axile placentas (x6). **8** *Sibthorpia europeae* dehiscing fruit—a capsule (x10). **9** *Penstemon lyallii* leafy shoot with irregular flowers and young fruits (x⅔).

Figwort and Foxglove Family

A family of annual to perennial herbs, shrubs, or rarely lianes or trees. Many members of this family, including foxgloves, penstemons, and snapdragons, are widely cultivated by gardeners and horticulturalists.

Description Annual to perennial herbs, occasionally climbing (*Asarina*), shrubs, or rarely 30 m lianes (*Wightia*) or trees (e.g., *Paulownia, Halleria*), often holoparasitic or hemiparasitic, rarely epiphytic (*Dermatobotrys*), sometimes aquatic (*Limosella*), sometimes resurrection plants (*Craterostigma*).

The leaves are alternate or opposite or occasionally whorled, simple to pinnatisect, sometimes reduced (aquatic *Limosella*).

The inflorescence is a raceme or thyrse, or the flowers are solitary. The flowers are strongly zygomorphic to occasionally subactinomorphic, sometimes resupinate (*Nemesia, Pedicularis resupinata*, and others), bisexual, usually 4- to 5-merous.

The sepals are free or fused, regular or irregular. The corolla is usually strongly zygomorphic and 2-lipped, usually with the upper lip 2-lobed and lower 3-lobed, often gibbous to spurred on the abaxial side, with paired spurs in *Angelonia* and *Diascia*. The stamens are usually 4, sometimes 5, inserted on the corolla tube.

The ovary is superior, usually of 2 free carpels with a terminal style and 2 locules, each with 2 to many ovules on axile placentae, rarely the ovules reduced to 1 (*Globulariopsis*), but sometimes in Orobancheae with 3 carpels and parietal placentae. The fruit is a capsule or rarely a berry (*Dermatobotrys, Teedia*), sometimes ballistic (*Lathraea*), and the seeds are usually many and often winged.

Distribution Cosmopolitan and in a wide range of habitats, commonly in open grassy places, rarely (*Wightia* etc.) in tropical forests.

Economic uses The family is of major importance in horticulture, including such genera as *Antirrhinum, Calceolaria, Cymbalaria, Digitalis, Hebe, Linaria, Mimulus, Nemesia,* *Parahebe, Paulownia, Pedicularis, Penstemon, Scrophularia, Verbascum,* and *Veronica.* The drugs digoxin and digitalin are extracted from *Digitalis* for heart treatment. The parasitic genera may be negatively important, and *Striga* is a major scourge in tropical agriculture.

Scrophulariaceae.
1 *Erinus alpinus* habit showing rosette of leaves and terminal inflorescence of irregular flowers ($\times 2/3$).
2 *Rhinanthus minor* shoot with opposite leaves and inflorescence ($\times 2/3$).

Potato Family

A cosmopolitan, economically important family of herbs, shrubs, trees, and lianas, including the potato, tomato, eggplant (aubergine), and many alkaloid-containing species that are highly poisonous.

Description Trees (some *Cyphomandra*, *Solanum*) or shrubs (*Cestrum*, *Lycium*) to vines, lianas, epiphytes, and perennial or annual herbs. The leaves are alternate, usually simple, lamina entire or dissected, exstipulate. The flowers are usually bisexual, actinomorphic, sometimes slightly to markedly zygomorphic, in terminal or axillary cymose inflorcsecences or reduced to a single flower (*Solanum*). The sepals are (4)5(–7), in 1 whorl, partly fused, usually regular and persistent, and sometimes enlarged around the fruit (e.g., *Physalis*). The petals are (4)5(–10), usually contorted and plicate, imbricate or valvate, variously fused, making the corolla round and flat (e.g., *Solanum*), campanulate (e.g., *Mandragora*) or tubular (e.g., *Nicotiana*); rarely 2-lipped as in *Schizanthus*, where the abaxial petals form a keel. The stamens are usually 4 or 5, 2+2, or up to 8 or 10. The ovary is superior, usually of 2 fused carpels with a single style, and usually with 2 locules, sometimes 3–5 (*Datura*), generally with numerous axile ovules. The fruits show considerable diversity but are usually bicarpellate and a septicidal capsule or a berry, sometimes a drupe or pyrene (*Goetzea* group, *Capsicum*, *Lycium*), or a schizocarpic with up to 15(–30) single-seeded mericarps (*Nolana*).

Distribution The family is distributed worldwide but is mainly tropical and subtropical, especially in Central and South America (c. 63

genera and 1,200 spp.) and in Australia, but also in tropical Africa. The range of habitats includes deserts to tropical rain forests.

Economic uses Solanaceae contains many species of major economic importance, including the potato (*Solanum tuberosum*) from the Peruvian Andes and Bolivia (the fourth most important food crop in terms of tonnage produced), Eggplant or Aubergine (*S. melongena*), tomato (*Lycopersicon esculentum*), and the Peppers (various *Capsicum* spp.), including Paprika, Chillies, Cayenne, and Sweet or Bell peppers). Others include the Husk Tomato (*Physalis pubescens*), the Tomatillo (*P. ixocarpa*), the Cape Gooseberry (*P. peruviana*), the Tree Tomato (*Cyphomandra betacea*), and the Pepino (*Solanum muricatum*). Various species with showy flowers are grown as ornamentals, especially in the genera *Browallia*, *Brugmansia*, *Brunfelsia*, *Cestrum*, *Datura*, *Nicotiana*, *Nierembergia*, *Petunia*, *Salpiglossis*, *Schizanthus*, *Solanum*, and *Solandra*. Some *Capsicum* and *Solanum* species are widely grown for their colorful fruits. Some *Cestrum*, *Solanum*, and *Streptosolen* species are popular shrubs. The Chinese Lantern Plant (*Physalis alkekengi*) is used extensively in dried floral arrangements. Many Solanaceae members are famed for their alkaloid content and have been used since historic times for their medicinal, poisonous, or psychotropic properties. For example, tobacco (*Nicotiana tabacum*) contains the addictive and highly toxic alkaloid nicotine and is grown extensively for smoking, chewing, and snuff manufacture. It is a major world commodity, but the most harmful plant in the world through the diseases it causes. Other *Nicotiana* species also contain nicotine and are used to make insecticides. Several genera contain steroid alkaloids that have been used for centuries, including Deadly Nightshade (*Atropa belladonna*) and Black Henbane (*Hyoscyamus niger*).

Solanaceae. 1 *Salpiglossis atropurpurea* (a) flowering shoot (x⅔); (b) part of flower showing 2 pairs of unequal stamens and a single infertile reduced stamen (x1⅓); (c) fruit (x2). **2** *Datura stramonium* var. *tatula* (a) flowering shoot (x⅔); (b) fruit—a capsule (x⅔). **3** *Solanum rostratum* (a) flowering shoot (x⅔); (b) flower with 2 petals and 2 stamens removed (x2). **4** *Physalis alkekengi* (a) shoot showing fruits enclosed in a persistent orange-red calyx (x⅔); (b) calyx removed to show the fruit (x⅔).

Tamarisks

A family of small, heathlike, temperate and subtropical shrubs and small trees, usually with tiny pink or white flowers. The plants are halophytic, xerophytic, or rheophytic.

Description Small trees, shrubs, or subshrubs with woody stems bearing slender branches. The leaves are alternate, small, tapering or scalelike, without stipules. The inflorescence consists of one (*Hololachna, Reaumuria*) to many flowers in dense spikes or racemes (*Myricaria, Myrtama, Tamarix*). The flowers are minute, regular, bisexual, without bracts. The sepals and petals are 4 or 5, free. The petals and the 5–10(–many) stamens are inserted on a fleshy, nectar-secreting disk. The stamens are free or slightly fused at the base. The carpels are 2, 4, or 5, fused into a superior ovary with 1 locule; ovules are few to numerous on parietal or basal placentas. The styles are usually free, absent in some species, and the stigmas sessile (*Myricaria*). The fruit is a capsule containing seeds with or without endosperm. The seeds are sometimes winged but usually covered with long hairs.

Distribution Temperate and subtropical, growing in maritime or sandy places from the Mediterranean through North Africa and southeastern Europe via central Asia to India and China. It also occurs in Norway and in southwestern Africa. The family is halophytic, xerophytic, or rheophytic.

Economic uses The twigs of the shrub *T. mannifera* (from Egypt to Afghanistan) yield the white sweet gummy substance manna as a result of puncture by the insect *Coccus maniparus*. Insect galls on species of *Tamarix* (*T. articulata* and *T. gallica*) are a source of tannin, dyes, and medicinal extracts. *T. gallica* and *T. africana* are often grown as ornamental shrubs for their feathery appearance and their catkinlike inflorescences. *T. pentandra* is sometimes grown as a hedge or windbreak, as is *T. gallica* in Mediterranean coastal regions. Species of *Tamarix* have become widely naturalized in North and South America and in Australia and some have become serious invasives, particularly *T. parviflora* and *T. ramosissima* in the USA, and *T. aphylla* in Australia.

Tamaricaceae. 1 *Tamarix aphylla* (a) shoot with
minute leaves and dense raceme of flowers (x⅔); (b)
part of inflorescence (x4); (c) stamens and gynoecium
(x6); (d) 4-lobed gynoecium (x8); (e) vertical section
of ovary with basal ovules (x10). **2** *Reaumuria linifolia*
(a) leafy shoot with solitary flowers (x⅔); (b) gynoecium (x2); (c) petal (x1½). **3** *Tamarix africana* habit
(x⅒). **4** *Myricaria germanica* (a) flowering shoot (x⅔);
(b) flower (x2); (c) stamens united at the base (x4);
(d) fruit—a capsule (x2); (e) dehiscing capsule showing cluster of hairy seeds (x2); (f) seed, which is hairy
at the apex only (x4).

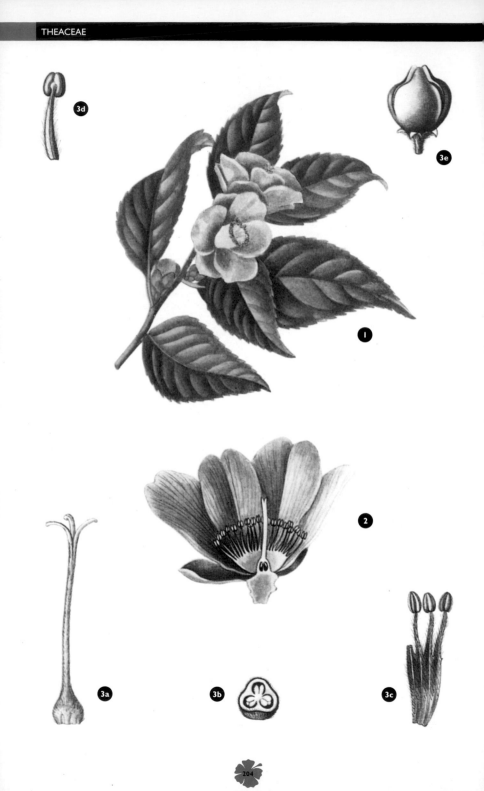

Tea, Camellia, and Franklinia

A small family of trees and shrubs, usually with simple evergreen leaves, including the economically important *Camellia sinensis*, the leaves of which are brewed to make tea.

Description Usually evergreen trees or shrubs, with unicellular indumentum and alternate leaves arranged spirally or distichously. *Camellia sinensis* can grow up to 17 m high but is usually kept below 2 m by pruning. The leaves are simple and coriaceous with a toothed (rarely entire) margin and no stipules. The leaves of *C. sinensis* are bright green and shiny and often have hairs on the underside.

The flowers are solitary, borne in the leaf axil, hermaphrodite, actinomorphic, large and showy, the outer bracts grading into the calyx of 5(6, rarely more) free, or basally connate, imbricate, usually thick, sepals that grade in to the 5 (rarely many) free or basally connate, imbricate petals. The flowers of *C. sinensis* are scented.

The stamens are 20 or more, free, rarely connate, frequently joined to the corolla base. The ovary is superior, of (3–)5(–10) fused carpels, each with 2 to few ovules usually on an axile placenta; the styles are simple or branched with a lobed stigma.

The fruit is usually a loculicidal capsule, but occasionally a drupe or with irregular dehiscence. The fruits of *C. sinensis* are brown to green and contain 1 to 4 spherical or flattened seeds.

Distribution The family is restricted mainly to tropical and subtropical regions and centered chiefly in America and Asia. There are close links between North American and Southeast Asian species dating from the Late Miocene.

Theaceae. I *Camellia rosiflora* flowering shoot (x⅔). **2** *C. japonica* "Kimberley" half flower with semi-inferior ovary and numerous stamens, united at their bases (x⅔). **3** *C. salicifolia* (a) gynoecium with 3-lobed stigma (x4); (b) cross section of 3-locular ovary (x6); (c) stamens with fused filaments (x3); (d) stamen (x4); (e) fruit—a capsule (x2).

Economic uses The genus *Camellia* accounts for almost all economic use of the family. *Camellia sinensis* yields tea from plantations primarily in India, Sri Lanka, China, and East Africa. Tea is drunk either black or green by about one half of the world's population.

Two varieties of *C. sinensis* are recognized: *C. sinensis* var. *sinensis* (China Tea) and *C. sinensis* var. *assamica* (Assam Tea, Indian Tea). China Tea is hardier than Assam Tea. Its leaves, which are narrower and smaller, are used to make green tea and China black tea. *C. sinensis* var. *assamica* can grow into a loosely branched tree, up to 17 m tall. Its large leathery leaves are used to make Assam (Indian) black tea.

Originally drunk in Myanmar and China, tea drinking then spread to adjoining countries. In the seventeenth century, its popularity spread to Europeans when they reached China. As the world's sole supplier of tea at that time, China established trade routes between itself and western Europe and Russia. Europe then sent tea on to the American colonies.

In 1773 there was a disagreement in Boston over the taxes levied on shipments of tea by the British government. This dispute became known as the Boston Tea Party. Rather than return three shiploads of taxed tea to Britain, colonists destroyed it by throwing it into Boston harbour. This key event contributed to the start of the American Revolutionary War in 1775.

Another economically important product is tea seed oil, which is extracted from the seeds of *Camellia sasanqua*. *Camellia japonica*, *C. reticulata*, and *C. sasanqua* are the parents of the roughly 30,000 cultivars of the garden camellia valued for its large flowers and glossy evergreen leaves. *Franklinia alatamaha*, originally distributed over a small area near Fort Barrington in Georgia in the southern USA, but now extinct in the wild, is still cultivated in North America and Europe.

Daphne Family

A medium-sized cosmopolitan family of mainly shrubs and trees but some lianas and herbs that have fibrous bark and phloem. The family grows in both temperate and tropical regions.

Description Trees, shrubs, or more rarely lianas or herbs, with long fibers in the bark and phloem giving the bark, stems, and leaves a certain toughness and flexibility. The leaves are simple, exstipulate, alternate or opposite, sometimes with the internodes closely spaced, making the alternate leaves appear opposite or whorled. The flowers are actinomorphic, bisexual or unisexual, sometimes polygamous (plants usually dioecious), in racemes, capitula, or fascicles. The flowers have a hollowed out receptacle, forming a deep tube (hypanthium) from the rim of which the floral parts are borne. The sepals are (3)4–5(6), united or rarely free, commonly petaloid, greenish white, cream, red, pink, or brown. The petals are as many as the sepals or twice as many, reduced to scales, or absent, free. The stamens are 3–5 or 8–10 or up to 100 (1–2 in *Pimelea*). The ovary is superior, at the base of the receptacular cup, and has 2–5(–8–12) fused carpels, containing as many locules, each with 1 pendulous ovule. The style is simple. The fruit is usually a drupe, an achene, berry, or occasionally a capsule (*Aquilaria*); the seed has little or no endosperm, and the embryo is straight.

Distribution The Daphne family is cosmopolitan, occurring in both temperate and tropical regions, and is especially well represented in Africa and Australia. It shows more diversity in the southern hemisphere than in the northern hemisphere.

Economic uses Some tree species (*Aquilaria, Gonystylus*) provide timber. Several species of *Daphne* are cultivated as ornamental shrubs, often with fragrant flowers. The bark of several genera, particularly *Wikstroemia*, yields fibers that are used locally in paper manufacture. The inner bark of the West Indian Lace-bark, *Lagetta lagetto*, is stretched to provide an ornamental textile in Jamaica.

Thymelaeaceae. 1 *Octolepis flamignii* (a) leafy shoot with flowers and flower buds (x⅔); (b) flower (x3); (c) half flower (x4); (d) hypanthial cup with stamens, and style and stigma (x4); (e) gynoecium (x5); (f) stamen (x5); (g) dehiscing fruit (x1⅓). **2** *Pimelea buxifolia* (a) leafy shoot with terminal inflorescences (x⅔); (b) flower (x3); (c) flower opened out (x3); (d) vertical section of ovary (x4). **3** *Daphne mezereum* (a) flowering shoot (x⅔); (b) leafy shoot with fruits (x⅔); (c) flower opened (x2); (d) fruit (x2). **4** *Gonystylus augescens* flower with 2 sepals removed (x4).

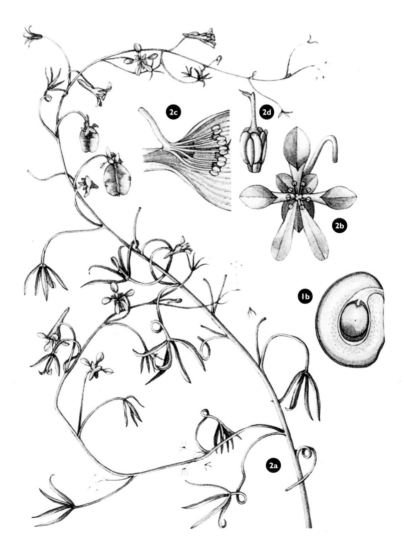

Tropaeolaceae. 1 *Tropaeolum majus* (a) prostrate stem bearing peltate leaves, solitary, spurred flowers, and fruit—a schizocarp comprising 3 mericarps (×1); (b) vertical section of mericarp containing a single seed (×2). **2** *T. porifolium* (a) stem with deeply palmate leaves, flowers, and fruits (×⅔); (b) irregular flower with 2 of the petals differing from other 3 and 8 stamens (×2); (c) base of flower opened out to show free stamens (×3); (d) gynoecium (×10); (e) winged fruits (×10).

Nasturtium, Canary Creeper, and Mashua

Climbing, fleshy herbs, including cultivated ornamentals and an important food crop, *Tropaeolum tuberosum*, which is cultivated throughout the Andean region for its tubers.

Description Twining fleshy herbs with an acrid mustard oil present in the sap, sometimes with root tubers. The leaves are alternate, peltate, sometimes deeply lobed, the petioles sometimes twining around supports and without stipules.

The showy flowers are bisexual, zygomorphic and spurred, and usually borne singly in the axils of leaves. The sepals are 5, free, 1 modified to form a long nectar spur. The petals are 5, free, usually clawed, the upper 2 smaller than the lower 3. The stamens are 8, free.

The ovary is superior, of 3 fused carpels, with 3 locules each containing 1 axile pendulous ovule; the single apical style has 3 stigmas.

The fruit is a 3-seeded schizocarp, each mericarp separating to become an indehiscent "seed" lacking endosperm. The embryo is straight and has thick, fleshy cotyledons.

Distribution The family is native mainly to the mountains from Mexico to southern Chile and across to eastern Argentina.

Economic uses About 8 spp. are cultivated for ornament; most commonly encountered are *Tropaeolum majus*, the Garden Nasturtium, and *T. peregrinum* (*T. canariense*), Canary Creeper or Canary-bird Flower. The unripe seeds of *T. majus* are occasionally pickled and used like capers. The tubers of *T. tuberosum* (commonly called Mashua, Mascho, and Cubio) are the fourth most important indigenous root crop in the Andean region. This perennial plant is grown for its edible tuber and is a major food source in this region.

1a

Elm Family

Trees with small apetalous flowers and winged or drupaceous fruits, related to Urticaceae (Nettle family). The genus *Ulmus* has been severely affected by a fungal disease called Dutch Elm disease.

Description Trees up to 40(–60) m high or occasionally shrubs or rarely lianes, armed with axillary spines in *Chaetacme* and some *Celtis*. The leaves are alternate or rarely (*Lozanella*) opposite, simple and unlobed, often asymmetrical, either with 3 main veins from the base or with pinnate venation, the margins crenate, toothed, or rarely entire. Stipules are inconspicuous and caducous. Dotlike cystoliths are sometimes present. The inflorescence is a terminal or axillary cyme, often aggregated into loose clusters, or the female flowers sometimes solitary. The flowers are unisexual (plants monoecious) or sometimes some are bisexual, actinomorphic, with a small and usually greenish, 4- to 5-merous, uniseriate perianth. The tepals are 4–5, free or shortly united. The stamens are as many or sometimes twice as many as the tepals, not inflexed in bud. The ovary is superior, of 2 united carpels, with 2 divergent styles, with 1(2) locules and a single ovule pendent from the apex. The fruit is a samara or fleshy drupe.

Distribution Widespread in tropical and temperate regions, from tropical forests to temperate woodland, but absent from some cool-temperate countries.

Economic uses *Ulmus* was formerly a plentiful source of good, decay-resistant timber and has been much planted in hedgerows and avenues but has been depleted in recent decades by Dutch Elm disease, a fungal disease spread by the elm bark beetle. *Zelkova* is planted for its colorful leaves in the fall and is more resistant to the disease. Other genera provide timber in the tropics, and bark has been used for fiber. *Celtis* sometimes has edible fruits (Hackberry) and is planted as a street tree.

Ulmaceae. **I** *Ulmus campestris* (a) habit; (b) leafy shoot (x⅔); (c) flowering shoot (x⅔); (d) flower with calyx, no petals, 5 stamens, and 2 styles (x8); (e) anther posterior (right) and anterior (left) view (x24); (f) gynoecium crowned by 2 styles with stigmas on inner faces (x12); (g) winged fruit (x1). **2** *Trema orientalis* (a) leafy shoot with flowers (x⅔); (b) fruit (x6). **3** *Celtis integrifolia* (a) male flower with 5 stamens and hairy vestige of ovary (x6); (b) bisexual flower with 5 stamens and gynoecium crowned by 2 styles forked at apices (x4); (c) vertical section of ovary with single pendulous ovule (x4).

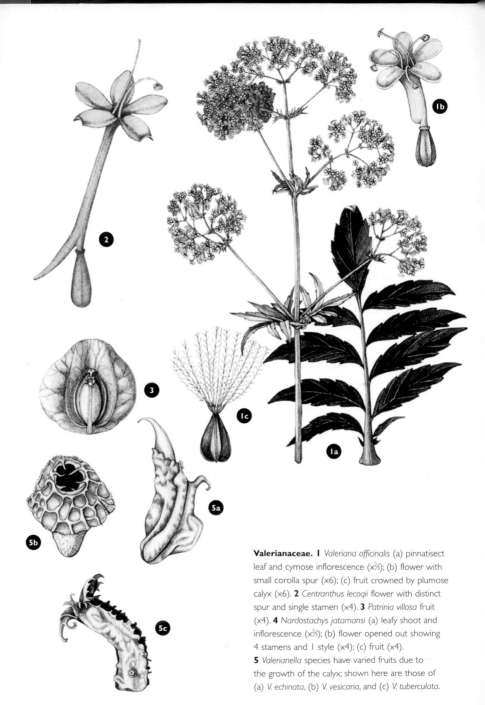

Valerianaceae. 1 *Valeriana officinalis* (a) pinnatisect leaf and cymose inflorescence (x⅔); (b) flower with small corolla spur (x6); (c) fruit crowned by plumose calyx (x6). **2** *Centranthus lecoqii* flower with distinct spur and single stamen (x4). **3** *Patrinia villosa* fruit (x4). **4** *Nardostachys jatamansi* (a) leafy shoot and inflorescence (x⅔); (b) flower opened out showing 4 stamens and 1 style (x4); (c) fruit (x4). **5** *Valerianella* species have varied fruits due to the growth of the calyx; shown here are those of (a) *V. echinata*, (b) *V. vesicaria*, and (c) *V. tuberculata*.

Valerian Family

An annual to perennial herbaceous family related to Caprifoliaceae (Honeysuckle family) and Dipsacaceae (Scabious and Teasle family), showing great variation in South America.

Description Mostly annual to perennial herbs, sometimes woody at the base, densely caespitose (*Phyllactis, Belonanthus, Stangea,* and *Aretiastrum* in the high Andes), microphyllous with imbricate leaves (*Aretiastrum*), or a herb climbing to several meters (*Valeriana scandens,* widespread in tropical America). The leaves are opposite or rarely alternate, simple and entire, to 3-foliate or pinnately compound. The inflorescence is a terminal dichasial cyme, usually lax and pyramidal, sometimes compact and subcapitate but without an involucre, the bracts at each node usually small but large and scarious in *Nardostachys*. In *Fedia* and *Astrephia* the inflorescence axes are markedly swollen. *Patrinia* has 2 bracteoles, often scarious and accrescent, and persistent in fruit. The flowers are regular to weakly zygomorphic, rarely unisexual (plants polygamomonoecious). The calyx is usually either absent or reduced to small teeth, or forms a pappus persisting on the fruit, but in *Nardostachys* it has 5 well-developed, scarious, rounded lobes. The corolla is tubular to trumpet-shaped, almost regular, but sometimes weakly 2-lipped, with 3, 4, or 5 lobes, spurred in *Centranthus*. The stamens are 1 in *Centranthus* and *Patrinia monandra*, 2 in *Fedia*, 3 in most genera, but 4 in *Nardostachys* and other *Patrinia* spp. The ovary is inferior, 3-carpellate, but 2 of the carpels abort and leave a single locule with a single pendulous ovule. The style is slender with a 2- to 3-lobed stigma. The fruit is a dry cypsela, often with an accrescent or pappus-forming calyx.

Distribution Widespread distribution, but with centers of generic diversity in the Mediterranean and temperate Asia, and with greatest morphological diversity in the Andes, but poorly represented in Africa and tropical Asia and absent from Australasia.

Economic uses Roots and leaves of some species have medicinal properties for relieving stress. *Nardostachys jatamansi* (*N. grandiflora*) (Spikenard) produces essential oils used in perfumery. *Valerianella* (Lambs' Lettuce) is eaten as a salad vegetable. Cultivated ornamental plants include *Centranthus ruber* (Red Valerian) from the Mediterranean, *Patrinia triloba* (*P. palmata*) from Japan, and several species of *Valeriana* (Valerian).

Violaceae. **1** *Anchietea salutaris* shoot with alternate leaves and fruit (x⅔). **2** *Rinorea* sp. half flower showing stamen filaments fused at the base and the anthers with a membranous extension to the connective (x10). **3** *Viola hederacea* (a) habit (x⅔); (b) vertical section of flower showing irregular petals and anthers in a close ring around the ovary (x4). **4** *Corynostylis arborea* (a) shoot with leaf and inflorescence (x⅔); (b) cross section of ovary with 1 locule containing numerous ovules on parietal placentas (x4). **5** *Hybanthus enneaspermus* var. *latifolius* dehiscing fruit—a capsule (x4). **6** *Melicytus obovatus* leafy shoot with fruit (x⅔).

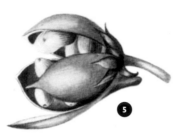

Violet Family

Tropical trees, shrubs, vines, and lowland herbs, and temperate montane and alpine herbs (*Viola*). The family grows mainly throughout the tropical regions of the world, and *Viola* is cosmopolitan.

Description Trees or treelets, shrubs or sub-shrubs, vines, and herbs. The leaves are alternate except in a few *Hybanthus* and some *Rinorea*, simple (infrequently dissected or lobed in *Viola*), linear to reniform, with entire to serrate margins, and bearing stipules. The inflorescence is mostly thyrsoid, dichasial, cymose, or racemose in woody genera, and mostly fasciculate or solitary in herbaceous ones, with flower pedicels usually bearing a pair of bractlets. The flowers are actinomorphic in around half of the genera (tribe Rinoreeae) or zygomorphic in the other half (tribe Violeae), bisexual or unisexual (some dioecious *Melicytus*), hypogynous or slightly perigynous. The sepals are 5 and small to conspicuous. The petals are 5 and linear to orbicular. The stamens are 5 (3 in 1 *Leonia* sp.), alternating with petals and free to variously fused, bearing separate nectariferous glands on 2 or 5 stamens or fused to the filament tube as an extended "collar," each anther connective tipped by a conspicuous to rudimentary dorsal scale (absent in *Leonia*, ventral only in *Fusispermum*). The ovary is superior, of 3 fused carpels (5 in some *Leonia*, 2–5 in *Melicytus*), each with 1 to many ovules with parietal placentation. The fruit is a 3-valved capsule in most genera (6-valved in one *Agatea*), sometimes somewhat woody, rarely a fleshy berry (*Gloeospermum* and *Melicytus*), nut (*Leonia*), follicle (*Hybanthopsis*), or papery bladder (*Anchietea*). The seeds are mostly globose to ovoid (flattened in *Corynostylis*, winged in *Anchietea* and *Agatea*, with basal projections in *Hybanthopsis*), bearing an elaiosome in most genera.

Distribution The family is predominantly pantropical in distribution, excepting 1 *Hybanthus* species (in temperate North America) and *Viola*, which is cosmopolitan

and has centers of diversity in the mountains of western South America, western North America, eastern Asia, and southern Europe.

Economic uses A few *Hybanthus* species are used for birdlime; certain larger *Rinorea* species provide some timber. Some *Rinorea* species in Southeast Asia take up heavy metals and may prove useful in bioremediation. *Rinorea* and *Viola* are used in traditional medicine owing to methyl salicylate. *Viola* leaves may be used for a potherb, and the flowers as a jelly, syrup, or confection. Numerous *Viola* species are grown as ornamentals (Pansies, Violets, Violas).

Grapevine and Virginia Creeper

Vitaceae is a family of mainly lianas with tendrils, rarely shrubs, renowned for the grapevine, *Vitis vinifera*, which grows mainly in the tropics and subtropics in both the northern and southern hemispheres.

Description Mostly lianas climbing by simple or branched leaf-opposed tendrils, but some are shrubs, small trees, or herbs. The leaves are alternate, simple (the lamina palmately lobed or veined, often coarsely dentate, rarely entire, with pellucid glands), or compound (3-foliate, palmate, 1- to 3-pinnate). Stipules are usually small, caducous, sometimes persistent. The inflorescence is usually leaf-opposed or terminal, cymose or racemose. The flowers are actinomorphic, bisexual, rarely unisexual (plants usually monoecious, dioecious in *Tetrastigma*), small. The sepals are (3)4–5, connate, forming a collar or tube. The petals are (3) 4–5, free, valvate, often deciduous. The stamens are as many as and opposite the petals, very small. A ringlike or lobed intrastaminal disk is usually present, absent in *Parthenocissus*. The ovary is superior, of 2 carpels and 2 locules, with 2 ovules per locule. The style is simple with a minute stigma. The fruit is a berry with 1(–4) seeds.

Distribution The Vitaceae grow mainly in the tropics and subtropics and are widely distributed in both the northern and southern hemispsheres. *Cissus* (200–350 spp.) is entirely tropical, *Cyphostemma* (150–250 spp.) is warm temperate and tropical, *Ampelocissus* (100 spp.) is widespread in the tropics, *Vitis* (c. 70 spp.) grows mainly in the northern hemisphere, and *Leea* (c. 70 spp.) ranges from Africa to northern Australia and the Pacific Islands.

Economic uses The grapevine is widely cultivated across the world for the production of table grapes, wine, fruit juice, and dried fruit (raisins, currants, sultanas). Globally, more than 6.5 million hectares are devoted to grape cultivation, the main producers being in Europe (c. 50%), Asia (22%), and the USA (18.5%). Most table wine is produced from *Vitis vinifera* but *V. labrusca*, *V. rotundifolia*,

V. amurensis, and hybrids with these and other species are also used on a smaller scale. World production of wine is nearly 3,000 million hectoliters, 79% of which is produced in Europe. Some *Cissus* species are used in traditional medicines. Species cultivated as ornamental climbers include *Parthenocissus quinquefolia* (Virginia Creeper), *P. tricuspidata* (Boston Ivy), *Vitis amurensis*, *V. davidii*, *Ampelopsis arborea*, and *Cissus* spp.

Vitaceae 1 *Vitis thunbergii* (a) inflorescence (x⅔);
(b) flower bud (x3); (c) flower with petals removed
showing cuplike calyx and 5 stamens (x3); (d) gynoecium (x3); (e) part of shoot with leaf and immature
and mature fruits —berries (x⅔). **2** *Tetrastigma obtec-
tum* (a) leafy shoot with axillary inflorescences (x⅔);
(b) flower bud (x4); (c) flower viewed from above
showing 4 petals and 4 stamens (x3); (d) stamens
(x6). **3** *Cissus velutinus* (a) leafy shoot with axillary
inflorescence and unbranched, coiled tendrils (x⅔);
(b) flower (x4); (c) vertical section of gynoecium
showing erect ovules and short style with a discoid
stigma (x4).

Vochysiaceae

A small, mainly neotropical family of medium to large trees with attractive and distinctive flowers, which is confined mainly to tropical Central America and South America.

Description Medium to large trees, sometimes shrubby, and an occasional climber. The leaves are opposite or whorled, simple, with small, paired, usually deciduous stipules and sometimes with pairs of stipular extrafloral nectaries at the base of the petiole.

The inflorescence is terminal or axillary, usually racemose, or reduced to a few axillary flowers in (some *Qualea, Callisthene*). The flowers are zygomorphic, bisexual.

The calyx is often showy, the sepals 5, connate at the base, the fourth spurred and sometimes elongate. The petals are usually 3, rarely 5 (*Salvertia* and *Erismadelphus*), sometimes 1 (*Callisthene, Erisma, Qualea*, some *Vochysia*), or absent (some *Vochysia*).

The stamens are only 1 fertile, antepetalous except in *Callisthene* and *Qualea*. The ovary is superior and 3-locular (Vochysieae) or inferior, 1-locular (Erismeae), with marginal (Erismeae) or axile placentation, the ovules 2 to many per locule; the style is simple, the stigma usually terminal.

The fruit is a loculicidal capsule (Vochysieae) or indehiscent and usually winged (Erismeae). The seeds are 1-numerous, winged or not.

Distribution The family is confined mainly to tropical Central and South America, with a few species present in West Africa (*Erismadelphus* and the recently discovered *Korupodendroni*). They grow in lowland rain forests and savannas.

Economic uses The timber of some species is used locally. Some species are used medicinally or as a source of gums or infusions.

The seeds of several species of *Erisma* are used as food or a source of oil, including Jaboty

Butter from *E. calcaratum* (which is used for making candles and soap), as well as *E. japura* and *E. splendens*.

Vochysiaceae. 1 *Vochysia divergens* (a) leafy shoot and inflorescence (x⅔); (b) winged fruit (x1⅓). **2** *V. guatemalensis* (a) vertical section of flower (x1⅓); (b) stamen (x2); (c) staminode (x4); (d) cross section of ovary (x2); (e) vertical section of ovary (x2). **3** *V. obscura* winged seed (x1). **4** *Salvertia convallariodora* part of inflorescence (x⅔). **5** *S. convallariodora* flower showing single fertile stamen (x⅔). **6** *Erismadelphus exsul* var. *platiphyllus* (a) flower (x4); (b) vertical section of flower base (x6); (c) winged fruit (x⅔).

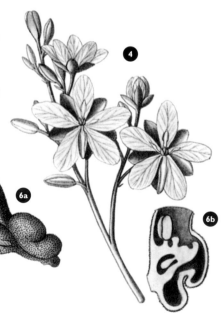

Amaryllidaceae. 1 *Cyrtanthus* sp. (a) habit showing bulb, linear leaves, umbel-like inflorescence with 2 bracts, borne on a leafless stalk (scape) and tubular flowers (x⅔); (b) longitudinal section of flower, showing the inferior ovary (1⅓). **2** *Narcissus bulbocodium* var. *citrinus* (a) solitary flower showing subtending bracteole, linear tepals, and the large tubular corona (x⅔); (b) longitudinal section of flower (1⅓). **3** *Leucojum vernum* (a) solitary flower with 2 whorls of free perianth segments subtended by fused bracts (x⅔); (b) longitudinal section of flower (1⅓). **4** *Clivia miniata* (a) umbel-like inflorescence (x½); (b) fruits—berries (x½).

Daffodil Family

A family of usually bulbous, perennial herbs frequently with distichous, simple, often linear leaves and scapose, umbel-like inflorescences. They grow worldwide but mainly in the tropics and subtropics.

Description Mostly bulbous, perennial geophytes, but sometimes aquatics (e.g., *Crinum*) or epiphytes, with distichous or spirally arranged, linear or elliptic leaves, which occasionally have a sheathing base that forms a pseudostem. The inflorescence is often scapose and umbel-like, but sometimes almost sessile (e.g., *Gethyllis*, *Sternbergia*) with 2 bracts that enclose the flowers in bud.

There are 1 to many, often large and showy, sessile or pedicellate flowers. The flowers are actinomorphic or zygomorphic, with 3+3 petaloid tepals, the inner smaller than the outer, usually fused into a tube at the base (e.g., *Crinum*, *Zephyranthes*, *Sternbergia*, *Cyrtanthus*, *Stenomesson*) or free (e.g., *Galanthus*, *Leucojum*, *Amaryllis*, *Nerine*). In some genera, there is a conspicuous (e.g., *Narcissus*) or inconspicuous corona (e.g., *Hippeastrum*, *Lycoris*). Generally, there are 3+3 more or less equal stamens, rarely fewer or more, inserted at the base of the tepals.

The stamens are occasionally connate into a cup or paracorona (e.g., *Pancratium*, *Nerine*). The ovary is inferior, 3-carpellate and usually 3-locular, with septal nectaries and axile or basal placentas with anatropous ovules. The style is filiform with a capitate, 3-lobed or 3-fid stigma. The fruit is a loculicidal capsule, rarely baccate (e.g., *Haemanthus*).

The seeds are frequently numerous, black or dark brown, and have a small, straight embryo and an endosperm consisting of hemicellulose and lipids or starch.

Distribution The family is cosmopolitan but grows mainly in the tropics and subtropics, although there are several representatives in temperate areas in Europe and a few in Asia. Most species in the family are adapted to seasonally dry habitats.

Economic uses The main economic importance of the family is for ornamental use. Several species of *Narcissus* (daffodils, jonquil; 30–60 spp.) are important as cut flowers, and more than 10,000 cultivars are known. Most important as garden plants in temperate areas are cultivars of *N. pseudonarcissus* (Daffodil) and *N. poeticus* (Pheasant's-eye Daffodil), but many wild species are also grown. *Galanthus* (snowdrops, c. 12–15 spp.) and *Leucojum* (snowflakes; c. 10 spp.) are also extremely important. Species of *Clivia* (4 spp.), especially *C. miniata*, *Crinum* (crinum lilies, c. 65 spp.), *Hippeastrum* ("amaryllis," c. 50–60 spp.) are cultivated as pot plants or in greenhouses. *Hippeastrum*, with its very large flowers, has been extensively hybridized and is an important bulb crop in the Netherlands. Some species of *Crinum* are sold as aquarium plants. Several genera are of local medical importance and have attracted attention for their possible anticancer alkaloids.

Water Hawthorn

This family comprises a single genus of rhizomatous or aquatic plants with a spicate inflorescence and more or less conspicuous tepals. They grow in the warm, tropical parts of the Old World and northern Australia.

Description Perennial aquatics with short, tuberlike corms or, rarely, elongated and branched rhizomes. Many species survive dry periods as dormant tubers. The usually distinctly petiolate leaves have intervaginal scales and are spirally arranged at the base of the stems. Submerged leaves are linear to oblong/elliptic, often undulate or contorted, whereas floating leaves are ovate to lanceolate, mostly with a distinct midrib and 1 or more pairs of parallel main nerves connected by numerous cross veins. Both leaves and stems have oil or tannin-containing articulated laticifers. In the Madagascan Lace Plant, *A. madagascariensis* (*A. fenestralis*), the whole blade is fenestrated and consists of a lattice of veins and nerves. Several species develop thick, leathery, floating leaves. In some species (e.g., *A. junceus*), the leaves are reduced to elongated midribs and resemble rushes. Flowers are usually bisexual; some species are agamospermous. The inflorescences are spikelike and borne on long stalks, which emerge above the water surface. In bud, each spike is enveloped in a spathe. In all Asian and most Australian species the spikes are single; in most African species they are bifurcating; in some Madagascan species there are up to 10 spikes on 1 stalk. The flowers are usually small and zygomorphic.

There are usually 2 tepals, often white. The 6 stamens are in 2 or more whorls of 3 each (up to 16 in *A. distachyos*). Between 2 and 9 ovaries are free, sessile, and superior. The usually 3 free carpels have 2 to numerous anatropous ovules on a basal placenta. The carpels may mature under water into free, leathery follicles with 2 to numerous seeds. The seeds have a straight embryo and no endosperm; the testa is usually single but can be split in two.

Distribution Restricted to warm and tropical parts of the Old World and northern Australia, almost all species are exclusively aquatics, although a few grow in marshy habitats. Most species are present in Africa and Madagascar. The South African *Aponogeton distachyos* (Water Hawthorn or Cape Pondweed) is naturalized in southern Australia, western South America, and Western Europe.

Economic uses Tubers and leaves are eaten locally by humans and livestock. Several species are popular aquarium plants. Owing to large-scale trade, the Madagascan Lace Plant (*A. madagascariensis*) has become extinct in many localities.

Aponogetonaceae. I *Aponogeton mada-gascariensis* (a) habit, showing rhizome bearing leaves in which the blade is merely a lattice of veins and nerves, and a bifurcating inflorescence born on a long stalk (x⅔); (b) portion of inflorescence (x4); (c) flower, consisting of 2 tepals, 6 stamens, and 3 sessile carpels (x6). **2** *Aponogeton distachyos* (a) aerial leaf (x⅔); (b) flower with a single tepal (x2); (c) inflorescence (x⅔); (d) infructescence with persistent tepals (x⅔). **3** *Aponogeton junceus* (a) habit showing tuberlike corms, tufts of straplike leaves, and bifurcating inflorescence (x⅔); (b) vertical section of carpel showing sessile ovules (x16); (c) fruit—a leathery follicle (x6).

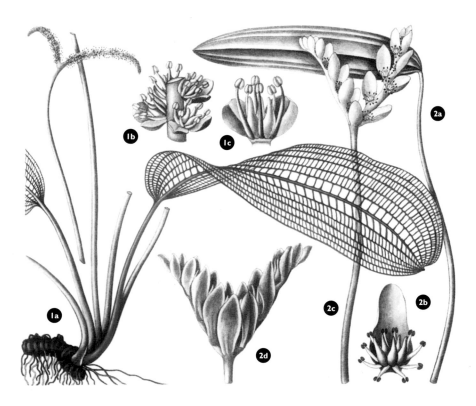

Aroids and Duckweeds

A family of terrestrial herbs with flowers in a spadix (aroids) and minute floating aquatic herbs with reduced flowers (duckweeds) that grow world-wide, although fewer species are present in temperate and boreal zones.

Description Perennial, mainly terrestrial, herbs, including geophytes, epiphytes, and climbers, rarely free-floating aquatics, with either rosulate leaves (*Pistia*) or platelike fronds (*Lemna*). Both raphides and laticifers, with a milky or watery sap (latex), are common. The roots are adventitious, often thickened, rhizomes or subglobose tubers. Most climbers and epiphytes have root dimorphism e.g., some roots are absorbent, growing downward toward the soil, while the others, not influenced by gravity, grow away from light and clasp firmly as they grow into crevices in the branches of the supporting tree. Many aerial roots develop an outer, water-absorbing tissue similar to the velamen of orchids. A few genera e.g., *Anthurium* and *Philodendron*, include species that are truly epiphytic and collect water and mineral salts in their leaf rosettes. The aquatics sometimes lack roots (*Wolffia*) or develop simple roots (*Lemna*). The leaves are usually differentiated in petiole sheath, petiole, and an expanded leaf blade of variable shape. Some species e.g., the Swiss Cheese Plant (*Monstera deliciosa*) develop fenestrated or holed leaves during development.

The inflorescence usually consists of a dense spadix with numerous, ebracteate flowers and is usually subtended by a conspicuous spathe that is often green but sometimes elaborately colored. In the aquatics (e.g., *Lemna*), the inflorescence is reduced to a single flower, almost hidden in a cavity of the fronds. The flowers are sessile and bi- or unisexual. The inflorescence is usually bisexual, with male flowers borne above female flowers. There are usually 2 whorls of 2 or 3 stamens opposite the tepals, if present. The ovary is superior or embedded in the spadix and usually composed of 1 to 3 carpels with a comparable number of locules with 1 to numerous ovules on basal, apical, axile, or parietal placentas. The style is usually inconspicuous with a lobed stigma. The fruit is a berry, sometimes a utricle, a drupe, or nut-like, with 1 to many seeds, which usually have endosperm. The embryo is usually straight. Nearly all species, except some aquatics (e.g., *Lemna*), are insect-pollinated. The inflorescence of many species emits a fetid odor that attracts carrion flies to effect pollination.

Distribution Cosmopolitan, with most species in tropical Southeast Asia, Africa, and America, fewer in temperate and boreal zones.

Economic uses The family is of considerable importance as it includes several species with edible tubers (e.g., taro, cocoyam, dasheen, *Colocasia esculenta*) or stems (tannia, *Xanthosoma sagittifolium*), which are a subsistence food crop locally and throughout the tropics. In some countries, cultivation has reached a commercial scale. More locally grown are species of *Amorphophallus* (e.g., elephant yam, *A. paeoniifolius*, in tropical Asia, and konjaku, *A. konjac*, in Japan), *Cyrtosperma*, and *Alocasia* (e.g., swamp taro, babai, *C. merkusii*, gigant taro, cunjevoi, *A. macrorrhizos* in Southeast Asia and Oceania). The inflorescence of *Monstera deliciosa* (cheese plant) is sometimes used fresh as food. Many aroids are poisonous and must be cooked before they are eaten. Some species are of medicinal use or are used as arrow poisons. Many genera contain species widely grown as garden ornamentals, house or aquarium plants, or as cut flowers, e.g., *Arum*, *Arisaema*, *Anthurium*, *Dieffenbachia* (poisonous and containing highly irritant raphides), *Monstera*, *Philodendron*, *Spathiphyllum*, and *Zamioculcas*. The genus *Cryptocoryne* is widely used in aquaria, and *Zanthedeschia aethiopica* (Arum Lily), *Anthurium andraeanum*, and *A. scherzerianum* (Flamingo Flowers) and their hybrids are important cut flowers. Members of the Lemnoideae are used to remove nutrients and heavy metals from waste water.

Araceae. 1 *Spirodela polyrhiza* (a) fronds with adventitious roots and prominent root caps (x 2⅔); (b) underside of frond with 2 daughter fronds (x2⅔); (c) vertical section of frond with multilayered air spaces (x5⅔). **2** *Wolffia arrhiza* (a) frond with several daughter fronds (x26); (b) section of frond with a daughter frond budding off from a lateral pouch and a flower (sometimes interpreted as a reduced inflorescence) in a single cavity (x52). **3** *Lemna gibba* (a) fronds (x12); (b) vertical section of frond with a single layered air space (x8); (c) inflorescence of 2 male flowers and 1 female flower enclosed by a scalelike leaf (x20); (d) opened fruit showing several seeds (x20); (e) cross section of fruit with 4 seeds (x20); (f) vertical section of seed with embryo at the top (x40). **4** *L. minor* opened fruit with with a single seed. **5** *L. trisulca* (a) frond with several daughter fronds (x2⅓); (b) seedling showing first frond and suspensor (x6); (c) fruit enclosed in scalelike leaf (x26).

Palm Family

Arecaceae consists of tree- or shrublike plants, or lianas, with woody stems and often large, tough, plicate, split leaves; axillary inflorescences with a characteristic prophyll; and single-seeded fruits.

Description The life-form of palms is highly variable. Some are tree- or shrublike, others are nearly stemless or climbing but all have woody stems that terminate in a crown of leaves. The leaves are usually spirally arranged and may have spines or prickles and generally a distinct petiole, which is unarmed or armed with spines or teeth. The blade is palmate, pinnate, rarely bipinnate (*Caryota*), bifid (*Asterogyne*), or entire (*Johannesteijsmannia*), tough, and usually plicate (folded like a fan). Palm leaves vary enormously in size from less then 15 cm in species of *Chamaedora* to 25 m in *Raphia*. The leaves may be undivided (e.g., *Licuala grandis*) or frequently split along the folds (e.g., *Phoenix*).

Palm inflorescences are axillary, simple or huge panicles, often emerging among the leaves, but sometimes below or above the crown (*Corypha*, *Metroxylon*), usually solitary. Species of *Corypha* have treelike inflorescences that carry up to 10 million flowers. The flowers occur individually, 2 or 3 together, in cincinnate clusters or are 2-ranked. The flowers may be bisexual or unisexual, basically 3-merous. There are 3 sepals; 3 petals; 3+3 stamens; and a superior ovary with 3 carpels, each with a single ovule. The carpels are either free (apocarpous) or wholly or partly fused (syncarpous). The ovules are erect or pendulous, anatropous. Male flowers occasionally have both 4 sepals and petals; the female flower may have up to 10 carpels. More than 6 stamens per flower are common. Palms are wind- or animal-pollinated (by ants, bees, beetles, or flies), or both.

The fruits are mostly one-seeded berries or drupes with a single seed, or rarely 2 to 10. They vary in size from 4.5 mm in diameter to a length of 50 cm and a weight of 18 kg (*Lodoicea maldivica* [double coconut]—the world's largest fruit and seed). The fruit surface is usually smooth but may be covered with geometrically arranged scales, prickles, hairs, or warts. The mesocarp is fleshy or dry and variously fibrous. The endocarp is mostly thin. Many fruits are brightly colored, and virtually all are indehiscent. The storage tissue is endosperm, which is oily or fatty rather than starchy.

Distribution Palms are distributed mainly in the tropics, with many species in Central America, northern South America, and East Asia; Africa has a surprisingly low number of species. Palms grow in many habitats, from mangrove swamps to lowland rain forests. There are a few subtropical and temperate outliers, including the European *Chamaerops humilis*, which attains latitude 44°N.

Economic uses The economic importance of palms is immense; only a limited range of well-known uses are mentioned below. The Coconut Palm (*Cocos nucifera*) yields coconuts and copra (the dried kernels that yield coconut oil). Oil is extracted from *Elaeis guineensis* (Oil Palm) and *Orbigyna* species. Dates, the fruits of *Phoenix dactylifera*, are a major crop in the Middle East, where they have been cultivated for at least 5,000 years. Other species of *Phoenix* yield fibers, sugar, and fuel, or are used as pot plants (*P. roebelenii*). Sago (a major carbohydrate source) is processed from the pith of palms of the genus *Metroxylon sagu* (Sago Palm). Palm wine (toddy) is another useful product of many palms, including *Borassus* and *Caryota*. Palms also yield useful fibers, including coir (from coconut husks) and raffia fiber (from the surface of young leaflets of the genus *Raphia*). Rattan cane comes mainly from *Calamus* spp.; waxes come from *Copernicia* (carnauba wax) and *Ceroxylon*. Vegetable ivory, from *Phytelephas* (Ivory Nut Palm) and others, was once important and used for buttons and as a substitute for real ivory. The betel nut (from *Areca catechu)* is rich in alkaloids and is used as a masticatory in betel-chewing.

Arecaceae. **1** *Livistona rotundifolia* part of branch bearing indehiscent fruit (x⅔). **2** *Chamaedorea geonomiformis* habit showing bifid leaves and male inflorescences. **3** *Caryota mitis* part of bipinnate leaf (x⅔). **4** *Raphia vinifera* fruit covered with shiny scaly fruit, a distinctive feature of the Calamoideae (x⅔). **5** *Chamaedorea fragrans* male inflorescence (x⅔). **6** *Elaeis guineensis* vertical section of the fruit, containing a single seed in a hollow cavity surrounded by a thick mesocarp.

Pineapple or Bromeliad Family

A family of frequently epiphytic, herbaceous rosette plants with spirally arranged leaves, often with serrate margins and inflorescences usually comprising showy bracts.

Description Most bromeliads are herbaceous epiphytes, but a few have elongated stems or are rosette trees. They vary in size from few centimeters in some epiphytic species of *Tillandsia* to 3 m in *Puya raimondii*. The main function of the roots in epiphytic species is to anchor the plant, whereas the terrestrial species (e.g., *Pitcairnia*, *Puya*) have fully developed root systems. The most specialized epiphytic genera (e.g., *Tillandsia*) lack roots (except as young seedlings) and leaf-base tanks and absorb water from the atmosphere by means of multicellular, peltate hairs.

The leaves are spirally arranged, often creating a basal rosette of stiff, usually evergreen, leaves, with spiny margins. There is seamless transition between the sheath and the blade, but often a characteristic difference in color. In the terrestrial species, the leaves have unexpanded leaf-bases and leaf hairs that serve only to reduce transpiration. In some tank-forming species (e.g., *Ananas*), the overlapping leaf-bases act as reservoirs for water and humus, which are utilized by adventitious roots growing up between the leaf-bases. The majority of genera have larger leaf-base tanks, and absorption from the tanks is mainly carried out by specialized peltate hairs (trichomes) composed of a foot, a stalk of living cells, and a shield of dead cells. These hairs are often positioned at the bottom of a pit and expand when wetted, so water is drawn into the dead cells of the hair and thence osmotically through the living cells of the stalk of the trichome into the leaf. The scales collapse when dry, closing the pit like a lid and permitting gas exchange through the stomata (almost entirely confined to the underside of the leaves) but reducing water loss from the surface of the plant. The plants can thus survive in extremely arid habitats, but not in very humid habitats such as rain forests. The tanks may hold up to 5 liters of water and serve as a water reservoir for canopy-dwelling animals. The tanks contain a highly specialized flora and fauna, including species of *Utricularia* (bladderworts), tree frogs (*Syncope antenori*), and various insects.

The inflorescence is terminal, produced out of the center of the tank in tank-forming species and may be a spike, raceme, or panicle, often with brightly colored, conspicuous bracts, rarely with solitary flowers (*Tillandsia*). Many bromeliads die after flowering, including some of the genera cultivated for their inflorescence, but these produce suckers and can be readily propagated. The flowers are bisexual or rarely functionally unisexual (*Hectia*), usually actinomorphic, although slightly zygomorphic in some genera (*Pitcairnia*). The flowers are 3-merous, with a greenish calyx and a showy petaloid corolla. The 6, free stamens are often attached to the base of the perianth or more or less fused. The ovary is superior to inferior and consists of 3 fused carpels. There are 3 locules, each with numerous ovules on axile placentas. The stigmas are 3-lobed and borne on a slender style. The fruit is a berry or capsule. The seeds contain a small embryo and a starchy endosperm. In several genera, the seeds have wings, are plumose, or have tailed appendages. In most genera, the showy inflorescences and the nectaries on the septa of the ovaries are adaptations to pollination by birds (hummingbirds and honeycreepers), bats, or insects.

Distribution Almost exclusively native to the Americas, growing from Virginia in the USA to Patagonia in South America. A single species (*Pitcairnia feliciana*) is native to Africa.

A few species are present on islands in the Pacific e.g., *Racinaea insularis* of the Galápagos Islands and *Greigia berteroi* and *Ochagavia elegans* of the Juan Fernandez Islands. *Tillandsia usneoides* is supposed to be one of the world's widest-ranging plants. Bromeliads grow in a variety of different

Bromeliaceae. 1 *Aechmea nudicaulis* inflorescence, with large showy bracts and leaf with spiny margin (x⅔).
2 *Pitcairnia integrifolia* (a) leaf (x⅔); (b) inflorescence, with reduced bracts (x⅔); (c) vertical section of semi-inferior ovary, showing numerous ovules on axile placentas (x4).

habitats and are a characteristic element in
Neotropical forests, but they are also common
in arid areas. They grow at altitudes of up to
4,500 m in the Andes mountain range.

Economic uses *Ananas comosus* (Pineapple)
is an extremely important edible fruit of tropical and subtropical regions. In 2005, the world
production exceeded 16 million tonnes,
accounting for the largest part of the world's
export in tropical fruits. Most commercially
grown pineapples are canned or made into
juice rich in vitamins A and B. Pineapple
stems and fruits are a possible commercial
source of enzymes. Bromelain, which has anti-
inflammatory properties, is a mixture of 5 different proteolytic enzymes. Other species with
edible fruits are found in the genera *Aechmea*,
Bromelia, and *Greigia*. They are consumed
locally. A range of species produce fibers used
locally for cloth-making and cordage, notably
the pineapple in the Philippines, *Aechmea
magdalenae* (Pita) in Colombia, and *Neoglaz-
iovia variegata* (Caroa) in Brazil. *Tillandsia
usneoides* (Spanish Moss) was previously widely used as a substitute for horsehair in uphol-
stery. Various genera are grown as ornamentals
in the open in frost-free regions, under glass,
or as house plants in temperate regions. The
foliage alone may be attractive, as in variegated forms of the pineapple, the striped leaves
of certain species of *Billbergia*,
Cryptanthus, and *Guzmania*,
and the dense rosettes of
Dyckia, *Nidularium*,
and *Aregelia*.

Additionally, sev-
eral genera include
species that produce
inflorescences with
showy bracts, for
example *Pitcairnia*,
Billbergia, *Aechmea*, and *Vriesea*.

In parts of the dry tropics, bromeliads
have hampered malaria control since the
water retained in the leaf tanks of certain
native species may serve as a breeding ground
for malaria-carrying *Anopheles* mosquitoes.
These leaf tanks cannot easily be sprayed for
mosquito control.

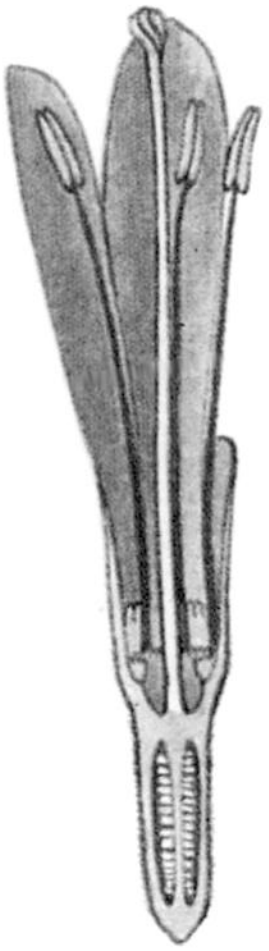

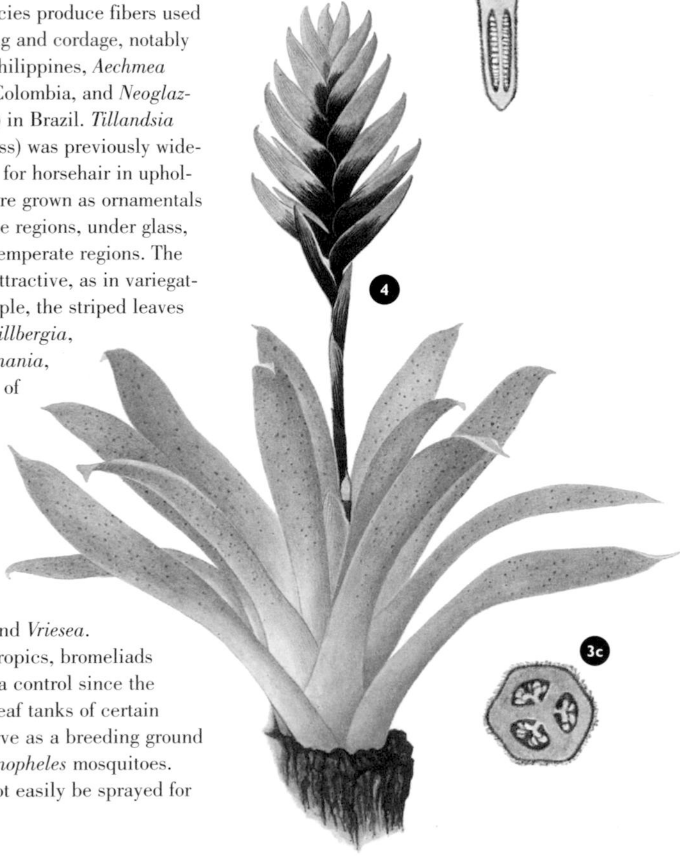

Bromeliaceae. 3 *Billbergia pyramidalis* (a) leaf with spiny margins and inflorescence with large red bracts (x⅔); (b) dissected flower with an inferior ovary crowned by a single style with a lobed stigma and stamens inserted at the calyx base (x1½); (c) cross section of the 3-locular ovary showing axile placentas (x4). **4** *Vriesia carinata* habit (x⅔). **5** *Ananas comosus* (pineapple) a multiple fruit (produced from the entire inflorescence) and "crown" of leaves produced by continued growth of the axis (x⅓).

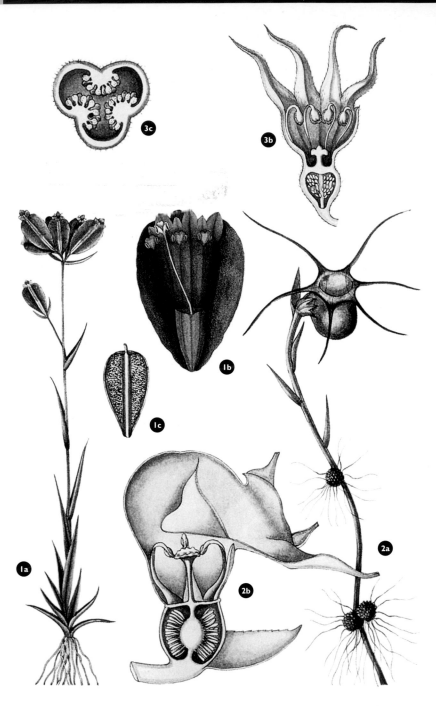

Burmannia Family

The Burmanniaceae is a family of mostly small, achlorophyllous, saprophytic or hemisaprophytic, annual or perennial herbs, which are often tinted reddish, yellowish, or white.

Description Mostly small, saprophytic or hemisaprophytic, annual or perennial herbs with slender, upright, unbranched stems produced from often tuberous rhizomes. The saprophytic species are achlorophyllous, often white, yellow, or red, with alternate, sessile, and scalelike leaves. Hemisaprophytic species (*Burmannia* spp.) are green, often with well-developed, basally aggregated, alternate leaves. The inflorescence is a terminal many-flowered cyme, often a bifurcate, bracteate circinnus. The flowers are bisexual, actinomorphic, usually pedicellate, and often white, bright blue, or rarely yellow. There are usually 6 tepals in 2 whorls, rarely only 3 or 1. They are basally fused into a tube, which often has longitudinal wings or ribs. The outermost whorl encloses and protects the inner whorl in the bud. The stamens are 6 or 3 on short filaments, often fused with the tube and opposite the inner tepals. The thecae open transversely or longitudinally and often bear various appendages or are fused into an anther tube (*Thismia*). The ovary is inferior, consisting of 3 carpels and 3- or 1-locular. The placentation is axile, parietal, or free, with numerous small, anatropous ovules. The style is cylindrical with 3 apical

branches or the stigma is capitate. The fruit is a capsule, rarely fleshy, often winged, and variously dehiscent. The tiny seeds have endosperm of just a few cells and containing a few starch grains that are replaced by protein and fat.

Distribution The Burmanniaceae is largely pantropical but also reaches warm-temperate regions. Most species grow in the moist understory of lowland and montane forests, but some inhabit open areas such as savannas and swampland. Several species are extremely rare.

Burmanniaceae. 1 *Burmannia coelestis* (a) habit (×1); (b) part of perianth opened to show 6 tepals and enlarged perianth tube expanded below the ovary, 3 anthers, and style with 3 stigmas (×4); (c) capsule (×4). **2** *Afrothismia winkleri* (a) saprophytic species, with scalelike leaves, rhizome with tubers, flower with nearly equal tepals, and an urnlike perianth tube (×⅔); (b) longitudinal section of flower showing inferior ovary containing ovules on parietal placentas, and a sterile column in the middle (×8). **3** *Haplothismia exannulata* (a) saprophytic species, with scalelike leaves and 3–6 flowered monochasial inflorescences, with nodding flowers (×⅔); (b) longitudinal section of flower showing pendant stamens and 1-locular ovary; (c) cross section of ovary with numerous ovules (×6).

Canna Family

A family of large, upright, rhizomatous herbs with alternate, petiolate, simple leaves and large, asymmetric flowers with petal-like staminodes that grows in the tropical parts of the Americas.

Description Large, erect plants, with starchy, tuberous rhizomes and distichously or spirally arranged leaves with sheathing bases that gradually taper into the petiole, no ligule, and a lamina that is rolled up from one side and with a distinct compound midrib and pinnately arranged lateral veins. The inflorescence is terminal with 3-ranked bracts, each subtending either few-flowered cymes or single flowers. The flowers are short-lived, large, and showy, bisexual with 5 whorls, but strongly asymmetric. The perianth comprises 3, imbricate, basally connate sepals, which are usually green or purple, much smaller than the petals, and persistent in fruit. The 3 petals, 1 of which is usually smaller than the other, are often yellow or white and basally fused. The 6 stamens are petal-like and brightly colored, 1 of which bears a bithecal anther along the edge, the remaining 1–5 being staminodes. The staminodes are all of different form and size, the 1 opposite the functional stamen, which is reflexed and rolled back on itself, is called the labellum, and the others called wings. The ovary is inferior, of 3 fused carpels, and has 3 locules each containing 2 rows of numerous ovules on axile placentas. The fruit is usually a hard, tuberculate or bristly, irregularly splitting capsule, containing many small seeds with a tuft of hairs and straight embryos surrounded by a thin starchy and a copious, extremely hard, starchy endosperm.

Distribution Restricted to the tropical parts of the Americas, where it grows on riverbanks.

Economic uses *Canna edulis*, the source of purple or Queensland arrowroot, has been cultivated in the Andes for around 4,500 years and is now grown all over the tropics for its starchy rhizomes, although it is most important in Australia and India. The starch is easily digestible, the grains of which are among the largest known and are visible to the naked eye. More than 1,000 horticultural varieties of cannas are known, often with showy leaves and large flowers that vary from yellow (*Canna x generalis*) to red and orange (*C. x orchidoides*) and are widely grown as tropical ornamentals or in greenhouses. The seeds are used locally in the production of necklaces.

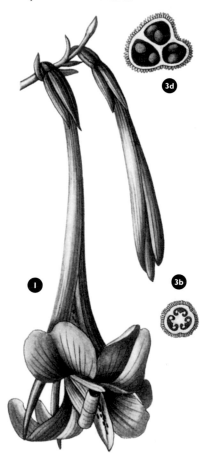

Cannaceae. 1 *Canna indica* fin tip of simple inflorescence with flowers showing 3 sepals at the base, 3 connate petals and the staminodes (x⅔). **2** *Canna glauca* (a) base of plant showing swollen rhizome and sheathing leaf-bases (x⅔); (b) sheathing leaf with distinct petiole (x⅔); (c) compound inflorescence (x⅔); (d) flower; shown from base upward are: tuberculate, inferior ovary, 2 of the 3 green sepals, 2 of the 3, lanceolate, orange petals, outer whorl of staminodes, 2 broader wings plus the curved labellum, inner staminode whorl of winglike staminode plus slightly coiled staminode with coiled half-anther attached, and central petaloid style (x1). **3** *Canna* x *generalis* (a) half section of flower base (x1); (b) cross section of ovary (x2); (c) tuberculate capsules with attached sepals fruits (x⅔); (d) cross section of fruit (x⅔).

Commelinaceae. 1 *Commelina erecta* shoot, showing sheathing leaf-bases, flowers with 3 petals, 3 stamens, and 3 staminodes (x⅔). **2** *Gibasis graminifolia* (a) leafy shoot and inflorescence, each flower with 6 stamens (x⅔); (b) capsule (x1⅓). **3** *Tradescantia zebrina* (= *Zebrina pendula*) leafy stem and solitary flower (x⅔). **4** *Tradescantia sillamontana* leafy shoot with inflorescence subtended by boat-shaped, leafy bracts (x⅔). **5** *Tradescantia* (= *Rhoeo*) *spathacea* shoot showing rosette of bromeliad-like leaves and inflorescence partly hidden by boat-shaped bracts (x⅔). **6** *Tradescantia navicularis* (a) juvenile plant and (b) adult shoot (x⅔).

Spiderwort Family

A family of perennial or annual herbs, often somewhat succulent, with a mucilaginous sap and alternate, entire leaves with a sheathing base that grows throughout warm-temperate, subtropical, and tropical regions.

Description Most species are stoloniferous, rhizomatous, terrestrial perennial herbs, but some species are annual (*Commelina*) or epiphytic (*Cochliostema*), and a few are climbers (e.g., *Dichorisandra*). Usually they have jointed, succulent aerial stems, but are sometimes almost stemless, with alternate leaves. The leaves are distichous or spirally arranged, often somewhat succulent, entire, frequently narrowing into a pseudopetiole, and with a closed basal sheath. The inflorescence is essentially a cyme with cincinate components and is borne either at the end of the stem or in the leaf axils. The flowers are bi- or unisexual, usually actinomorphic, but occasionally zygomorphic. The perianth consists of a calyx of 3 free or partly fused sepals and a corolla of 3 free or basally fused white or colored petals. When fused, the corolla may have a basal tube (*Coletrype, Cyanotis, Tradescantia*). The flowers often are of a short duration, typically no more than a day. The stamens are in 2 whorls of 3, usually free, but in some genera only 2 or 3 of the stamens are fertile, the others being reduced to staminodes. Several genera have brightly colored, often beadlike hairs on the filaments. The ovary is superior and has 3 fused carpels with 3 locules (rarely 2), each containing 1 to many atropous ovules on axile placentas. The style is terminal and simple, terminating in 3 branches or capitate. The flowers are strongly scented in some genera (e.g., *Palisota, Tripogandra*) but always without nectar. The fruit is usually a dehiscent capsule, rarely indehiscent and berrylike. The seeds have a distinct, caplike enlargement (embryostega) that covers the embryo. They contain a copious, starchy endosperm.

Distribution The family grows throughout warm-temperate, subtropical, and tropical regions. In temperate regions, it is best represented in North America and Asia. No species are native to Europe. Commelinaceae grows in most habitats but prefers humid conditions and is typically found in grassland and forests.

Economic uses Some genera are important pot or garden plants, e.g., *Commelina* (170 spp.), *Tradescantia* (including *Rhoeo* and *Zebrina*, 70 spp.), *Cyanotis* (50 spp.), and *Dichorisandra* (25 spp.). *Tradescantia* species are sold under the Tradescantia, Wandering Jew, Wandering Sailor, or Spiderwort (*T. virginiana*). The leaves and stems of the tropical African perennial herb *Aneilema beninense* is used as a laxative. The sap of several species is used to treat eye inflammation (e.g., *Commelina* spp.) in Africa, Asia, and South America.

Panama Hat Family

The Cyclanthaceae is a small family of perennial epiphytes, root-climbers, or terrestrial herbs, with alternate, simple leaves, usually with a bifid apex or, rarely, palmlike.

Description Monoecious, perennial, rhizomatous plants that may be terrestrial, epiphytic, or climbing lianas, with or without lignified aerial stems. The leaves are distichous or spirally arranged, sheathing at the bases, and in most species, petiolate, rarely fan- or palmlike. The inflorescence is an unbranched, axillary, or terminal, usually cylindrical to ellipsoid, spadix, subtended by 2 to 11, mostly 3 to 4, bracts or spathes. Usually 1 female flower is surrounded by 4 male flowers in a spiral along the spadix, or the individual flowers are not discernable. The flowers are unisexual. The ovary has apical or subapical placentas with numerous ovules. The fleshy fruit has numerous seeds, with minute, straight embryos surrounded by copious endosperm of fat.

Distribution The family grows in lowland and montane rain forests (up to 3,000 m), ranging from southern Mexico through Central America, the West Indies, the Amazonian part of South America, to subtropical coastal areas of Brazil.

Economic uses This family is economically important for *Carludovica palmata* (the Panama Hat Plant). The young petioles and leaves are made into fibers (paja toquilla) from which Panama hats are weaved. These hats have been produced for centuries and were sold and shipped from Panama in the 1800s, giving rise to their name. Ecuador is the main producer, exporting more than 1 million hats every year. Older, coarser leaves are used to make mats and baskets. The leaves of species of *Carludovica*, *Asplundia*, and some other genera are used as thatching material. Species of *Asplundia* are used to treat snakebites.

Cyclanthaceae. 1 *Asplundia vagans* habit, with bifid leaf apices and lateral inflorescence (x⅔). **2** *Stelestylis stylaris* female flower with 1 perianth segment removed (x4½). **3** *Evodianthus funifer* (a) half male flower in bud, with numerous stamens, and asymmetric position of the pedicel (x4½); (b) male flower (x6); (c) young fruit, with 1 perianth segment (x4). **4** *Cyclanthus bipartitus* (a) tip of spadix with alternating whorls of male and female flowers (x1½); (b) section of spadix showing male and female flowers (x4). **5** *Sphaeradenia chiriquensis* portion of spadix showing the characteristic arrangement of male and female flowers (x2). **6** *Carludovica rotundifolia* (a) habit, with spadices and fanlike leaves (½); (b) female flower, with a long staminodes (the others removed) (x2); (c) young fruit, inside the tepals, and with the staminodes removed (x4½); (d) male flower, with numerous stamens (x2); (e) inflorescence with connate female flowers, cut open to show the stalk (pink) into which bases of the fleshy (orange) fruits are partially imbedded (x⅔).

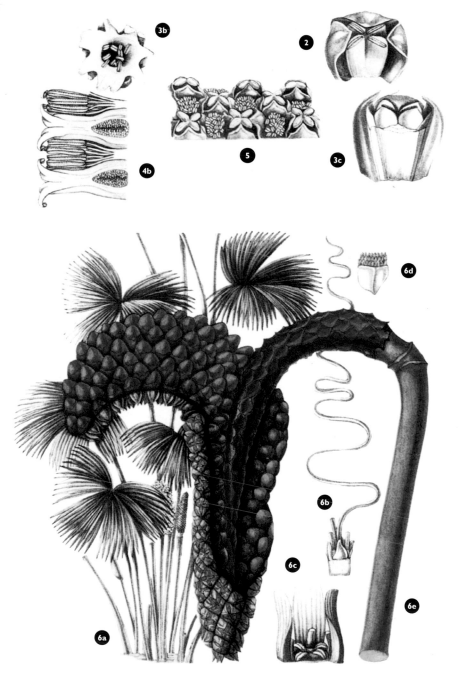

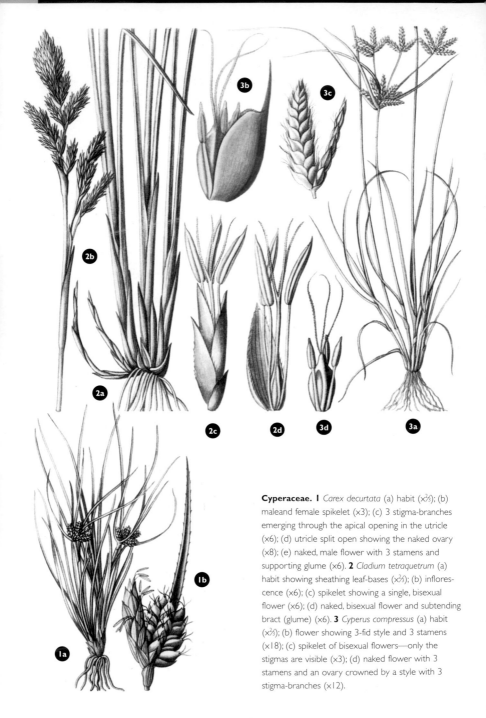

Cyperaceae. **1** *Carex decurtata* (a) habit (x⅔); (b) male and female spikelet (x3); (c) 3 stigma-branches emerging through the apical opening in the utricle (x6); (d) utricle split open showing the naked ovary (x8); (e) naked, male flower with 3 stamens and supporting glume (x6). **2** *Cladium tetraquetrum* (a) habit showing sheathing leaf-bases (x⅔); (b) inflorescence (x6); (c) spikelet showing a single, bisexual flower (x6); (d) naked, bisexual flower and subtending bract (glume) (x6). **3** *Cyperus compressus* (a) habit (x⅔); (b) flower showing 3-fid style and 3 stamens (x18); (c) spikelet of bisexual flowers—only the stigmas are visible (x3); (d) naked flower with 3 stamens and an ovary crowned by a style with 3 stigma-branches (x12).

Sedge Family

A large family of mainly perennial, grasslike herbs, with trigonous, solid stems and 3-ranked leaves, with the tepals being reduced to bristles or scales, or being entirely absent.

Description Mostly perennial, rhizomatous, or caespitose herbs, rarely annuals, shrubs (e.g., *Microdracoides*), or lianas (e.g., in *Scleria*), generally with solid culms that are trigonous in cross section, but hollow and terete culms are not uncommon. The leaves are usually tristichous, rarely distichous (e.g., *Oreobolus*), and basal, occasionally absent, with closed sheaths (rarely open) and with or without a ligule at the junction with the linear blade. The leaf epidermis has cells with 1 or more, conical silica bodies with their base resting on the inner surface of the cell. The inflorescence is terminal and composed of spikelets that are arranged in a large variety of compound, usually open inflorescences, often with erect branches, e.g., spikes, panicles, or corymbs, but may be condensed, e.g., headlike, or even reduced to a single spikelet. The spikelets consists of 1 to many, spirally or distichously arranged glumes (bracts), the lateral spikelets often with a sterile glume (prophyll) at the base, and the remaining glumes support small, inconspicuous bisexual or unisexual flowers (plants usually monoecious). The perianth is typically represented by 3 to 6 scales, bristles, or hairs but may be absent in some genera (e.g., *Carex*). There are 3 stamens, rarely only 1 or numerous. The ovary is superior, 2- or 3-carpellate, with a single locule and a single, basal, anatropous ovule. The style is divided into 2 or 3 branches and often persistent on the ripe fruit, which is an achene, or rarely a drupe. In *Carex* and related genera, the fruit is completely enclosed by a prophyll (utricle). The seed contains a small embryo surrounded by copious mealy or oily endosperm.

Distribution The Cyperaceae has a worldwide distribution and is absent only from Antarctica. Members of the family are especially abundant in damp, wet, or marshy regions of the temperate and subarctic zones, where species can dominate the vegetation entirely.

Economic uses The Cyperaceae is of limited economic importance, but several species are used for human food, notably *Eleocharis dulcis* (Chinese Water Chestnut) and *Cyperus esculentus* (Tigernut, Chufa), which are cultivated in Southeast Asia. In Africa, especially, species are used as fodder (e.g., *C. involucratus*) for livestock. Several species are noxious weeds in rice fields e.g., *C. rotundus* (Nut Sedge) and *C. esculentus*. The stems of a number of other *Cyperus* spp., such as *C. malacopsis* and *C. tegetiformis* (Chinese Mat Grass), are used to make mats, as are the stems of *Eleocharis austrocaledonica*. *C. dispalatha* is cultivated in Japan for its leaves, which are used to make hats. Stems of *Cladium mariscus* are used for thatching material for houses in Europe and parts of North Africa.

The stems of *Scirpus totara* are used to make canoes and rafts in tropical South America, and those of *S. lacustris* (Bulrush) of Europe and North and Central America in basketwork, mats and chair seats. *Cyperus papyrus* (Papyrus or Paper Reed) was used by the ancient Egyptians, and later by the Greeks, to make papyrus more than 5,000 years ago. The word *paper* is derived from the Egyptian "papyrus." Now, *C. papyrus* is gaining importance as a fuel. Some species of *Carex*, *Caustis*, *Cyperus*, and *Scirpus* are also cultivated as pot plants and water-garden ornamentals.

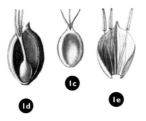

Pipewort Family

A small family of mainly tropical herbs, often with the spirally arranged leaves forming dense rosettes and bearing characteristic head- or button-like inflorescences at the ends of long, leafless peduncles.

Description Rhizomatous, perennial, or annual herbs, usually with rosettes of spirally, rarely distichously arranged, usually linear grasslike leaves or filiform when submerged in aquatic species; rarely, thick and coriaceous.

Some species have large trunks covered in adventitious roots or large (up to 4 m high) leafy stems (*Paepalanthus*); others, especially the aquatics, have leafy, floating stems.

The inflorescence is a single, indeterminate, headlike spike borne at the end of a leafless peduncle or composed of up to 100 such heads in an umbel-like inflorescence.

The peduncles usually extend beyond the leaves, which may sheathe them at the base. Each head is subtended by an involucre of bracts and is composed of 10 to more than 1,000 flowers. The bracts subtending the individual flowers are very different from the involucral bracts.

The flowers are usually unisexual, rarely bisexual (e.g., in *Rondonanthus* and *Syngonanthus*), and within each head the male and female flowers are mixed, or the male flowers are in the center surrounded by female flowers (plants monoecious); occasionally, the male and female flowers are on separate plants (plants dioecious).

The flowers are usually small, actinomorphic, 3-merous (most genera) or 2-merous (e.g., *Eriocaulon*, *Syngonanthus*). The sepals are free or fused at the base, while the petals are commonly fused into a tube.

There are 1 or 2 whorls of 3 or 2 stamens, rarely only 1. The ovary is superior, with 2 or 3 fused carpels and 2 or 3 locules and a single terminal style bearing 2 or 3 elongate stigmas, occasionally with appendices that may be longer than the stigmas. There is a solitary, atropous, pendulous ovule in each locule. The fruit is a membranous, loculicidal capsule. The seeds contain copious starchy endosperm and a small embryo.

Distribution Mainly tropical and subtropical, with species concentrations in South America and Africa, but with a few outliers in North America and Europe.

Members of the family often grow in seasonally wet, marshy, and boggy habitats. A few genera include true aquatics (e.g., *Eriocaulon*, *Tonina*) and some even grow in temporarily dry habitats.

Economic uses Apart from their use as everlasting flowers, which has made some species endangered, there are no reported economic uses. However, *Syngonanthus chrysanthus* has become a common pot plant in Europe and elsewhere within the last 7 to 8 years.

Species of *Eriocaulon* occur as weeds in rice fields, e.g., *E. aquaticum* in Europe and North America and *E. cinereum* in northern Italy, but they are not overly troublesome.

Eriocaulaceae. I *Eriocaulon aquaticum* (a) habit, showing dense head- or buttonlike inflorescence and basal rosette of leaves (x⅔); (b) male flower with 2 free sepals and 2 fused petals, and 4 stamens (x8); (c) inner perianth segment from male flower, showing rudimentary stamen and fertile stamen with gland behind (x12); (d) female flower with 2 free sepals and petals (x8); (e) head- or buttonlike inflorescence (x3); (f) vertical section of fruit (a capsule), showing pendulous seeds (x12). **2** *Syngonanthus laricifolius* (a) habit; note the internodes between the rosettes from different growth seasons (x⅔); (b) male flower with 2 bracts and 3 free sepals and 3 fused petals (x15). **3** *Paepalanthus riedelianus* (a) habit, each inflorescence supported by a leaf (x⅔); (b) gynoecium with 3 brushlike stigmas and elongated appendices (x16); (c) female flower with free sepals and petals (x8); (d) the fused petals of a male flower opened out to show 3 stamens and rudimentary ovary (x10); (e) male flower with free sepals (x8).

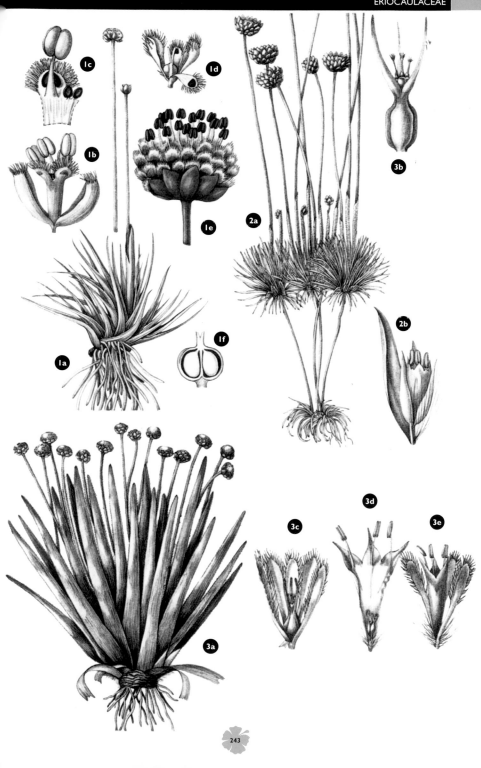

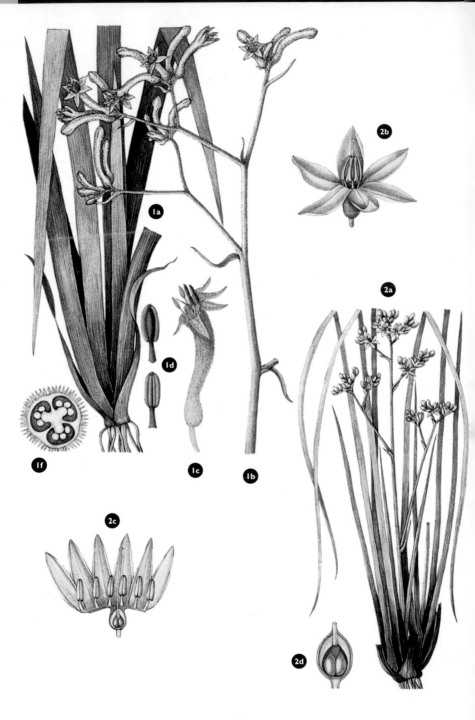

Bloodwort or Kangaroo Paw Family

A small herbaceous family of perennial plants with rhizomes, corms, or bulbs and with distinctive red-colored roots and ensiform leaves covered in simple, stellate, or dendritic hairs.

Description Perennial herbs with rhizomes, corms or bulbs, which are often—as are the roots—red or reddish (e.g., *Haemodorum*).

The inflorescences, flowers, and bracts are often more or less densely covered in simple, stellate, or dendritic hairs. The leaves are 2-ranked ensiform, narrowly linear or acicular, glabrous or hairy, with a sheathing base. The inflorescences are terminal, variable, but often a raceme or a panicle, with bracts and composed either of 1- to 3-flowered clusters or bi- or trifurcate helicoid cymes.

The flowers are bisexual, actinomorphic or slightly zygomorphic, often conspicuously colored, consisting either of 3+3 free (*Phlebocarya*), or basally fused, tepals, or the tepals united into a straight or curved tube with 6 free, valvate lobes. The flowers vary in length from 5 mm in *Barberetta* to more than 9 cm long in *Anigozanthos*.

The stamens are 3 or 6, rarely only 1, free or adnate to the tepals or tube. Species with 3 stamens may have staminodes.

The ovary is either superior or inferior, of 3 fused carpels, with 3 locules, each locule containing 1 to many anatropous or atropous ovules usually on axile placentas. The style is usually filiform, with a capitate stigma or 3-lobed. The fruit is a capsule, opening by 3 valves. The seeds have a tiny embryo and a starchy endosperm.

Distribution The Haemodoraceae is distributed in temperate to tropical Australia, northern South America, and Africa, although a few species are found along the Atlantic coast of North America and on New Guinea.

Economic uses Several species of Haemodoraceae, especially *Anigozanthos* (Kangaroo Paw), but also species of *Blancoa*, *Conostylis*, *Haemodorum*, *Tribonanthes*, and *Xiphidium*, are cultivated as garden and pot plants. *Anigozanthos manglesii* is the State emblem of Western Australia.

Lachnanthes caroliniana is an agricultural pest in commercial cranberry bogs.

Some species have been used locally as medicines or dyes e.g., *Haemodorum corymbosum* produces a red pigment with antitumor and antibacterial qualities.

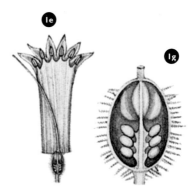

Haemodoraceae. 1 *Anigozanthos flavidus* (a) habit (x⅔); (b) inflorescence (x⅔); (c) flower showing curved green perianth tube and 6 stamens (x1); (d) stamen front (lower) and back view (upper) (x3); (e) flower dissected showing epipetalous stamens (x⅔); (f) cross section of 3-locular ovary with 3 axile placentas (x6); (g) vertical section of ovary (x6). **2** *Phlebocarya ciliata* (a) habit (x⅔); (b) flower showing perianth in 2 whorls and 6 stamens (x6); (c) flower dissected showing epipetalous stamens (x6); (d) vertical section of ovary (x14).

Canadian Waterweed and Frog-Bit

The Hydrocharitaceae is a family of cosmopolitan, perennial or aquatic marine and freshwater aquatics with an inflorescence that often has 2 fused bracts at the base.

Description Perennial or annual aquatic herbs, having either a creeping rhizome with leaves arranged in rosettes or an erect main stem with roots at the base and spirally arranged or whorled leaves. The leaves are simple, highly variable in shape, usually submerged, sometimes floating, rarely emergent, with or without sheathing bases.

The inflorescence is initially enclosed in 1 to 2 free or fused bracts, with between 1 and 100 or more flowers. The flowers are usually unisexual (plants dioecious), actinomorphic, rarely slightly irregular (e.g., *Vallisneria*), and either bisexual or unisexual (male and female then being borne on separate plants). The perianth segments are in 1 or 2 series of 3 (rarely 2) free segments; the inner series when present are usually showy and petal-like. The stamens are usually numerous, in up to 6 or more series; the inner stamens are sometimes sterile (in *Lagarosiphon* the staminodes function as sails for the free-floating male flowers). The pollen is inaperturate, globular, and free or in tetrads. In the marine genera *Thalassia* and *Halophila*, the pollen grains are liberated in chains. The ovary is inferior with between 2 and 20 incompletely united carpels, and with a long hypanthium in many genera. The numerous ovules are scattered over the inner surface of the carpel walls, with as many styles as there are carpels. The fruits are globular to linear, dry or pulpy, usually indehiscent, and splitting up irregularly. Usually, the seeds have straight embryos and lack endosperm.

The family has a spectacular variety of pollination mechanisms. Some genera, such as *Hydrocharis* (Frogsbit), *Ottelia*, and *Stratiotes*, have relatively large, showy flowers that are insect-pollinated. Several genera

are pollinated at the water surface. In *Elodea*, the pollen is liberated at or below the water surface and floats to the stigmas of the female flowers. In *Lagarosiphon, Maidenia, Nechamandra*, and *Vallisneria*, the male flowers become detached as buds from the parent plant and rise to the surface, where they expand and drift or sail to the female flowers, where pollination takes place above the water surface. In *Hydrilla*, male flowers are also released, but

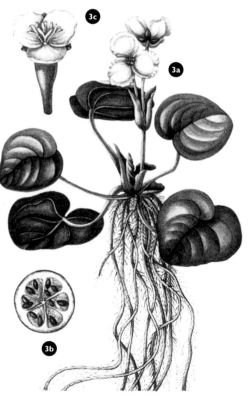

pollen is liberated from the anthers by an explosive mechanism. In *Halophila* and *Thalassia*, pollination takes place below water.

Distribution Cosmopolitan but mainly tropical, the family grows in a wide range of marine and freshwater habitats.

Economic uses Several species are used in aquaria, and a number of introduced species have become pernicious weeds, e.g., *Egeria densa* and *Hydrilla verticillata* in southern USA, *Hydrocharis morsus-ranae* (Frog-bit) in eastern Canada, and *Elodea canadensis* (Canadian Waterweed) in Europe.

Hydrocharitaceae. 1 *Vallisneria spiralis* (a) habit, showing stolons bearing new plants, ribbon-shaped leaves, and the long-stalked female flowers that reach the water surface (x⅔); (b) male flower, which separates from the parent plant and floats to the surface (x12); ovary (c) in cross section (x8) and (d) in vertical section (x4); (e) female flower, at pollination it remains attached but floats horizontally on the surface (x4). **2** *Elodea canadensis* (a) habit showing female flowers on long hypanthia (x⅔); (b) vertical section of ovary (x5); (c) female flower with 3 forked styles (x5). **3** *Hydrocharis morsus-ranae* (a) general habit of this free-floating plant, shown here with male flowers (x⅔); (b) cross section of fruit (x2); (c) female flower (x⅔).

Iris Family

The Iridaceae is a cosmopolitan family of perennial, rarely annual, herbs with rhizomes, corms, or bulbs, and flowers with conspicuous, petaloid tepals. Although most species are deciduous, a few are evergreen.

Description Perennial, rarely annual (e.g., *Sisyrinchium*) herbs, with rhizomes, corms, or bulbs. Most species are deciduous, although a few are evergreen. *Geosiris* is achlorophyllous. The leaves are mostly distichous, sometimes ensiform, basal, or cauline, with an imbricate, open or closed sheathing base, usually appearing with the flowers, or scalelike in *Geosiris*. The inflorescence varies considerably but is usually bracteate and either composed of terminal, 1 to many flowered, umbellate, monochasial cymes, or spicate, more rarely paniculate, or reduced to a single, almost sessile, flower (e.g., *Crocus*).

The flowers are bisexual, actinomorphic, or zygomorphic (e.g., *Gladiolus*) and frequently with a large conspicuous perianth of 2 whorls of 3 petaloid tepals, although the inner whorl is sometimes reduced (e.g., *Iris*) or missing; when zygomorphic, the flowers are more or less bilabiate. The tepals are free or united at the base into a straight or curved, tubular or funnel-shaped tube. The 3, rarely only 2 (*Diplarrhena*), stamens are opposite the outer tepals. The ovary is inferior, very rarely superior (*Isophysis*), with septal nectaries, and consists of 3 fused carpels, with 3 locules and axile placentas, or more rarely 1 locule with 3 parietal placentas. The ovules are usually numerous, rarely 1 or few, anatropous or campylotropous, in 1 or 2 rows in each locule.

The style is terminal and usually 3-branched or 3-lobed. The branches are filiform or expanded and petaloid, with the stigmatic surface facing the tepals. In several genera (e.g., *Iris*, *Moraea*), the style is a 3-branched, flattened, petaloid structure, which has enlarged showy "crests" overtopping the stigmatic surface. In *Iris*, these style branches curve outward, away from the axis of the flower, and form, with 3 of the perianth segments, a protective tunnel-like organ over each anther. The fruit is a loculicidal capsule, usually with many brown seeds, with a small embryo in an endosperm that contains hemicellulose, oil, and protein but rarely starch.

Distribution The family is cosmopolitan and grows in tropical and temperate regions, but South Africa and Central and South America are especially rich in species. Most species inhabit open scrub, deserts, and grassland, but the family is conspicuously absent from the Indian subcontinent, Sahara, and the interior of Australia, and few species appear in forests.

Economic uses The family is of great horticultural importance and includes numerous garden and indoor ornamentals. Genera cultivated in temperate areas include *Crocus* (85 spp.), *Iris* (225 spp.), *Sisyrinchium* (60–80 spp.), and *Tigridia* (35 spp.). *Crocosmia* (*Montbretia*; 9 spp.), *Gladiolus* (255 spp.), *Iris*, and *Freesia* (14 spp.) are important as cut flowers. The stigmas of the triploid *Crocus sativus* provide the spice saffron, grown commercially in Europe, the Middle East, and India. It is harvested manually and is exceedingly expensive. Its use was known in ancient Greece. The powdered, fragment rhizome of *Iris germanica* (German Iris) is a source of orris, used in perfumes and potpourris. A few South African species are serious weeds in Australia, e.g., *Sparaxis*, *Romulea*, and *Watsonia*.

Iridaceae. 1 *Crocus flavus* (a) capsule (×⅔); (b) tip of trilobed style (×4). **2** *Crocus* sp. flower with perianth opened (×⅔). **3** *Gladiolus papilio* (a) spicate inflorescence, with bract and large prophyll (×⅔); (b) cross section of 3-locular ovary with 2 rows of ovules in each locule (×2⅔). **4** *G. melleri* (a) longitudinal section through "bilabiate" flower (×⅔); (b) tip of style (×3). **5** *Iris laevigata* (a) apex of rhizome and leaf-bases of the ensiform leaves (×⅔); (b) inflorescence with fully opened flower consisting of three reflexed "falls," three erect inner "standards," and three petaloid style branches behind the stamens (×⅔); (c) bearded standard (×1); (d) stamen (×1); (e) petaloid style branch, the stigmatic surface is on the small triangular crest (×1). **6** *I. germanica* cross section of ovary with 2 rows of ovules in each locule (×2⅔). **7** *I. foetidissima* loculicidally dehiscing capsule, with seeds (×⅔).

Juncaeae. 1 *Luzula nodulosa* habit showing, ciliate leaf margins and sheathing leaf-bases (x⅓). **2** *L. alpinopilosa* (a) a perfect flower, with 5 whorls (x20); (b) cross section of 3-locular ovary (x100). **3** *Distichia muscoides* a low-growing cushion plant with distichous leaves and solitary flowers (x⅔). **4** *Juncus bufonius* habit showing erect linear leaves with loosely sheathing bases and flowers in dense cymose heads subtended by leaflike bracts (x⅔). **5** *J. acutiflorus* inflorescence (x⅔). **6** *J. bulbosus* half flower (x14). **7** *J. capitatus* dehiscing capsule consisting of 3 valves (x18).

Rush Family

A small cosmopolitan family of mainly perennial, rarely annual, grasslike, predominantly terrestrial herbs, usually with tristichous, rarely distichous, simple sheathing leaves.

Description Most species are perennial, rarely annuals (e.g., in *Juncus* and *Luzula*), with erect or horizontal rhizomes and erect or ascending stems. The leaves are usually tristichous, but some species have distichous leaves, linear or filiform, with open or closed sheaths, usually flat, dorsiventral but occasionally terete, or the blade is reduced. The inflorescence is terminal or apparently lateral, many-flowered (*Juncus* and *Luzula*), compound, and consist of open panicles and head- or spikelike inflorescences. In the remaining genera, the flowers are solitary and either terminal (*Rostkovia*) or lateral (*Oxychloe*). The flowers are actinomorphic, typically bisexual, or rarely female. The tepals are small, similar, glumaceous or herbaceous, arranged in 2 whorls of 3. They are dull in color, often green, brown, or black but sometimes also white or yellowish. There are usually 6 stamens in 2 whorls, alternating with the tepals. Occasionally, the inner whorl is missing. The ovary is superior, terminated by a style with 3 branches, consisting of 3 carpels, and usually 3-locular, rarely 1-locular. There are 3 (e.g., *Luzula*) to many anatropous ovules on central, axile, or parietal placentas. The fruit is a loculicidal capsule, and the seeds have a copious starchy endosperm and a straight embryo.

Distribution The family is cosmopolitan but present mainly in cold temperate or montane regions in wet or damp, occasionally saline, habitats. A few genera (e.g., *Distichia*, *Oxychloe*, and *Patosia*) consist of cushion-forming species adapted to the harsh diurnal freezing and thawing in the High Andes of South America and reaching the limit of vegetation.

Economic uses Generally, the family is of very limited commercial value. However, some species of *Juncus* and *Luzula* are important components in pastures. *Distichia muscoides* is used as fuel in the treeless Andes Mountains. Split rushes used in basket-making and the manufacture of chair bottoms are taken from the stems of *Juncus effusus* (Soft Rush) and *J. squarrosus* (Heath Rush).

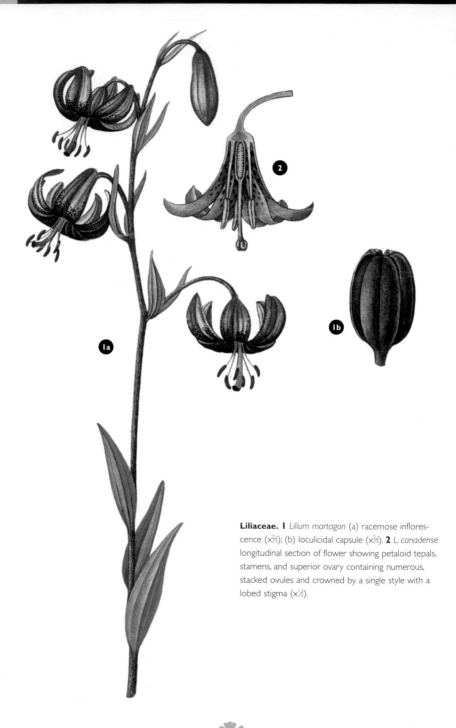

Liliaceae. I *Lilium martagon* (a) racemose inflorescence (x⅔); (b) loculicidal capsule (x⅔). **2** *L. canadense* longitudinal section of flower showing petaloid tepals, stamens, and superior ovary containing numerous, stacked ovules and crowned by a single style with a lobed stigma (x½).

Lily Family

A family of perennial geophytes with large, often conspicuously colored, typical monocot flowers that grows mainly in the temperate zone of the northern hemisphere.

Description Perennial, upright, unbranched, or rarely branched geophytes, with bulbs or rhizomes. The bulb is often tunicate and composed of a single or numerous fleshy scales. Lilies are the classic representatives of the monocotyledons, or plants with only one seed leaf.

The leaves are alternate but may appear opposite or verticillate, usually sessile, and sometimes sheathing. They vary in number from one to many. The leaves are flat, linear to lance-shaped, without teeth along the margins, and lack stalks.

The inflorescence is a raceme, occasionally umbel-like (e.g., *Gagea*, *Fritillaria*), but often the flowers are solitary. The flowers are often large, bisexual, actinomorphic, or slightly zygomorphic, with 2 whorls of 3, usually similar, free, and conspicuously colored tepals that are nectariferous. There are 3+3, rarely only 3, free stamens.

The ovary is superior, consists of 3 carpels, and is usually 3-locular, with 3 free, or more or less fused, styles and numerous, anatropous ovules on axile placentas.

The fruit is a loculicidal capsule, rarely a septicidal capsule (*Calochortus*) or a berry (e.g., *Clintonia*), usually with numerous, often flattened seeds in each locule, each with a minute embryo.

Fritillaria meleagris (Snake's Head Fritillary, Checkered Daffodil, Frog-cup) has a small round bulb (2 cm in diameter) that contains poisonous alkaloids. The flower is chequered, with reddish-brown, purple, white, and gray. The plant grows between 15 and 40 cm in height and is commonly found in grasslands in damp soils and river meadows. Native to Europe, it is an endangered species in many places, including France and Slovenia.

In the genus *Tulipa*, most of the cultivated species, subspecies, and cultivars are derived from *T. gesneriana* (Didier's tulip).

Distribution Distributed mainly in the temperate zone of the northern hemisphere, although a few genera reach the subtropics. They are present mostly in forests, grassland, and alpine meadows, reaching 4300 m, but rarely in deserts (*Calochortus*) or alpine tundra (*Lloydia*).

Economic uses The family includes some of the oldest-known ornamentals of the western world. Some species of lilies are famous for their large, showy flowers. *Lilium candidum* (Madonna Lily, Bourbon Lily) is depicted on a 5,000-year-old tablet from Sumeria and on wall paintings at the Minoan palace of Knossos, Crete. Native to the Balkans and western Asia, this true lily has a basal rosette of leaves through the winter, which dies back in the summer. Its leafy flower stems can reach up to 2 m tall. Many *Lilium* species (lily; 150 spp.) and hybrids are now in cultivation in gardens and as cut flowers.

Tulipa (tulip; 150 spp.) was introduced to Vienna in 1554 via Turkey (where the flowers were first cultivated commercially), and to Holland in 1571, where it created a veritable "tulipomania." Between 1634 and 1637, these newly introduced flowers triggered a speculative frenzy, and tulip bulbs were then considered to be a form of currency. The bulbs were exchanged for houses, livestock, and land and traded on stock exchanges.

Tulips are still very popular. Tulip festivals are held in the Netherlands, parts of England (Spalding), and in North America. The term "Dutch tulips" is often used for the cultivated forms. Now, more than 2,600 cultivars are in cultivation, and around 300 cultivars are grown on a commercial scale.

Fritillaria (130 spp.) is also widely cultivated, and in China more 18 spp. are known to possess medicinal properties. Species of all 3 genera have edible bulbs.

Prayer Plant Family

A small tropical family of terrestrial herbaceous perennials, with underground rhizomes or tubers and distichous, simple, often asymmetric leaves and flowers.

Description Terrestrial, perennial herbs, with underground rhizomes or tubers and distichous, sheathing leaves, with or without a petiole, and the lamina with a strong midrib and closely set, parallel, lateral veins. The inflorescence is lateral or terminal, simple, or consisting of spike-like or capitate partial inflorescences, with distichously or spirally arranged bracts. The flowers are not very conspicuous, bisexual, and asymmetric, usually in pairs and mirror images of each other. The 3 free sepals are rarely connate at the base (*Megaphrynium*) and distinct. The 3 petals, stamens, and style are fused below into a corolla tube of variable length. The outer whorl of the androecium usually consists of between 1 and 2 petaloid staminodes; the inner whorl has 1 fertile often petaloid and monothecal staminode, 1 hoodlike staminode, and 1 firm and fleshy staminode. The ovary is inferior, of 3 fused carpels, 3-locular, but usually 2 of the locules are aborted. The fertile locule contains 1 basal, anatropous ovule. There is a single style fused to the corolla tube at the base. Until pollination, the style is enclosed in the hood-shaped staminode and bent backward under tension, but when touched it curls up. The fruit is usually a loculicidal capsule, more rarely berrylike. The seeds have an aril and abundant starchy endosperm surrounding a horseshoe-shaped embryo.

Distribution The Marantaceae is pantropical but absent from Australia. With the exception of 2 genera (*Halopegia* and *Thalia*), the family is restricted to either Africa, Asia, or the neotropics. They grow mainly in disturbed areas in tropical rain forests, usually below 1,000 m.

Economic uses Economically, the most important crop plant is *Maranta arundinacea* (West Indian Arrowroot), which has rhizomes that produce a high-quality, easily digestible starch. The species is cultivated commercially in the West Indies and the tropical Americas. Several species are used in temperate zones as greenhouse ornamentals and houseplants mainly for their attractive foliage, e.g., *Calathea lancifolia*, *Maranta bicolor*, and *M. leuconeura*. The tough, durable leaves of *Ischnosiphon* are used to make basketry, and those of some species of *Calathea* for roofing, lining baskets, and food wraps. The inflorescences of some *Calathea* spp. are cooked and eaten as a vegetable; the tubers of *C. allouia* (Topee-tampoo) are eaten as potatoes in the West Indies.

Marantaceae. I *Calatheu villosa* (a) leaf, showing basal sheath, petiole, blade, and characteristic venation (x⅔); (b) a simple inflorescence with flowers subtended by green bracts (x⅔). **2** *C. concolor* (a) flower comprising free sepals, 3 irregular petals, 1 outer petaloid staminodes, and 1 petaloid stamen, with a fertile anther, and the hooded and fleshy staminode (x1); (b) the opened corolla tube, with fertile stamen and staminodes, 1 of which is hooded (x1). **3** *Stromanthe sanguinea* (a) upper rolled leaf and complex inflores- cence (x⅔); (b) flower the corolla tube almost hidden (x2); (c) open corolla tube (x3). **4** *Maranta arundi- nacea* (a) shoot with leaves and inflorescence (x⅔); (b) tuber (x⅔); (c) flower (x1); (d) hooded petaloid staminodes, dorsal view of fertile stamen and style (x1½); (e) cross section of 1-locular ovary (x3); (f) fruit with style (x2).

Orchid Family

The largest family of flowering plants, characterized by their often showy, strongly zygomorphic flowers and numerous dustlike seeds. These perennial plants have a cosmopolitan distribution.

Description Terrestrial or epiphytic, often rhizomatous, perennial herbs, or rarely scramblers, climbers, or achlorophyllous. The root system consists of an adventitious root, which in most terrestrial species is rather unspecialized. In many terrestrial orchids, however, the roots function as storage organs and become swollen or tuberous. Most of the epiphytic species have 2 types of roots—flattened roots that attach the plant to the substrate and long, tangled, and dangling, dull gray or white, velamen-covered, aerial roots with a green, densely meristematic apex. The velamen is a sheathing layer of dead cells that develops around the root as it matures and absorbs moisture and nutrients. Mycorrhizal (and nonmycorrhizal) fungi enter the plant through the roots, remaining concentrated in the roots but can also be found in the vegetative tissues. Many orchids are partly or entirely mycotrophic. In the achlorophyllous mycotrophic orchids, the root system is often reduced and more or less coralloid (e.g., *Neottia*).

Many tropical and subtropical orchids, both terrestrial and epiphytic, possess special swollen structures, called pseudobulbs, which consist of a single or several stem internodes to store water and nutrients. Pseudobulbs are especially common in orchids that suffer periodic drought. Pseudobulbs vary in size from mere pinheads in 1 Australian species to thick cylinders up to 3 m tall in another Asian species. The leaves of most orchids are alternate, distichous, rarely opposite (e.g., *Isotria*), sometimes reduced to a single leaf or scales, varying in size from 1 mm to more than 1 m, simple, linear, lanceolate, ovate or obovate, thin, leathery, or, in species that occur in dry habitats, more or less succulent, and with a sheathing base, which usually clasps the stem.

The inflorescence is either lateral or terminal, and frequently a bracteate raceme, but sometimes a spike, a panicle, or the flowers are solitary. Basically the flowers are bisexual, though unisexual flowers are sometimes found (plants monoecious or dioecious, e.g., *Catasetum*), and strongly zygomorphic. They have 2 whorls of 3 tepals, 3 sepals, and 3 petals. The sepals are usually rather similar, but the 2 laterals or the single dorsal may be elongated or bear a longitudinal crest. In some genera, the lateral sepals are partially or completely united (e.g., *Cypripedium*). However, the petals are usually clearly different with the 2 laterals being quite similar to the sepals but distinct from the dorsal and the lip, or labellum. The labellum is highly modified, variously lobed or divided, often with characteristic raised ridges, lamellae, or with hairs and glands, and often extended at the base to form a spur, which may contain nectar. The spur, which may be bilobed apically, can be up to 30 cm long in *Angraecum sesquipedale* from Madagascar. Although technically seen dorsally in the flower, the labellum is very often facing downward as the whole flower is turned or bent over, because the inferior ovary is twisted lengthwise or bent downward at the apex. As a result, the flower is turned 180° (i.e., upside down) in most terrestrial orchids.

The flowers are ephemeral to very long-lasting, often fragrant, the scent varying from the smell of rotting carrion through sickly sweet vanilla-like odor to unquestionably very pleasing perfumes. Opposite the labellum in the floral whorl are the sexual organs, which are reduced and always united to form a single structure called the column (gynostemium). In its simplest, basic form, the column is surmounted by the anther with the receptive stigmatic surface just underneath, usually separated from each other by a flap of sterile tissue (the rostellum). The column is often winged subapically and with a foot that is often fused to the sepals. There are usually 1, rarely 2 or 3, stamens with 2-locular anthers and 3 stigmas, one of which is usually sterile and transformed

Orchidaceae. 1 *Bulbophyllum barbigerum* habit, showing pseudobulbs, single leaf, inflorescence, and flowers with strongly dissected labellum (x⅔). **2** *Dendrobium pulchellum* habit showing creeping stem rooting at the nodes, distichous, spotted leaves, and single flowers (x⅔). **3** *Sophronitis coccinea* habit (x⅔).

into the rostellum. The anther many be parallel to the column or bent, lying as a cap at the end of the column. The huge variations of columnar structures provide the basis for much orchid classification. The pollen are often agglutinated into 2, 4, 6, 8 discrete masses (pollinia) that are sessile or on short, sticky stalks, grouped 1 or 2 together.

The simplest form of pollinating mechanism is the accidental removal, by a bee, of 1 or more, or all, of the pollinia, which attach themselves to the bee's head or thorax during its search for nectar. Bees, wasps, flies, fungus gnats, ants, beetles, hummingbirds, bats, and frogs have all been observed as pollinating agents for orchids. The attachment of the pollinia to the insect is helped by a variety of additional mechanisms such as a quick-setting glue on the pollinia stalks or an explosive device that can project the pollinia up to 60 cm from the flower (e.g., *Catasetum*), and by the development of features, both visual and olfactory, that attract the insect to the right position on the right flower. A well-known mechanism is called pseudocopulation (e.g., *Ophrys*).

The ovary is inferior, usually 3-carpellate, 1-locular with parietal placentas, or rarely 3-locular with axile placentas. There are numerous anatropous ovules in each locule. The fruit is a capsule, which opens by 6 lateral, longitudinal slits. The seeds are dustlike, without endosperm. A single fertilized flower spike may produce 1 million or more seeds. In most species, they contain a more or less undifferentiated embryos. After association with the appropriate fungus, the seeds develop an ephemeral tubercle, a protocorm, and only later is the first seedling leaf and roots developed. This symbiosis appears to persist in terrestrial, but not in epiphytic, orchids.

Distribution The family has a cosmopolitan distribution, and orchids may grow under nearly all conditions: as understory plants in dark, tropical lowland forests; at the top of tall trees in the rain forest, where they are baked by the sun and then showered by torrential rain; in grassy and marshy areas; along the sides of the street; and as pioneering plants on landslides. They are absent only from extreme environ-

ments, such as the sea, the driest deserts, and the tops of the coldest mountains. The terrestrial habit prevails in temperate regions; in the tropics most species are epiphytes.

Economic uses Excepting the flavoring essence vanillin, orchids have little direct economic importance other than as the basis for a vast floricultural industry. Vanilla beans are the cured, unripe fruits of *Vanilla planifolia* (Bourbon Vanilla) or *V. tahitensis* (Tahiti Vanilla). The main source of vanilla is the islands of Madagascar, the Comores, and Réunion, which together account for about 75% of the world production. The characteristic aroma is developed by enzymatic actions during curing, and the cured capsules contain 2% vanillin. Owing to their alkaloid content, several orchid species are used medicinally in China and India.

The modern orchid industry is based in the USA, but it is also a major export earner in countries such as Australia, Britain, Germany, Hawaii, Holland, Indonesia, Malaysia, Singapore, and Thailand. Orchids are cultivated in the controlled environment of greenhouses in the temperate regions of the world; elsewhere they are grown outdoors in the same way as other plants. The last decade has witnessed a vast increase in the production of orchids as pot plants. Many orchids are now endangered, and avid collecting of rare species has brought many to the brink of extinction, as growers are willing to pay exorbitant amounts for such species. However, orchid trade is among the most controlled and regulated.

Orchidaceae. 4 *Oncidium tigrinum* (a) flowers borne in a wiry, spikelike partial inflorescence, the "pedicels" are the inferior ovary (x⅔); (b) column (united sexual organs), note the caplike anther and the stigmatic surface in the center (x⅓). **5** *Paphiopedilum concolor* (a) an evergreen, terrestrial orchid, with distichous leaves and a single flower—the labellum is pointing downward as the ovary has been bent (x⅔); (b) column side view, from above are seen the shieldlike staminodium, one of the 2 anthers and the stigma (x1); (c) column front view of staminodium (x1). **6** *Coelogyne parishii* (a) aerial shoot with pseudobulbs (x⅔); (b) column, with caplike anther, stigmatic surface, and winged apex (x1⅓).

Orchidaceae. 7 *Neottia nidus-avis* (Bird's Nest Orchid), an achlorophyllous, mycotrophic plant, with scale leaves and coralloid roors. **8** *Anoectochilus roxburghii* net-veined leaf and flowering spike, with flowers with a clearly twisted inferior ovary making the labellum point downward. **9** *Apostasia nuda* (a) almost symmetrical flower (×4); (b) column with stigma and 2 anthers (×8). (right:) **10** *Disa hamatopetala* spike. **11** *Ophrys bertolonii* habit, with the characteristic, egg-shaped tuberous roots (×⅔). **12** *Cypripedium calceolus* (Lady's Slipper) flower section, showing the staminodium, the stigmatic surface, and the inner hairy part of the labellum (×1). **13** *Cypripedium impeanum* solitary flower and leaves (×⅔).

Grass Family

A large and, economically, the most important family of flowering plants. A milestone in human development was reached with the adoption of the grasses as a principal source of food.

Description Mostly rhizomatous, stoloniferous, or caespitose perennial or annual herbs, although sometimes woody in the tropics. The roots are fibrous and often supplemented by adventitious roots from the lower nodes of the stem such that each new shoot has its own root system. It has been estimated that a single plant of *Festuca rubra*, which spreads by rhizomes, may be 250 m in diameter and up to 400 years old, and that a large tussock of *F. ovina* (8 m across) could be 1,000 years old.

The upright stems are cylindrical, usually hollow but sometimes solid, pithy, and mostly unbranched. A few species develop bulbs or corms. The leaves emerge from the nodes, and are composed of a sheath and a blade. The node has an intercalary meristem that extrudes the stem from the sheath and remains active. Differential growth at this meristem enables the stem to bend upright again after being flattened by rain or trampling. The blade is long and narrow but may be broad, lanceolate to ovate. The base of the blade has a meristematic zone, permitting the blade to continue growth despite the removal of its distal parts by grazing or cutting. The leaves of the South American bamboo *Neurolepis nobilis* are up to 5 m long.

The inflorescence is a specialized leafless branch system, which usually surmounts the stem and may be a spike or raceme. Extremes of size range from the spectacular 2 m plume of *Gynerium sagittatum*, to the solitary single-flowered spikelet of *Aciachne pulvinata*. The basic unit of the inflorescence is the spikelet, which consists of an often elongated axis (rhachilla) that may extend beyond the last floret and have 2-ranked scales. The 2 lowest scales (glumes) are empty, but the remainder (lemmas) each form part of a floret, whose floral parts are enclosed between the lemma on the outside and a delicate membranous scale (palea) on the inside. Glumes or lemmas are often produced into 1 or more long, stiff,

straight, or bent bristles (awns). The floral parts usually consist of 2 tiny, membranaceous scales, 3 stamens, and 2 styles and feathery stigmas surmounting the ovary. The basic pattern is uniform throughout the family, but there are an extraordinary number of variations. Bisexual spikelets are the rule, although some florets are often unisexual, mostly male, or barren.

The pollen is viable for less than a day—the shortest-lived of all angiosperm pollens—and of a distinctive type, monoporate, operculate, with a very finely granular surface. In some mountain or arctic species, the spikelets are transformed into bulbils, which can propagate.

The ovary is superior with a single locule containing 1 ovule. In the embryo, the cotyledon (scutellum) is attached to the starchy endosperm. The fruit is a caryopsis (fruit wall fused to the seed); some bamboos have a berrylike fruit (*Melocanna*) and a few genera (*Sporobolus*) have a nut. At germination, a special organ (coleoptile) protects the shoot meristem while it penetrates the surface. Awns, windborne plumes, hooks, barbs, and occasionally an adhesive often play a part in seed dispersal.

Distribution The family is truly cosmopolitan, ranging from the polar circles to the equator (1 of the 2 flowering plants on Antarctica is a grass, *Deschampsia antarctica*), and from mountain summits to the sea. Grasses are the main component in some 25% of Earth's vegetation cover. Native grassland has developed on most continents; prairie and plains in North America, pampas and llanos in South America, veldt in South Africa, and steppe in Eurasia. Savannah (grassland interspersed with trees and bushes) has developed in Africa, Australia, India, and South America.

Economic uses The adoption of the grasses as a principal source of food was a milestone in human development, with many of the great

Poaceae. **I** *Arundinaria japonica* tip of shoot, showing leaves with pseudopetiole and spicate inflorescence arranged in a panicle (x⅔). **2** *Phleum pratense* spikelike inflorescence (x⅔). **3** *Stipa capillata* dispersal unit—lemma with enclosed caryopsis and long, twisted, feathery awn (x⅔). **4** *Aristida kerstingii* dispersal unit—lemma with enclosed caryopsis and apically 3-branched awn (x⅔). **5** *Tristachya decora* paniculate inflorescence, with the spikelets arranged in groups of 3 mimicking a single spikelet (x⅔). **6** *Poa annua* junction between blade and sheath, a long membranaceous ligule inserted where the blade and base meet (x6).

civilizations being founded on the cultivation of grass crops. In many areas of the world, humans shifted from foraging to farming some 8,000–10,000 years ago. Evidence suggests that Stone Age people in Israel collected wild grass seed around 23,000 years ago, including wild emmer wheat and barley—forerunners of the crops now grown.

In the Near East, in the area known as the Fertile Crescent (parts of Iran, Iraq, Turkey, Syria, Lebanon, and Israel), wild species of *Triticum* and *Hordeum* yielded the cereals wheat and barley. *Hordeum vulgare* subsp. *vulgare* (barley) is one of the oldest crops to be domesticated in this region, from its wild progenitor *H. vulgare* subsp. *spontaneum*. Domestication of barley is likely to have taken place around 9,000 years ago. From the Fertile Crescent, domestication spread westward in the Mediterranean area and eastward through Tibet to China. *Triticum aestivum* (Common Wheat) arose from hybridization between *Aegilops tauschii* (diploid) and *Triticum turgidum* (Wild Emmer; triploid), itself a hybrid between *Aegilops speltoides* and *Triticum uraruix*. The domestication of common wheat took place around 8,000 years ago.

Secale cereale (Rye) is most likely a domesticated form of *S. strictum* (Mountain Rye), from Morocco to Iran and Iraq. Cultivated rye is known from the Neolithic age in Austria, but cultivation seems to have become widespread in Europe only after the Bronze Age. *Avena sativa* (Oat) is a domesticated form of *A. sterilis* (Wild Oat), which became widespread in Europe after the Bronze Age. Hybrids between *S. cereale* and *Triticum aestivum* have now resulted in *Triticale*, which has resistance to several diseases and is now widely grown.

The origins of *Oryza sativa* (Rice) are unknown but the earliest evidence for its domestication in Southeast Asia is from remains found in Thailand, dating back at least 4,000 years. Signs of early cultivation of rice have been found in the Yangtze valley dating back to about 8500 BCE. *Oryza glaberrima* (African Rice) has been cultivated for 3,500 years.

The cultivation of *Zea mays* (Maize, Corn) is thought to have started from 7500 to 12,000 BCE. Archaeological remains of the earliest

maize cob, found in the Oaxaca Valley of Mexico, date back around 6,250 years. Many other species of grasses are cultivated, including Foxtail Millet (*Setaria italica*) and Proso (*Panicum miliaceum*) in Asia, and Sorghum (*Sorghum bicolor*) and Bulrush or Pearl Millet (*Pennisetum glaucum*) in Africa.

Saccharum officinarum (Sugarcane) originated in New Guinea, where it has been known since about 6000 BCE. From about 1000 BCE, sugarcane spread with human migrations to Southeast Asia, India, and east into the Pacific. It spread westward to the Mediterranean between 600 and 1400 CE, and the crop was then taken to Central and South America from the 1520s onward, and later to the West Indies. It was the only sugarcane grown in the New World for more than 250 years, until it was replaced by the noble cane "Otaheite" ("Bourbon") at the end of the eighteenth century.

The second facet of humankind's dependence on the grasses springs from the domestication of animals, which was roughly contemporaneous with the advent of agriculture. Until recent times, livestock rearing was based upon the exploitation of natural grasslands, although the preservation of fodder as hay had been introduced by the Roman era. Sown pastures, based on rye grass, date from the twelfth century in northern Italy and from the late sixteenth century in northern Europe.

Bamboos are used for housing and furnishings, for tools, hunting weapons and utensils, in basketry, for fuel, and even for food. Young bamboo shoots, especially of *Phyllostachys*, are eaten as vegetables, either cooked or pickled. On an industrial scale, bamboos are used as timber for construction and as a source of pulp for the production of paper and cardboard.

An aromatic oil is distilled from the leaves of lemon grass (*Cymbopogon* spp.), imparting a citronella scent to soaps and other perfumery and it is also used as a spice. Among a host of minor uses are necklace beads (*Coix involucres*), brush bristles (*Sorghum inflorescence* branches), pipe bowls (*Zea* cobs), clarinet reeds (*Arundo donax* stems), and corn dollies or various garishly dyed inflorescences sold as house decorations. Lawns grasses (especially species of *Festuca* and *Cynodon*) have a place in horticulture, and several are used as ornamentals e.g., *Festuca* spp. (Fescue) and *Arundo donax* for their foliage, *Cortaderia selloana* (Pampas Grass) and *Miscanthus* spp. and hybrids for their impressive foliage and silvery inflorescences, *Briza* spp. (Doddering-dillies, Jiggle-joggies) for their characteristic nodding

spikelets, a large variety of *Pennisetum* spp. for their showy inflorescences, and varieties of *Phalaris arundinacea* for the often variegated leaves. Many grass species are serious weeds, including *Elytrigia repens* (Common Couch), *Imperata cylindrica*, *Avena fatua* (Wild Oat), and *Poa annua* (Annual Meadowgrass).

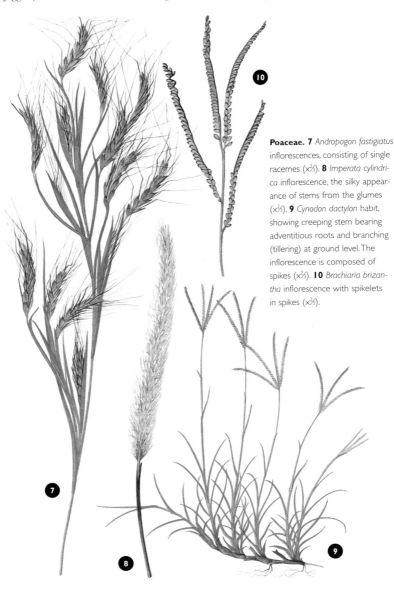

Poaceae. 7 *Andropogon fastigiatus* inflorescences, consisting of single racemes (x⅔). **8** *Imperata cylindrica* inflorescence, the silky appearance of stems from the glumes (x⅔). **9** *Cynodon dactylon* habit, showing creeping stem bearing adventitious roots and branching (tillering) at ground level. The inflorescence is composed of spikes (x⅔). **10** *Brachiaria brizantha* inflorescence with spikelets in spikes (x⅔).

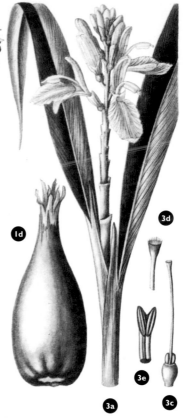

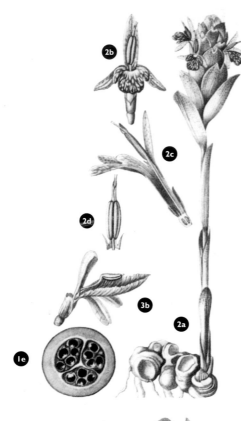

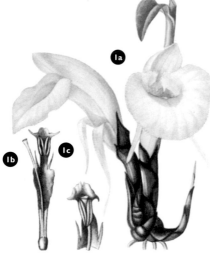

Zingiberaceae. 1 *Aframomum melegueta* (a) flowering, leafless shoots (x⅔); (b) opened flower, with inferior ovary, with 2 glands, the style freed from the embracing thecae (x⅔); (c) style in place between the thecae, stigma protuding (x1); (d) fruit (x⅔); (e) cross section of fruit, with many seeds (x⅔). **2** *Zingiber officinale* (Ginger) (a) flowering leafless shoot (x½); (b) flower, with clearly visible labellum and anther with style in place between the thecae (x1); (c) longitudinal section of flower (x1); (d) thecae, with extended connective folded around the style (x10). **3** *Alpinia officinarium* (a) leafy shoot and inflorescence (x⅔); (b) flower, with clearly visible labellum and anther (x1); (c) gynoecium, with glands at base of the style (x1 1/3); (d) cup-shaped stigma (x4); (e) anther (x1½).

Ginger Family

A tropical family of aromatic, perennial, rhizomatous herbs, with distichous, simple, sheathing leaves and often showy flowers. The Ginger family is distributed mainly in the humid, tropical lowlands of Indo-Malaysia.

Description Aromatic, perennial herbs, with branched, thick, and fleshy rhizomes, frequently possessing tuberous roots. The aerial stems are largely unbranched pseudostems, may vary considerably in size (up to 8 m high), but usually the stems are short.

The leaves are distichous or tufted, often without blades at the bases. The leaf sheath is often open, with or without a ligule, and a petiole of varying length, sometimes absent. The lamina is usually entire; elliptical; with a prominent midrib; and parallel, pinnate, lateral veins, diverging obliquely from the midrib.

The inflorescence terminates a leafy shoot or emerges from a separate, sheath-covered, leafless shoot directly from the rhizome. The inflorescence is often more or less cylindrical or globose and usually a thyrse in which each bract subtends a short cincinnate partial inflorescence, rarely only a single flower, a spike, or raceme.

The flowers are zygomorphic and bisexual and last only a day. The calyx is 3-lobed or 3-dentate, and the corolla tubular at the base, 3-lobed, the lobes varying in size and shape, the median, posterior lobe often larger than the others.

Only the median, posterior stamen of the inner whorl is fertile; the 2 others of the inner whorl are petaloid staminodes that are fused into a conspicuous 2- or 3-lobed labellum. The 2 lateral stamens of the outer whorl are petaloid or absent, whereas the median, anterior stamen of the outer whorl is always reduced. The fertile stamen has a long or short filament but is occasionally sessile.

The ovary is inferior, of 3 carpels, and either 3-locular with axile placentas or 1-locular with parietal or basal, many, anatropous ovules. The style is often extremely thin, almost always embedded in a furrow in the filament of the fertile stamens, emerging between the thecae. The fruit is a dry or fleshy capsule, usually dehiscing loculicidally, with few to many seeds, with a distinctive white or red aril, straight embryos, and scanty, often starchy endosperm.

Distribution Zingiberaceae has a pantropical distribution, chiefly occurring in Indo-Malaysia. The majority of species are found in the humid, tropical lowlands, but several occur in montane forests or drier dipterocarp forests, and a few more are epiphytes.

Economic uses The Zingiberaceae are rich in aromatic, volatile oils and are widely used as condiments, herbs, dyes, and medicinal plants. The rhizomes of *Zingiber officinale* (Ginger) and *Curcuma* spp. are important on the world market.

Bombay or East Indian Arrowroot is derived from the tubers of *Curcuma angustifolia*, whereas *C. longa* yields turmeric, one of the main coloring and aromatic ingredients of curry powder, which is also used as a yellow dye. *C. longa* is native to tropical Southeast Asia and needs high temperatures and a great deal of annual rainfall to grow well.

Elettaria cardamomum from Indonesia yields the important eastern spice cardamom, while the seeds of *Aframomum melegueta* are marketed as Melegueta pepper or grains of paradise.

Other important products include abir—a perfumed powder obtained from the rhizome of *Hedychium spicatum*—and zedoary—a spice, tonic, and perfume extracted from the rhizomes of *C. zedoaria*.

Alpinia officinale and *A. galanga* yield the medicinal and flavoring rhizome galangal.

Many species have beautiful flowers and are cultivated in the tropics and as greenhouse ornamentals in temperate countries, including *Hedychium coronarium* (Ginger Lily), *Alpinia purpurata* (Red Ginger), and *A. zerumbet* (Shell Ginger). *Roscoea* is cultivated as a garden plant in temperate areas.

CLASSIFICATION

In the last 20 years, DNA-sequencing technology has allowed botanists to review the classification of flowering plants (angiosperms), specifically which families should be recognized and how they should be clustered into larger groups. A group of botanists from around the world, the Angiosperm Phylogeny Group (APG), published the first DNA-based classification for angiosperms in 1998. Two slightly modified versions, APG II and APG III, were published in 2003 and 2009.

The APG system has gained wide acceptance, and its "linear" version (LAPGIII), published by Haston *et al.* in 2009, as shown below, now forms the basis for how a number of botanical organizations around the world classify and organize their collections and publish their research.

In the following table superorders and other higher groups are shown in capital letters; those in italic type are naturally related groups that have not been formalized within the APGIII system. Orders are shown in boldface. Orders and families given in italics are still "unplaced" within the system but their position and numbers show that they are closely related to surrounding families.

Three families in the main section of the book do not appear below; Durionaceae are now included in Malvaceae. Dipsacaceae and Valerianaceae are included in Caprifoliaceae.

AMBORELLANAE

Amborellales
1 Amborellaceae

NYMPHAEANAE

Nympheales
2 Hydatellaceae
3 Cabombaceae
4 Nymphaeaceae

AUSTROBAILEYANAE

Austrobaileyales
5 Austrobaileyaceae
6 Trimeniaceae
7 Schisandraceae

Chloranthales
8 Chloranthaceae

MAGNOLIANAE

Cannelales
9 Canellaceae
10 Winteraceae

Piperales
11 Saururaceae
12 Piperaceae
13 Lactoridaceae
14 Hydnoraceae
15 Aristolochiaceae

Magnoliales
16 Myristicaceae
17 Magnoliaceae
18 Degeneriaceae
19 Himantandraceae

20 Eupomatiaceae
21 Annonaceae

Laurales
22 Calycanthaceae
23 Siparunaceae
24 Gomortegaceae
25 Atherospermataceae
26 Hernandiaceae
27 Monimiaceae
28 Lauraceae

LILIANAE

Acorales
29 Acoraceae

Alismatales
30 Araceae
31 Tofieldiaceae
32 Alismataceae
33 Butomaceae
34 Hydrocharitaceae
35 Scheuchzeriaceae
36 Aponogetonaceae
37 Juncaginaceae
38 Zosteraceae
39 Potamogetonaceae
40 Posidoniaceae
41 Ruppiaceae
42 Cymodoceaceae

Petrosaviales
43 Petrosaviaceae

Dioscoreales
44 Nartheciaceae
45 Burmanniaceae
46 Dioscoreaceae

Pandanales
47 Triuridaceae
48 Velloziaceae
49 Stemonaceae
50 Cyclanthaceae
51 Pandanaceae

Liliales
52 Campynemataceae

53 Melanthiaceae
54 Petermanniaceae
55 Alstroemeriaceae
56 Colchicaceae
57 Philesiaceae
58 Ripogonaceae
59 Smilacaceae
60 Corsiaceae
61 Liliaceae

110 Circaeasteraceae
111 Lardizabalaceae
112 Menispermaceae
113 Berberidaceae
114 Ranunculaceae

115 *Sabiaceae*

PROTEANAE

Proteales
116 Nelumbonaceae
117 Platanaceae
118 Proteaceae

TROCHODENDRANAE

Trochodendrales
119 Trochodendraceae

BUXANAE

Buxales
120 Haptanthaceae
121 Buxaceae

MYROTHAMNANAE

Gunnerales
122 Myrothamnaceae
123 Gunneraceae

124 *Dilleniaceae*

Saxifragales
125 Peridiscaceae
126 Paeoniaceae
127 Altingiaceae
128 Hamamelidaceae
129 Cercidiphyllaceae
130 Daphniphyllaceae
131 Iteaceae
132 Grossulariaceae
133 Saxifragaceae
134 Crassulaceae
135 Aphanopetalaceae
136 Tetracarpaeaceae
137 Penthoraceae
138 Haloragaceae

139 *Cynomoriaceae*

ROSANAE

Vitales
140 Vitaceae

FABIDS

Zygophyllales
141 Krameriaceae
142 Zygophyllaceae

Fabales
143 Fabaceae
144 Quillajaceae
145 Surianaceae
146 Polygalaceae

Rosales
147 Rosaceae
148 Barbeyaceae
149 Dirachmaceae
150 Elaeagnaceae
151 Rhamnaceae
152 Ulmaceae
153 Cannabaceae
154 Moraceae
155 Urticaceae

Fagales
156 Nothofagaceae
157 Fagaceae
158 Myricaceae
159 Juglandaceae
160 Casuarinaceae
161 Ticodendraceae
162 Betulaceae

163 *Apodanthaceae*

Cucurbitales
164 Anisophylleaceae
165 Corynocarpaceae
166 Coriariaceae
167 Cucurbitaceae
168 Tetramelaceae
169 Datiscaceae
170 Begoniaceae

Celastrales
171 Lepidobotryaceae
172 Celastraceae

Oxalidales
173 Huaceae
174 Connaraceae
175 Oxalidaceae
176 Cunoniaceae
177 Elaeocarpaceae
178 Cephalotaceae
179 Brunelliaceae

Malpighiales
180 Pandaceae
181 Rhizophoraceae
182 Erythroxylaceae
183 Rafflesiaceae
184 Euphorbiaceae
185 Centroplacaceae
186 Ctenolophonaceae
187 Ochnaceae
188 Picrodendraceae
189 Phyllanthaceae
190 Elatinaceae
191 Malpighiaceae

Asparagales
62 Orchidaceae
63 Boryaceae
64 Blandfordiaceae
65 Asteliaceae
66 Lanariaceae
67 Hypoxidaceae
68 Tecophilaeaceae
69 Doryanthaceae
70 Ixioliriaceae
71 Iridaceae
72 Xeronemataceae
73 Xanthorrhoeaceae
74 Amaryllidaceae
75 Asparagaceae

COMMELINIDS

Arecales
76 Arecaceae

Commelinales
77 Hanguanaceae
78 Commelinaceae
79 Philydraceae
80 Pontederiaceae
81 Haemodoraceae

Zingiberales
82 Strelitziaceae
83 Lowiaceae
84 Heliconiaceae
85 Musaceae
86 Cannaceae
87 Marantaceae
88 Costaceae
89 Zingiberaceae

90 *Dasypogonaceae*

Poales
91 Typhaceae
92 Bromeliaceae
93 Rapateaceae
94 Xyridaceae
95 Eriocaulaceae
96 Mayacaceae
97 Thurniaceae
98 Juncaceae
99 Cyperaceae
100 Anarthriaceae
101 Centrolepidaceae
102 Restionaceae
103 Flagellariaceae
104 Joinvilleaceae
105 Ecdeiocoleaceae
106 Poaceae

CERATOPHYLLANAE

Ceratophyllales
107 Ceratophyllaceae

RANUNCULANAE

Ranunculales
108 Eupteleaceae
109 Papaveraceae

192 Balanopaceae
193 Trigoniaceae
194 Dichapetalaceae
195 Euphroniaceae
196 Chrysobalanaceae
197 Lophopyxidaceae
198 Putranjivaceae
199 Passifloraceae
200 Lacistemataceae
201 Salicaceae
202 Violaceae
203 Goupiaceae
204 Achariaceae
205 Caryocaraceae
206 Humiriaceae
207 Irvingiaceae
208 Linaceae
209 Ixonanthaceae
210 Calophyllaceae
211 Clusiaceae
212 Bonnetiaceae
213 Podostemaceae
214 Hypericaceae

MALVIDS

Geraniales
215 Geraniaceae
216 Vivianiaceae
217 Melianthaceae

Myrtales
218 Combretaceae
219 Lythraceae
220 Onagraceae
221 Vochysiaceae
222 Myrtaceae
223 Melastomataceae
224 Crypteroniaceae
225 Alzateaceae
226 Penaeaceae

Crossosomatales
227 Aphloiaceae
228 Geissolomataceae
229 Strasburgeriaceae
230 Staphyleaceae
231 Guamatalaceae
232 Stachyuraceae
233 Crossosomataceae

Picramniales
234 Picramniaceae

Sapindales
235 Biebersteiniaceae
236 Nitrariaceae
237 Kirkiaceae
238 Burseraceae
239 Anacardiaceae
240 Sapindaceae
241 Rutaceae
242 Simaroubaceae
243 Meliaceae

Huerteales
244 Gerrardinaceae
244a Petenaeaceae
245 Tapisciaceae
246 Dipentodontaceae

Malvales
247 Cytinaceae
248 Muntingiaceae
249 Neuradaceae
250 Malvaceae*
251 Sphaerosepalaceae
252 Thymelaeaceae
253 Bixaceae
254 Sarcolaenaceae
255 Cistaceae
256 Dipterocarpaceae

Brassicales
257 Akaniaceae
258 Tropaeolaceae
259 Moringaceae
260 Caricaceae
261 Limnanthaceae
262 Setchellanthaceae

263 Koeberliniaceae
264 Bataceae
265 Salvadoraceae
266 Emblingiaceae
267 Tovariaceae
268 Pentadiplandraceae
269 Gyrostemonaceae
270 Resedaceae
271 Capparaceae
272 Cleomaceae
273 Brassicaceae

BERBERIDOPSIDANAE

Berberidopsidales
274 Aextoxicaceae
275 Berberidopsidaceae

SANTALANAE

Santalales
276 Balanophoraceae
277 Olacaceae
278 Opiliaceae
279 Santalaceae

280 Loranthaceae
281 Misodendraceae
282 Schoepfiaceae

CARYOPHYLLANAE

Caryophyllales
283 Frankeniaceae
284 Tamaricaceae
285 Plumbaginaceae
286 Polygonaceae
287 Droseraceae
288 Nepenthaceae
289 Drosophyllaceae
290 Dioncophyllaceae
291 Ancistrocladaceae
292 Rhabdodendraceae
293 Simmondsiaceae
294 Physenaceae
295 Asteropeiaceae
296 Caryophyllaceae
297 Achatocarpaceae
298 Amaranthaceae
299 Stegnospermataceae
300 Limeaceae

301 Lophiocarpaceae
302 Barbeuiaceae
303 Gisekiaceae
304 Aizoaceae
305 Phytolaccaceae
306 Sarcobataceae
307 Nyctaginaceae
308 Molluginaceae
309 Montiaceae
310 Didiereaceae
311 Basellaceae
312 Halophytaceae
313 Talinaceae
314 Portulacaceae
315 Anacampserotaceae
316 Cactaceae

ASTERANAE

Cornales
317 Hydrostachyaceae
318 Curtisiaceae
319 Grubbiaceae
320 Cornaceae
321 Hydrangeaceae
322 Loasaceae

Ericales
323 Balsaminaceae
324 Marcgraviaceae
325 Tetrameristaceae
326 Fouquieriaceae
327 Polemoniaceae
328 Lecythidaceae
329 Sladeniaceae
330 Pentaphylacaceae
331 Sapotaceae
332 Ebenaceae
333 Primulaceae
334 Theaceae
335 Symplocaceae
336 Diapensiaceae
337 Styracaceae
338 Sarraceniaceae
339 Roridulaceae
340 Actinidiaceae
341 Clethraceae
342 Cyrillaceae
343 Mitrastemonaceae
344 Ericaceae

LAMIIDS

345 *Oncothecaceae*
346 *Metteniusaceae*
347 *Icacinaceae*

Garryales
348 Eucommiaceae
349 Garryaceae

Gentianales
350 Rubiaceae

351 Gentianaceae
352 Loganiaceae
353 Gelsemiaceae
354 Apocynaceae

355 *Vahliaceae*
356 *Boraginaceae*

Solanales
357 Convolvulaceae
358 Solanaceae
359 Montiniaceae
360 Sphenocleaceae
361 Hydroleaceae

Lamiales
362 Plocospermataceae
363 Carlemanniaceae
364 Oleaceae
365 Tetrachondraceae
366 Calceolariaceae
367 Gesneriaceae
368 Plantaginaceae
369 Scrophulariaceae
370 Stilbaceae
371 Linderniaceae
372 Pedaliaceae
373 Lamiaceae

374 Phrymaceae
375 Paulowniaceae
376 Orobanchaceae
377 Lentibulariaceae
378 Acanthaceae
379 Bignoniaceae
380 Thomandersiaceae
381 Schlegeliaceae
382 Verbenaceae
383 Byblidaceae
384 Martyniaceae

CAMPANULIDS

Aquifoliales
385 Stemonuraceae
386 Cardiopteridaceae
387 Phyllonomaceae
388 Helwingiaceae
389 Aquifoliaceae

Asterales
390 Rousseaceae
391 Campanulaceae
392 Pentaphragmataceae
393 Stylidiaceae
394 Alseuosmiaceae
395 Phellinaceae

396 Argophyllaceae
397 Menyanthaceae
398 Goodeniaceae
399 Calyceraceae
400 Asteraceae

Escalloniales
401 Escalloniaceae

Bruniales
402 Columelliaceae
403 Bruniaceae

Paracryphiales
404 Paracryphiaceae

Dipsacales
405 Adoxaceae
406 Caprifoliaceae*

Apiales
407 Pennantiaceae
408 Torricelliaceae
409 Griseliniaceae
410 Pittosporaceae
411 Araliaceae
412 Myodocarpaceae
413 Apiaceae

Footnote
* Durionaceae as listed in the main section of the book is included in Malvaceae (250).
   Dipsacaceae and Valerianaceae are included in Caprifoliaceae (406).

Further Resources

APG. An ordinal classification for the families of flowering plants. *Annals of Missouri Botanical Garden 85*: 531–553 (1998).

APG II. An update of the Angiosperm Phylogeny Group classification for orders and families of flowering plants: *APG II. Bot. J. Linn. Soc. 141*: 399–436 (2003).

APG III. An update of the Angiosperm Phylogeny Group Classification for the orders and families of flowering plants: *APG III. Bot. J. Linn. Soc. 161*: 105–121 (2009).

Bentham, G. & Hooker, W. J. *Genera Plantarum*. London: L. Reeve & Co. (1862–1883).

Brummitt, R. K. *Vascular Plant Families and Genera*. Richmond: Royal Botanic Gardens, Kew (1992).

Cronquist, A. *The Evolution and Classification of Flowering Plants*. Boston: Houghton Mifflin (1968).

Cronquist, A. *An Integrated System of Classification of Flowering Plants*. New York: Columbia University Press (1981).

Dahlgren, R. M. T., Clifford, H. T., & Yeo, P. F. *The Families of the Monocotyledons: Structure, Evolution, and Taxonomy*. Berlin & New York: Springer (1985).

Haston E, Richardson J. E, Stevens P. F, Chase M. W, Harris D. J. LAPG III: a linear sequence of the families in APG III. *Bot. J. Linn. Soc. 161*: 128–131 (2009).

Heywood, V. H., Brummitt, R. K., Culham A, Seberg O. *Flowering Plant Families of the World*. Kew: Royal Botanic Gardens (2007).

Hultén, E. *The Circumpolar Plants*. Uppsala: Almqvist & Wiksells (1971).

Hutchinson, J. *The Families of Flowering Plants Arranged According to a New System Based on their Probable Phylogeny*. 3rd edn. Oxford: Clarendon Press (1973).

Judd W. S., Stevens P. F., Campbell C. S., Kellogg E. A., Donoghue M. J. *Plant Systematics: a phylogenetic approach*. Sunderland: Sinauer Associates (2007).

Kubitzki, K. *et al.* (eds), *The Families and Genera of Vascular Plants*. Berlin: Springer-Verlag (1990 onward).

Mabberley, D. J. *Mabberley's Plant-Book. A Portable Dictionary of Plants, their Classification and Uses.* 3rd edn. Cambridge: Cambridge University Press (2008).

Smith, N. *et al.* (eds), *Flowering Plants of the Neotropics.* Princeton: Princeton, University Press (2004).

Soltis, D. E. *et al. Phylogeny and Evolution of Angiosperms.* Sunderland, Mass: Sinauer Associates (2005).

Stevens, P. F. (2001 onward). Angiosperm Phylogeny Website. Version 7, May 2006.
www.mobot.org/MOBOT/research/APweb *or* seedplants.org

Takhtajan, A. *Diversity and Classification of Flowering Plants.* New York: Columbia University Press (1997).

Takhtajan, A. *Systema Magnoliophytorum.* Leningrad: Nauka (1987) [in Russian].

Thorne, R. F. The classification and geography of the flowering plants: dicotyledons of the class Angiospermae (subclass Magnoliidae, Ranunculidae, Caryophyllidae, Dilleniidae, Rosidae, Asteridae, and Lamiidae). *Bot. Rev.* 66: 441–647 (2000).

Thorne. R. F. 1983. Proposed new alignments in the angiosperms. *Nordic Journal of Botany 3*: 85–117.

Thorne. R. F. *An Updated Classification of the Class Magnoliopsida ("Angiospermae").*
rsabg.org/angiosperms

273

GLOSSARY

abaxial On side facing away from stem or axis.

achene A small, dry, single-seeded fruit that does not split open.

acute Having a sharp point.

adaxial On the side facing the stem or axis.

adnate Joined to or attached to; applied to unlike organs, e.g., stamens adnate to perianth; cf connate.

adventitious Arising from an unusual position, e.g., roots from a stem or leaf.

aerial root A root that originates above the ground level.

aestivation Arrangement of parts of a flower within the bud, usually referring to sepals and petals.

alternate (of leaves) One leaf at each node of the stem; (of stamens) between the petals.

androecium All the male reproductive organs of a flower; the stamens; cf gynoecium.

androgynophore A column on which stamens and carpels are borne.

angiosperm A plant producing seeds enclosed in an ovary. A flowering plant.

annual A plant that completes its life cycle from germination to death within one year.

annular Ringlike.

anther The terminal part of the male organs (stamen), usually borne on a stalk (filament) and developing to contain pollen.

anthocyanin Pigment usually responsible for pink, red, purple, violet, and blue in plants.

antipetalous Occurring opposite the petals, on the same radius, as distinct from alternating with the petals.

antisepalous Occurring opposite the sepals, on the same radius, as distinct from alternating with the sepals.

aperturate (of pollen) Having one or more apertures.

apetalous Without petals.

apex Tip of an organ; usually the growing point.

apical Pertaining to the apex.

apocarpous With carpels free from each other.

aquatic Living in water.

aril A fleshy or sometimes hairy outgrowth from the hilum or funicle of a seed.

asepalous Without sepals.

auricle (adj. auriculate) Small earlike projections at the base of a leaf or leaf blade or bract.

awn A stiff, bristlelike extension to an organ, usually at the tip.

axil The upper angle formed by the union of a leaf with the stem.

axile placentation A type of placentation in which the ovules are borne on placentas on the central axis of an ovary that has two or more locules.

axillary Pertaining to the organs in the axil, e.g., the buds, flowers, or inflorescence.

axis The main or central stem of a herbaceous plant or of an inflorescence.

baccate Berrylike.

basal placentation Having the placenta at the base of the ovary.

berry A fleshy fruit without a stony layer, usually containing many seeds.

bicarpellate (of ovaries) Derived from two carpels.

biennial A plant that completes its life cycle in more than one, but less than two years and which usually flowers in the second year.

bifid Forked; having a deep fissure near center.

bilabiate Two-lipped.

bipinnate (of leaves) A pinnate leaf with the primary leaflets themselves divided in a pinnate manner; cf pinnate.

bisexual (of flowers) Containing both male and female reproductive organs in a single flower; cf unisexual.

blade The flattened part of a leaf; the lamina.

bract A leaf, often modified or reduced, which subtends a flower or inflorescence in its axil.

bracteole A small leaflike organ, occurring along the length of a flower stalk, between a true subtending bract and the calyx.

bulb An underground organ comprising a short disklike stem, bearing fleshy scale leaves and buds and surrounded by protective scale leaves; it acts as a perennating organ and is a means of vegetative reproduction; cf corm, tuber.

bulbil A small bulb or bulblike organ often produced on aboveground organs.

calyx Collective term for all a flower's sepals.

cambium A layer of cells that occurs within the stem and roots which divides to form secondary permanent tissues.

campanulate Bell-shaped.

capitate Headlike.

capitulum An inflorescence consisting of a head of closely packed stalkless flowers.

capsule A dry fruit that normally splits open to release its seeds.

carnivorous plant A plant that is capable of catching and digesting small animals such as insects.

carpel One of the flower's female reproductive organs, comprising an ovary and a stigma, and containing one or more ovules.

caryopsis A dry fruit (achene) typical of grasses.

catkin A pendulous inflorescence of simple, usually unisexual flowers.

ciliate (of margins) Fringed with small hairs.

circumscissile Opening all round by a transverse split.

claw Narrow basal part of some petals and sepals.

colpate (of pollen) Having one or more colpi (oblong-elliptic apertures in the pollen wall).

column (of a flower) Combined stamen and style (in orchids) or united staminal filaments (hibiscus).

compound Consisting of several parts, e.g., a leaf with several leaflets or an inflorescence with more than one group of flowers.

connate Joined or attached to; applied to similar organs fused during development, e.g., stamens fused into a tube; cf adnate.

connective (of stamens) The tissue connecting the pollen sacs of an anther.

contorted (of sepals and petals) Twisted in the bud so that they overlap on one side only; spirally twisted.

cordate (of leaves) Heart-shaped.

corm A bulbous, swollen, underground, stem base, bearing scale leaves and adventitious roots; cf bulb, tuber.

corolla All the petals of a flower; normally colored.

corona A series of petal-like structures in a flower, either outgrowths from the petals, or modified from the stamens, e.g., a daffodil "trumpet."

cotyledon(s) The first leaf, or pair of leaves, of an embryo within the seed.

crenate (of leaf margins) Round-toothed.

crenulate Finely crenate.

cross-fertilization, cross-pollination See fertilization, pollination.

cupule (adj. cupulate) A cup-shaped sheath, surrounding some fruits.

cyme An inflorescence in which each terminal growing point produces a flower. Subsequent growth is from a lateral growing point, the oldest flowers being at the apex, or center, if flat.

cymose Arranged in a cyme; cymelike.

deciduous The shedding of leaves seasonally.

declinate (of stamens) Curving downward.

decussate (of leaves) Arranged in opposite pairs on the stem, with each pair at 90 degrees to the preceding pair.

dehiscence The method or act of opening.

dehiscent Opening to shed pollen or seeds.

dehiscing In the act of shedding pollen or seeds.

dentate Having a toothed margin.

denticulate Having a finely toothed margin.

dichasium (of inflorescences) A form of cymose inflorescence with each branch giving rise to two other branches.

didymous In pairs.

didynamous Having two long and two short stamens.

dimorphism (adj. dimorphic) Having two distinct forms.

dioecious Having male and female flowers borne on separate plants.

disk Fleshy outgrowth developed from the receptacle at the base of the ovary or from stamens surrounding the ovary; it often secretes nectar.

distichous Arranged in two vertical rows.

dorsal Upper.

drepanium (of inflorescences) A cymose inflorescence with successive branches on one side only, flattened in one plane, and curved to one side.

drupe A fleshy fruit containing one or more seeds, each of which is surrounded by a stony layer.

elliptic(al) (of leaves) Oval, with narrowed ends.

embryo The rudimentary plant within the seed.

embryo sac The central portion of the ovule; a thin-walled sac within the nucellus containing the egg nucleus.

endocarp The innermost layer of the ovary wall (pericarp) of a fruit. In some fruits it becomes hard and "stony"; cf drupe.

endosperm In some seeds, fleshy nutritive material derived from embryo sac.

entire (of leaves) With an undivided margin.

epicalyx A whorl of sepal-like appendages resembling the calyx but outside the true calyx.

epidermis Usually a single layer of living cells forming the protective covering to many plant organs, particularly leaves, petals, sepals, and herbaceous stems.

epigynous (of flowers) With sepals, petals, and stamens inserted near top of ovary.

epipetalous Attached to petals or corolla.

epiphyte A plant that grows on the surface of another, without deriving food from its host.

erect (of an ovule) Upright, with its stalk at the base.

exine Outer layer of a pollen grain's wall.

exocarp Outermost layer of fruit wall.

exserted Protruding.

exstipulate Without stipules.

female flower A flower containing functional carpels but not stamens.

fertilization The fusion of male and female reproductive cells (gametes) in the ovary after pollination. *Cross-fertilization* occurs between flowers from separate plants; *self-fertilization* occurs between flowers on the same plant or within the same flower.

filament The anther-bearing stalk of a stamen.

filiform Threadlike.

fimbriate (of margins) Fringed, usually with hairs.

flower Structure concerned with sexual reproduction in angiosperms, consisting of male organs (androecium, i.e., the stamens) and female organs (gynoecium, i.e., the ovary, style(s), and stigma(s), usually surrounded by a whorl of petals (corolla) and a whorl of sepals (calyx). The male and female parts may be in the same flower (bisexual) or in separate flowers (unisexual).

follicle A dry fruit that is derived from a single carpel and which splits open along one side only.

fruit Strictly, the ripened ovary of a seed plant and its contents. Loosely, the whole structure containing ripe seeds, which may include more than the ovary; cf achene, berry, capsule, drupe, follicle, nut, samara.

funicle The stalk of an ovule.

gamopetalous/gamosepalous With petals/sepals fused, at least at the base.

gland (adj. glandular) Secreting organ producing oil, resin, nectar, water, etc.; cf nectary.

gynoecium All the female reproductive organs of a flower, comprising one or more free or fused carpels.

gynophore Stalk of a carpel or gynoecium.

habit The characteristic mode of growth or occurrence; the form and shape of a plant.

halophyte A plant that tolerates salty conditions.

hardy Able to withstand extreme conditions, usually of cold.

haustorium A peglike fleshy outgrowth from a parasitic plant, usually embedded in the host plant and drawing nourishment from it.

head A dense inflorescence of small, crowded, often stalkless, flowers; a capitulum.

helicoid (of cymose inflorescences) Coiled like a spring.

herb (adj. herbaceous) A plant that does not develop persistent woody tissue above ground and either dies at the end of the growing season or overwinters by means of underground organs, e.g., bulbs, corms, rhizomes.

heterophylly Having leaves of more than one type on the same plant.

heterostyly Having styles (and usually stamens) of two or more lengths in different flowers within a species.

hilum The scar left on a seed marking the point of attachment to the stalk of the ovule.

hirsute Covered in rough, coarse hairs.

honey-guide Markings (e.g., lines or dots) on the perianth that direct insects to the nectar.

hydrophyte An aquatic plant.

hypanthium A cup-shaped enlargement of the floral receptacle or the bases of the floral parts, which often enlarges and surrounds the fruits, e.g., the fleshy tissue in rose hips.

hypha The threadlike part of a fungal body.

hypogynous (of flowers) With the sepals, petals, and stamens attached to the receptacle or axis, below and free from the ovary.

imbricate (of sepals and petals) Overlapping.

imparipinnate (of leaves) A pinnate leaf with a central unpaired terminal leaflet.

inaperturate (of pollen grains) Without an aperture; without any pores or furrows.

incised (of leaves) Sharply, deeply cut.

indehiscent Fruits not opening to release seeds; cf dehiscent.

indumentum A covering, usually of hairs.

inferior (of ovaries) An ovary with sepals, petals, and stamens attached to its apex.

inflorescence Any arrangement of more than one flower, e.g., bostryx, capitulum, corymb, cyme, dichasium, fascicle, panicle, raceme, rhipidium, spadix, spike, and thyrse.

infructescence A cluster of fruits, derived from an inflorescence.

integument (of ovules) The outer 1–2 protective layers covering the ovule.

internode The length of stem that lies between two leaf-joints (nodes).

introrse Directed and opening inward toward the center of the flower.

involucel A whorl of bracteoles; cf bracteole.

involucre A whorl of bracts beneath an inflorescence; cf bract.

irregular (of flowers) Not regular; not divisible into halves by an indefinite number of longitudinal planes; zygomorphic.

lacerate (of leaves) Irregularly cut.

lamina Thin, flat blade of leaf or petal.

lanceolate Narrow, as a lance, with tapering ends.

latex A milky, usually whitish fluid produced by the cells of various plants that is the source of, e.g., rubber, gutta percha, chicle, and balata.

laticiferous Producing a milky juice (latex).

leaf An aerial and lateral outgrowth from a stem (typically, a stalk or petiole and a flattened blade or lamina) that makes up the foliage of a plant.

leaflet Each separate lamina of a compound leaf.

liana A woody, climbing vine.

ligulate Strap- or tongue-shaped.

ligule (of leaves) A scalelike membrane on the surface of a leaf; (of flowers) the strap-shaped corolla in some Compositae.

limb The upper, expanded portion of a calyx or corolla with fused parts; cf tube.

linear (of leaves) Elongated and with parallel sides.

lithophyte A plant that grows on stones.

lobed (of leaves) With curved or rounded edges.

locule Chamber or cavity of an ovary that contains the ovules, or, within an anther, that contains the pollen.

male flower A flower containing functional stamens but no carpels.

marginal placentation A type of placentation in which the ovules are borne along the fused margins of a single carpel, e.g., pea seeds in a pod.

membranous Resembling a membrane; thin, dry, and semitransparent.

mericarp A one-seeded portion of a fruit that splits when the fruit is mature, e.g., the fruits of the Umbelliferae.

meristem A group of cells capable of dividing indefinitely.

mesocarp The middle layer of the fruit wall (pericarp). It is usually fleshy, as in a berry.

mesophyte A plant having moderate moisture requirements.

micropyle The opening through the integuments of an ovule, through which the pollen tube grows after pollination.

midrib Central or largest vein of a leaf or carpel.

mono- A prefix meaning single, one, or once.

monocarpic Fruiting only once and then dying.

monocolpate (of pollen) Having a single colpus (an oblong-elliptic aperture).

monoecious Having separate male and female flowers on the same plant.

monogeneric (of a family) Of only one genus.

monopodial (of stems or rhizomes) With branches or appendages arising from a simple main axis; cf sympodial.

monotypic A genus or family of a single species.

mucilage A slimy secretion that swells on contact with water.

multiseriate (of flower parts) Borne in many series or whorls.

mycorrhiza The symbiotic association of the roots of some seed plants with fungi.

naked (of flowers) Lacking a perianth.

nectar A sugary liquid secreted by some plants; it forms the principle raw material of honey.

nectary The gland in which nectar is produced.

node The point on a stem where one or more leaves are borne.

nucellus Central tissue of the ovule, containing the embryo sac and surrounded by, in angiosperms, 1–2 integuments.

numerous (of floral parts) Usually meaning more than 10.

nut A dry, single-seeded and nonopening (indehiscent) fruit with a woody pericarp.

obligate (of parasite) Plant unable to grow on its own; entirely dependent on a host for nutrition.

ochrea A cup-shaped structure formed by the joining of stipules or leaf-bases around a stem.

opposite (of leaves) Occurring in pairs on opposite sides of the stem; (of stamens) inserted in front of the petals.

ovary The hollow basal region of a carpel, containing one or more ovules and surmounted by the style(s) and stigma(s). It is made up of one or more carpels, which may fuse together in different ways to form one or more chambers (locules). The ovary is generally above the perianth parts (superior) or below them (inferior).

ovate (of leaves) Having the outline of an egg with narrow end above middle.

ovule The structure in the chamber (locule) of an ovary containing the egg cell within the embryo sac that is surrounded by the nucellus. It is enclosed by 1–2 integuments. The ovule develops into the seed after fertilization.

palmate (of leaves) With more than three segments or leaflets arising from a single point.

panicle (of inflorescences) Strictly, a branched raceme, with each branch bearing a further raceme of flowers. More loosely, applies to any complex, branched inflorescence.

parasite Plant that usually obtains its food from another living plant to which it is attached.

parenchyma Tissue made up of thin-walled living photosynthetic or storage cells that is capable of division even when mature.

paripinnate A pinnate leaf with all leaflets in pairs; cf imparipinnate.

pedicel The stalk of a single flower.

peduncle The stalk of an inflorescence.

perennating Living over from season to season.

perennial A plant that persists for more than two years and normally flowers annually.

perfect flower A flower with functional male and female organs.

perianth Floral envelope whose segments are divisible into an outer whorl (calyx) of sepals and an inner whorl (corolla) of petals. The segments of either or both whorls may fuse to form a tube.

pericarp The wall of a fruit that encloses the seeds and develops from ovary wall.

perigynous (of flowers) Having the stamens, corolla, and calyx inserted around the ovary, their bases often forming a cup-shaped disk.

perisperm The nutritive storage tissue in some seeds, derived from the nucellus.

persistent Remaining attached, not falling off.

petal Nonreproductive (sterile) flower part, usually colored; one of the units of the corolla.

petaloid Petal-like.

petiole The stalk of a leaf.

phloem Part of a plant's tissue that is concerned with conducting food material. In woody stems, it is the innermost layer of the bark; cf xylem.

photosynthesis The process by which green plants manufacture sugars from water and carbon dioxide by converting the energy from light into chemical energy with the aid of the green pigment chlorophyll.

phyllode A flattened leafstalk (petiole) that has assumed the form and function of a leaf blade.

pinnate (of leaves) Compound, with leaflets in pairs on opposite sides of the midrib; cf imparipinnate and paripinnate.

pinnatisect (of leaves) Pinnately divided, but not as far as the midrib.

pistil The female reproductive organ consisting of one or more carpels, comprising ovary, style, and stigma; the gynoecium as a whole.

pistillate A flower that has only female organs.

pistillode A sterile, often reduced pistil.

placenta Part of the ovary wall to which the ovules are attached.

placentation The arrangement and distribution of the ovule-bearing placentas within the ovary; cf axile, basal, and marginal.

plumule The rudimentary shoot in an embryo.

pollen Collective name for pollen grains (minute spores [microspores] produced in the anthers).

pollen sac The chamber (locule) in an anther where the pollen is formed.

pollination The transfer of pollen grains from stamen to stigma. *Cross-pollination* occurs between flowers of different plants of the same species; *self-pollination* occurs between flowers of the same plant, or within one flower.

polygamous Having separate male, female, and bisexual flowers on the same plant.

polypetalous With petals free from each other.

pseudo-whorled (of leaves) Arising close together and so appearing to arise at the same level, although not doing so.

pubescent Covered in soft, short hairs.

punctate Shallowly pitted or dotted, often with glands.

raceme An inflorescence consisting of a main axis, bearing single flowers alternately or spirally on stalks (pedicels) of approximately equal length. The apical growing point continues to be active so there is usually no terminal flower, and the youngest branches or flowers are nearest the apex. This mode of growth is known as monopodial.

racemose Arranged like a raceme; in general, any inflorescence capable of indefinite prolongation, having lateral and axillary flowers.

radical (of leaves) Arising from the base of a stem or from a rhizome; basal.

radicle The rudimentary root in an embryo.

receptacle Flat, concave, or convex part of stem from which all parts of a flower arise; floral axis.

recurved Curved backward.

reflexed Bent sharply backward at an angle.

regular (of flowers) Radially symmetrical, with more than one plane of symmetry; actinomorphic.

reticulate Marked with a network pattern, usually of veins.

rhachis The major axis of an inflorescence.

rhipidium (of inflorescences) A cymose inflorescence with branches alternating from one side of the vertical axis to the other; normally flattened in one plane and fan-shaped.

rhizome Horizontally creeping underground stem that lives over from season to season (perennates) and which bears roots and leafy shoots.

root Lower, usually underground, part of a plant.

rosette A group of leaves arising closely together from a short stem, forming a radiating cluster on or near the ground.

rotate (of corollas) Wheel-shaped; with the petals or lobes spreading out from the axis of a flower.

ruminate (of endosperm in seeds) Irregularly grooved and ridged; having a "chewed" appearance.

sagittate (of leaves) Shaped like an arrowhead; with two backward-directed barbs.

samara A dry fruit that does not split open and has part of the fruit wall extended to form a flattened membrane or wing.

saponins A toxic, soaplike group of compounds that is present in many plants.

saprophyte A plant that cannot live on its own, but which needs decaying organic material as a source of nutrition.

scale A small, often membranous, reduced leaf frequently found covering buds and bulbs.

scaled Covered by scale leaves.

scarious Dry and membranous, with a dried-up appearance.

schizocarp A fruit derived from a simple or compound ovary in which the locules separate at maturity to form single-seeded units.

sclerenchyma Tissue with thickened cell walls, often woody (lignified), and which give mechanical strength and support.

scrambler A plant with a spreading, creeping habit usually anchored with the help of hooks, thorns, or tendrils.

seed The unit of sexual reproduction developed from a fertilized ovule; an embryo enclosed in the testa which is derived from integument(s).

seedling The young plant that develops from a germinating seed.

self-fertilization *See* fertilization.

self-pollination *See* pollination.

semiparasite A plant that, although able to grow independently, is much more vigorous in a parasitic relationship with another plant.

sepal A floral leaf or individual segment of the calyx of a flower, usually green.

septate (of ovaries) Divided into locules by walls.

septicidal (of fruits) Splitting longitudinally through septa so that the carpels are separated.

septum (of ovaries) The wall between two chambers (locules) of an ovary made up of two or more fused carpels (syncarpous ovary).

serrate (of margins) Toothed, with the teeth pointing forward.

serrulate (of margins) Finely serrate.

sessile Without a stalk, e.g., leaves without petioles or stigmas without a style.

sheath (of leaves) The base of a leaf or leafstalk (petiole) that encases the stem.

sheathing (of leaves) With a sheath that encases the stem.

shoot The aboveground portions of a vascular plant, such as the stems and leaves; the plant part that develops from the embryo's plumule.

shrub A perennial woody plant with well-developed side branches that appear near the base, so that there is no trunk.

simple (of leaves) Not divided or lobed in any way.

simple umbel (of inflorescences) An umbel in which the stalks (pedicels) arise directly from the top of the main stalk.

solitary (of flowers) Occurring singly in each axil.

spadix A spike of flowers on a swollen, fleshy axis.

spathe A large bract subtending and often ensheathing an inflorescence. Applied only in the monocotyledons.

spatulate or spathulate (of leaves) Shaped like a spoon.

spicate Spikelike.

spike An inflorescence of simple racemose type in which the flowers are stalkless (sessile).

spine The hard and sharply-pointed tip of a branch or leaf, usually round in cross section.
spinose Spiny.
spur A hollow, usually rather conical, projection from the base of a sepal, petal, or fused corolla.
stamen Male reproductive organ of a flower (usually a bilobed anther on a stalk, or filament).
staminate Having stamens (male organs), but no carpels (female organs); cf pistillate.
staminode A sterile, often reduced or modified stamen.
stem Main supporting axis of a plant, bearing leaves with buds in their axils; usually aerial (but can be subterranean).
stigma Receptive part of the female reproductive organs on which pollen grains germinate; the apical part of a carpel.
stipitate Having a stalk or stipe.
stipulate Having stipules.
stipule A leafy appendage, often paired, and usually at the base of the leafstalk.
stomata The pores that occur in large numbers in the epidermis of plants and through which gaseous exchange takes place.
stooling (of plants) Having several stems arising together at the base.
style The elongated apical part of a carpel or ovary bearing the stigma at its tip.
subapical Below the apex.
succulent With fleshy or juicy organs containing reserves of water.
suffrutescent (of herbaceous plants) Having a persistent woody stem base.
superior (of ovaries) Occurring above the level at which the sepals, petals, and stamens are borne; cf inferior.
suture A line of union; the line along which dehiscence often takes place in fruits.
symbiosis The nonparasitic relationship between living organisms to mutual benefit.
sympodial (of stems or rhizomes) With the apparent main stem consisting of a series of usually short axillary branches; cf cyme and monopodial.
syncarpous (of ovaries) Made up of two or more fused carpels.
tendril Part or all of a stem, leaf, or petiole modified to form a delicate, threadlike appendage; climbing organ able to coil around objects.
tepal A perianth-segment that is not clearly distinguishable as either a sepal or a petal.
terminal Situated at the apex.
ternate (of leaves) Compound, divided into three parts more or less equally. Each part may itself be further subdivided.
tessellated (of leaves) Marked with a fine chequered pattern, like a mosaic.
testa Seed's outer protective covering.
thallus A type of plant body that is not differentiated into root, stem, or leaf.

theca Half of an anther containing two pollen sacs.
throat The site in a calyx or corolla of united parts where the tube and limbs meet.
thyrse (of inflorescences) Densely branched, broadest in the middle and in which the mode of branching is cymose.
trichome A hairlike outgrowth.
tricolpate (of pollen) Having three colpi.
trifoliolate (of leaves) Having three leaflets.
tube The united, usually cylindrical part of the calyx or corolla made up of united parts; cf limb.
tuber An underground stem or root that lives over from season to season (perennates) and which is swollen with food reserves; cf bulb, corm, rhizome.
umbel An umbrella-shaped inflorescence with all the stalks (pedicels) arising from the top of the main stem; sometimes compound, with all the stalks (peduncles) arising from the same point and giving rise to several terminal flower stalks (pedicels).
undershrub A perennial plant with lower woody parts, but herbaceous upper parts that die back seasonally.
undulate (of leaves) With wavy margins.
unifoliolate With a single leaflet that has a stalk distinct from the stalk of the whole leaf.
unilocular (of ovaries) Containing one chamber (locule) in which the ovules or seeds occur.
uniseriate Arranged in a single row, series or layer, e.g., perianth segments.
unisexual (of flowers) Of one sex.
utricle Small, bladderlike, single-seeded dry fruit.
valvate (of perianth-segments) With the margins adjacent without overlapping; cf imbricate.
vascular Possessing vessels; able to conduct water and nutrients.
vascular bundle A strand of tissue, consisting of phloem and xylem, involved in water and food transport.
vein Any of the visible strands of conducting and strengthening tissues running through a leaf.
venation The arrangement of the veins of a leaf.
ventral On the lower side.
verticillate Arranged in whorls.
vessels Tubelike cells arranged end to end in the wood of flowering plants and which form the principal pathway in the transport of water and mineral salts.
whorl The arrangement of organs, such as leaves, petals, sepals, and stamens so that they arise at the same level on the axis in an encircling ring.
xeromorphic Possessing characteristics such as reduced leaves, succulence, dense hairiness, or a thick cuticle, which are adaptations to conserve water and so withstand extremely dry conditions.
xerophyte A plant thath is adapted to withstand extremely dry conditions.
xylem The woody, fluid-conveying (vascular) tissue concerned with the transport of water about the plant; cf phloem; vessels.

INDEX

Page numbers in *italic* font refer to illustrations.

A
Abeliophyllum 147
Abelmoschus 126–127
Abrahamia 16
Abronia *142*
Abutilon 126, 127
Acacia 116, 118, *119*
Acaena 184
Acalypha *92, 93*
Acanthogilia 163
Acantholimon 160
Acanthopanax *28, 29*
Acanthosicyos 68, 70
Acanthus 12–13, *13*
Achillea 35
Aciachne 262
Aconitum 178–180, *181*
Acridocarpus 125
Actaea 178, 180
Adenia 157
Adenium 22
Adenophora 55
Adhatoda 12
Adina 189
Aechmea 229, 230
Aegialitis 160, *161*
Aegilops 264
Aeollanthus 112
Aeschynanthus 102, *103*
African Violet 102
Afrothismia 232
Agapetes 88, *89*
Agastache 112
Agatea 215
Ageratina 35
Ageratum 35
Agrimonia 186
Agrostemma 57
Ajuga 112
Albizia 117, 118
Alcea 127
Alchemilla 184, 185
Alder 38
Aldrovanda 82
Alfaroa 111

Alkanna 42
Allamanda 22, *23*, 24
Allanblackia 65
Almond 185
Alnus 38, *39*
Alocasia 224
Alstonia 25
Alternanthera 15
Alternifolia 147
Althaea 126
Altingia 105
Alyssum 44
Amaranthus 14–15, *14*
Amaryllis 221
Ambrosia 31, 35
Amelanchier 185
Amorphophallus 224
Ampelocissus 216
Ampelopsis 216
Amphipterygium 16
Anacampseros 168
Anacardium 16, *17*
Anagallis 170, 172
Ananas 228, 230, *231*
Anchietea *214, 215*
Anchusa 43
Ancylotropis 165
Andropogon 265
Androsace 172
Androsiphonia 157
Aneilema 237
Anemone 178–180, *181*
Anemopsis 196, *196*
Anethum 21
Angelica 21
Angelonia 199
Angraecum 256
Anigozanthos *244*, 245, *245*
Anise 21
Anoectochilus 260
Anthemis 35
Anthocephalus 189
Anthocleista 99
Anthriscus 21
Anthurium 224
Antigonon 166
Antirrhinum 199
Aphelandra 12

Aphylloclados 31
Apium 21
Apodostigma 58
Apodytes 108
Aponogeton 222, *222, 223*
Apostasia 260
Apple 185
Apricot 185
Apterokarpos 16
Aquilaria 206
Aquilegia 179, 180, *181*
Arachis 117
Aralia *28, 29*
Araujia 25
Arbutus 88, *89*
Archangelica 21
Arctostaphylos 89
Arctotis 35
Ardisiandra 172
Areca 226
Aregelia 230
Arenaria *56, 57*
Aretiastrum 213
Argemone 153, *154*
Argentine Trumpet Vine 41
Argylia 41
Argyranthemum 35
Ariocarpus *48*, 50
Arisaema 224
Aristida 263
Armeria 160, *160*, *161*
Arnica 35
Arracacia 20
Artedia 19, *21*
Artemisia 34–35
Arum 224
Arum Lily 224
Arundinaria 263
Arundo 264, 265
Asarina 199
Asclepias 25, *25*
Ash 147
Asperula 189
Aspidosperma 22, 24
Asplundia 238, *238*
Aster 35
Asterogyne 226
Asterolinon 170, 172
Astrantia 19, 21

Astrephia 213
Astronium 16
Asystasia 12
Atropa 201
Atroximia 165
Aubergine 201
Aucoumea 46
Australian Blackwood 118
Autograph Tree 64
Auxemma 42
Avena 264, 265
Avens 185
Averrhoa 148
Azorella 18

B
Babai 224
Baby's Breath 57
Baccharis 31
Balsam Apple 70
Bamboo 262, 264
Baneberry 180
Banisteriopsis 124
Banksia 174
Baptisia 117
Barbados Cherry 124
Barberetta 245
Barclaya 144, *145*
Barleria 12
Barley 264
Barnadesia 33
Barteria 157
Bartonia 99
Basananthe 157
Basil 112
Batrachium 178
Bauhinia 119
Bean 116–118
Bears' Breech 12
Beech 95–96
Begonia 36, 37
Begoniella 37
Bellflower 52
Bellis *32*, 35
Belonanthus 213
Beloperone 12, *13*
Benincasa 70
Bergamot 190
Bermuda Buttercup 148
Bersama *128, 129*